JIM
LANE

JIM LANE

SCOUNDREL, STATESMAN, KANSAN

ROBERT COLLINS

PELICAN PUBLISHING COMPANY
GRETNA 2007

*The word "Pelican" and the depiction of a pelican are trademarks
of Pelican Publishing Company, Inc., and are registered in the
U.S. Patent and Trademark Office.*

Library of Congress Cataloging-in-Publication Data

Collins, Robert, 1965-
 Jim Lane : scoundrel, statesman, Kansan / Robert Collins.
   p. cm.
 Includes bibliographical references and index.
 ISBN-13: 978-1-58980-445-6 (hardcover : alk. paper)
 1. Lane, James Henry, 1814-1866. 2. Politicians—Kansas—Biography.
3. Kansas—History—1854-1861. 4. Kansas—Politics and government—
1854-1861. 5. Legislators—United States—Biography. 6. United States.
Congress—Biography. 7. United States—Politics and government—
1849-1861. 8. United States—Politics and government—1861-1865. 9.
Generals—United States—Biography. 10. United States. Army—
Biography. I. Title.
 F685.L268C65 2007
 973.7092—dc22

                                    2007012834

Printed in the United States of America

Published by Pelican Publishing Company, Inc.
1000 Burmaster Street, Gretna, Louisiana 70053

Contents

Bleeding Kansas, 1854-1861

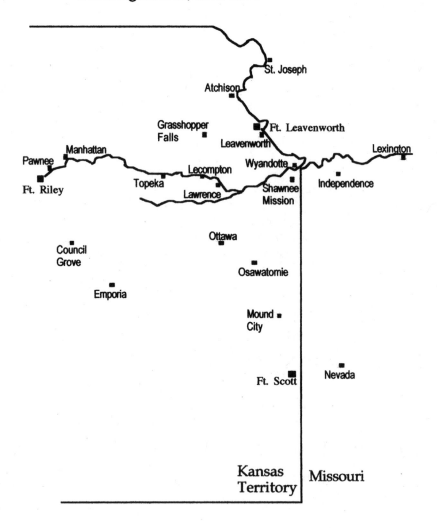

Introduction
Who Is the "Grim Chieftain"?

"He who would resurrect the 'Grim Chieftain' from the books, newspapers and manuscripts of the State Historical Society, will fail. He will obtain nothing more satisfactory than a dry, eyeless mummy."

—Noble L. Prentis, in "Jim Lane,"
Olathe Mirror, June 7, 1888

Speaking to the Kansas State Historical Society in 1938, the biographer and drama editor for the *Chicago Daily News,* Lloyd Lewis, said this about James Henry Lane: "Not long ago, at a luncheon in Chicago, your president, William Allen White, and I made the discovery that a certain Kansan, who has been dead down among the roots of your grass for more than seventy years, was a mutual favorite of our lives—and apparently of nobody else's."

By then James H. Lane had become an almost-forgotten figure in Kansas history. If he was known, it was as one of the "wild men" of Kansas Territory. It was said that Lane, along with John Brown, was one of the fanatics who made the territory into "Bleeding Kansas." Lane was one of the leaders of the Free State movement at the time, but he wasn't believed to have been either influential or respectable.

Digging a bit deeper at the time, one might have learned that Lane was the powerbroker in Kansas during the Civil War. He was one of the state's first two senators, had the ear of Pres. Abraham Lincoln, and led soldiers in the field. But a researcher of that period would not have thought these facts to be accomplishments worth elevating Lane. Instead, that researcher likely would have read that Lane got his seat through back-room deals and kept it by handing out favors to friends. Astonished, he would have found that the Great Emancipator actually listened to the Grim Chieftain. Most of all, he would have seen accusations that Lane's 1861 expedition into Missouri was one of the causes for the 1863 Lawrence "massacre."

As to Lane's character, the man would have been dismissed as a foul-mouthed, tobacco-chewing, dirty-dealing, divorced, frontier politician whose only talent was an ability to move crowds. And Lane did not die in his bed or in battle, but took his own life, a sure sign that he was not a man to admire.

Twenty years later, Jim Lane's standing in Kansas had not improved noticeably. In the late 1950s Albert Castel published *A Frontier State at War*, the first modern history of the Civil War in Kansas. Early in his book he wrote, "Vulgar, tempestuous, of fluctuating courage, and utterly unscrupulous, [Lane] was a cynic who posed as a zealot, a demagogue who claimed to be a statesman. His private life was that of a satyr, and he was utterly irreligious except at election time." Castel gave very little credit to Lane, even in the face of the spectacular blunders made by the senator's political foes. Lane might be "colorful and fascinating," but never in a positive way.

The most balanced picture given of Lane until recently was from Sen. John J. Ingalls. Ingalls had come to Kansas Territory during the time of Lane's ascendancy and began his political career just before the Civil War. He didn't know Lane personally, but he knew Lane's friends and his enemies. He wrote that Lane "was the object of inexplicable idolatry and unspeakable execration." In spite of such evenhanded writing, most historians from the 1920s to the 1990s believed the latter of Ingalls' comment and dismissed the former.

Today the view of Senator Lane might be changing. This evolution in thought is due in part to more modern biographies of President Lincoln, which have replaced the older, saintly image of "Father Abraham" with that of a tough war leader who did what he had to do so that the nation would survive the Civil War, but who, like Lane, was plagued with doubt and depression. Another factor is that there is an ever-increasing understanding of the time and place in which Jim Lane lived. He may well have been a man both of his time and ahead of his time. There is also an acknowledgment now that much of the negative writing about Lane was done by men who had their own motivations for demeaning him, thereby elevating their own images. And perhaps it is as Lane's close friend and biographer John Speer once said, "Falsehood will travel a mile while the truth is getting on its boots."

Lane was a controversial man while he was alive, of that there is no doubt. People either loved him or hated him. He was either a hero to them or a villain. The mere mention of his name could inspire pride, envy, fear, disgust, or hope, sometimes all at once. He was one of the key figures in the struggle over Kansas Territory and again in the Far West during the Civil War. While his actions were known, and sometimes famous, his motivations could be shrouded in mystery. Even the facts of his birth and early life are in dispute.

But Jim Lane certainly does not, as Lloyd Lewis said, deserve to be "crowded out of the schoolbooks and the histories of the nation." He must be better known if the story of "Bleeding Kansas" is to be properly understood. So let us go back and take a look at what turned an unknown politician of Indiana into one of the giants of Kansas history.

JIM
LANE

I.

Lane's Early Life

An incident from the life of James Henry Lane illustrates how difficult it has been to get a handle on the man. According to Lane biographer Kendall Bailes, Lane went to the town of Ozawkie, Kansas Territory, in 1858 to give a speech. His audience was composed of both those who wanted Kansas to become a state without slavery and those who favored its status as a Slave State. Lane was an antislavery man, and as he spoke he launched into attacks on his opponents.

At one point in Lane's harangue a man called him a liar and pulled out a pistol. "Hold the assassin!" Lane called out. He said to the man, "I am a Kentuckian and recognize the code. Now step off twenty paces and give me my choice of weapons!" Amid shouts of "fair play" the proslavery man backed down from the challenge to face Lane in a duel. The interruption over, Lane returned to his speech.

The only problem with the challenge, as Bailes wrote, was that Lane was not born in Kentucky but in Indiana. Bailes noted that Lane sometimes claimed to be from Kentucky when facing a crowd with plenty of proslavery men and would call Indiana the place of his birth before antislavery citizens. To this Bailes quoted an Ozawkie hotel owner who said that "when Old Jim was first discovered, he was standing astride the Ohio River, claiming both states."

William Elsey Connelley, another Lane biographer, noted this confusion in his 1899 book about the Grim Chieftain. "The majority of authorities say that he was born in Boone county [sic],

Kentucky," Connelley wrote. But John Speer, the man who could best be called Lane's closest friend, stated that Lane was born in the town he was raised in, Lawrenceburg, Indiana, on June 22, 1814.

Author and college professor Leverett Spring, in writing about Lane's political career, said that James H. Lane "was almost wholly a product of the border." His education was spotty, and Lane didn't like reading books, Spring claimed, because he "had none of the finer mental aptitudes" nor any "of the mysterious spiritual qualities which crave their ministry." "His education, such as it was, came from the public street and corner grocery, from the barrooms of country taverns and the political convention."

This evaluation sounds quite harsh, but Spring's comments have to be taken in context. His views reflected what many in "refined" New England thought about men born on the western frontier. They might admire frontier heroes like Daniel Boone or Davy Crockett. They might read for pleasure the frontier novels of authors like James Fenimore Cooper. But by and large, New Englanders saw Westerners as uncivilized and rowdy men with bad habits and low morals. In reviewing the life and actions of James Lane and how others saw them and him, it is important to keep that New England viewpoint in mind. This regional disconnect, more than probably anything else, shapes any attempt to consider Lane and his life.

William Connelley, who was far more sympathetic an author to Lane, phrased his frontier origins far differently. He wrote that the frontier was a school that taught "strength of character, self-reliance, [and] resource in emergency" and that Lane learned these lessons. He did have the faults that many other frontiersmen, including Abraham Lincoln, had but "they were not considered of so great consequence as in [an] older and better ordered society." Neither was Lane completely illiterate, as he was taught "the elementary branches of learning" by his mother.

Author William G. Cutler, quoting another historian, wrote of Lane's early life: "James' mother, who was a woman of superior intellectual and moral qualifications, superintended his early education. Always restive and unable to confine himself to books, he attained but the rudiments of school learning, even under the excellent tutorship of his mother."

Mrs. Lane kept a journal of her life and thoughts, and historian Richard Hinton wrote that she had a high moral character and a strong intellect, even going so far as to say she was "a poetess of no mean order." She ran two or three schools in her life, including one in Lawrenceburg. When she was eulogized in a Lawrenceburg newspaper in 1856, it was noted that Mrs. Lane had been born a Presbyterian. After she married and went west with her husband, she converted to the Methodist religion. Interestingly, her marriage to Amos Lane was reported to have been her second. Her first husband died only a year after their wedding, and seven years passed before she became betrothed to Mr. Lane.

William Connelley found an article from a Kentucky newspaper with many details about Lane's father, who was as influential as his mother. Amos Lane was apparently from New York and moved to Lawrenceburg, Indiana, in 1808. The elder Lane was a lawyer but initially was prevented from being admitted to the bar because he was an ardent Democrat, the local judge and county clerk both being Federalists. Unable to find a position in the city, Lane decided to move with his wife to a village in Kentucky across the Ohio River from Lawrenceburg and worked at odd jobs. Author and historian Wendell H. Stephenson in his 1930 biography of James Lane recognized that the new hometown of the Lane family was a prosperous place. The town, along the Ohio River and close to the mouths of two important Indiana rivers, was a river trading center of between one thousand and two thousand people with businessmen visiting from all over America.

The family's first child was born in 1810. There were at least two sisters and one more brother born into the family as well. In 1814, the year James Henry Lane was born, Amos Lane moved the family back to Lawrenceburg to practice law. Two years later he was elected to the Indiana House of Representatives. Amos Lane remained a Democrat despite most of the residents of his district being first Federalists and later Whigs.

It is not clear what Amos Lane did during the next decade, the 1820s, but according to the article Connelley quoted, the man was an active speaker for Democrats in southern Indiana. The elder Lane certainly had a commanding presence, standing some six feet tall, with "a voice of remarkable force and power." The man also was a "master of invective" who "could express more indignation and bitterness by his manner of speaking" than anyone in the area and could even be "heard to grit and grind his teeth together at fifty yards." But if Amos Lane could singe ears, he could also turn "soft and mellow" to the point of drawing his listeners to tears. The author of the article claimed that Lane never used tobacco or got drunk, avoided using "profanity or vulgarity," and though a partisan politician never had his integrity questioned by his opponents. Amos Lane was elected to Congress in 1833 and served at least two terms. By the time Amos Lane died around 1850, he was one of the most powerful politicians in Indiana.

Probably because of his upbringing and environment, young Lane decided on a career in law and politics. It seems that Mrs. Lane wanted James to enter the ministry, if the writing of Verres Smith (under the pen name Jacob Stringfellow) can be believed. The young man may have demonstrated great speaking ability at an early age, and his mother's desire was that he use that ability in the service of some church. However, according to Richard Hinton, James Lane was admitted to the Indiana bar in 1840. Smith claimed that during Lane's years as a lawyer he used his ability and an innate charisma to his advantage in winning trials and in gaining political supporters.

Before becoming a lawyer, William Connelley noted, Lane worked for one of his brothers-in-law at a "pork-packing establishment." One of Lane's duties apparently was to load the pork into flatboats and guide the boats down the Ohio and Mississippi Rivers to New Orleans for sale. It may have been on these trips that Lane gained firsthand experience with slavery and perhaps his distaste of the institution that would play such a large role in his later life. First, though, he would become a store owner and was to prove adept at keeping his business going, in spite of the fact that he was out of the country for an extended time during this period.

According to reporter Bob Markwalter, writing for a modern-day newspaper published in Lane's hometown, Lane cashed in what he had made as a lawyer in 1845 and ran for a seat in the state legislature. He came in third out of six candidates. As it happened, however, the candidate who placed fourth ended up getting the seat, due to what Markwalter called a "quirk in the law" and "some political maneuvering."

At this point in James Lane's life, national events took hold of his career. The United States plunged into a war with Mexico in 1846 that lasted two years and would add a great deal of territory to the nation. The war offered Lane a chance at military success and the glory that could result. That in turn would provide an opportunity to move from local to state politics, and that much closer to the position on the national stage his father held.

The cause of the Mexican War largely revolved around Texas and the conflicting internal and external politics of the United States and Mexico. Americans, who had started settling the Mexican province of Texas in the 1820s, revolted against Mexican rule in 1835 and 1836 over the issues of slavery, immigration, and federalization, and the nation of Texas was successfully established in 1836. Mexicans never recognized the new nation but did not attempt to reconquer the Republic of Texas.

From the start Texans had wanted to become part of the United States. Many Americans felt the same way as the notion of Manifest Destiny, an America from "sea to shining sea," swept into public popularity. Mexicans, however, opposed the idea of the United States annexing Texas and came to view their northern neighbor as an enemy. When Pres. John Tyler signed a treaty for the annexation of Texas in 1844, conflict between the United States and Mexico seemed inevitable. Tyler failed to get the treaty approved by the Senate, and presidential candidate James K. Polk made annexation a cornerstone of his platform. Polk won the election, an amended treaty passed before his inauguration, and the Texans rallied behind annexation. Polk was willing to pay Mexico up to $40 million for a secure border along the Rio Grande River and the territories of New Mexico and California, but Mexican popular opinion and a revolution sunk the effort. In the spring of 1846 the United States and Mexico went to war.

When the war started, the standing American army was too small to wage war successfully. It was a tiny force designed to protect the frontier from periodical Indian raids. Therefore, President Polk issued calls to the states for volunteers to fill the ranks. Lane's home state of Indiana and Lane himself responded to the call. James H. Lane was commissioned captain of the Dearborn Volunteer Company of June 1, the first such commission issued in the state. By the middle of the month the company was enrolled and designated part of the Ohio River Regiment, later known as the Third Regiment Indiana Volunteers. On June 24 the three Indiana regiments held elections for their senior officers; Lane was elected colonel of the Third.

The Third was one of many regiments from western states placed under the command of Gen. Zachary Taylor. Taylor was in command in Texas when war broke out, and his force had engaged in the first military actions. But his army remained largely inactive for some time while they assembled in northern Mexico. Disease and riots took many soldiers out of the war before they fired a shot.

James Lane himself almost came to blows with his superior days before his regiment was to go into battle. Joseph Lane (no relation) commanded the Second Indiana and was subsequently put in charge of the entire Indiana Brigade. General Lane continued to favor his old regiment, but in two marches the Third had moved before the Second, preempting the line of regimental march. While the Third was at the Mexican village of Buena Vista, Colonel Lane was outdoors discussing some matter with two of his officers while the general was nearby. According to an 1876 account of the dispute, the argument started during a "discussion of the relative merits of two companies" in General Lane's brigade. The general backed a company in the Second, and the colonel one in the Third. Edward Dickey, a veteran of the Third, wrote that at one point General Lane "said something that Colonel Lane didn't believe." The general told the colonel he didn't care if he was believed, and the colonel questioned the general's word.

General Lane asked Colonel Lane if he thought he was a man who "disregarded his word. 'I do, by ——, sir,'" James Lane replied. General Lane took a swing at him, Colonel Lane dodged, and the colonel slapped the general. The general went for a musket, and the two senior officers prepared to engage in a duel. Just before shots were fired, a guard escorted General Lane away.

Luckily the military campaign took the Lanes away from their dispute. In August 1846 the former Mexican general and president Santa Anna returned from exile. In January 1847, Santa Anna began moving his army against Taylor. Taylor moved cautiously back to a defensive position near Buena Vista, allowing a subordinate general who had scouted the area to arrange his forty-five hundred men to best counter the expected Mexican attack. Santa Anna's fifteen-thousand-man army arrived on February 23, and the battle of Buena Vista began early that morning.

The Third Indiana was posted in the rear of the American position, on a height along with a battery of artillery. Lane's men were ordered to support the position of a Mississippi regiment under Col. Jefferson Davis. The two regiments, backed by artillery, held off Mexican infantry and cavalry attacks. Accurate American cannon fire played havoc with Santa Anna's men. Taylor's force suffered between six hundred and seven hundred casualties, while Mexican losses came close to three thousand killed and wounded. Historian Jack Bauer noted that though Santa Anna still had a strong army, that army "lost its belief in itself" at Buena Vista. Santa Anna went on the defensive, and Zachary Taylor was later credited with a successful military campaign.

As far as the feud between the two Lanes went, the 1876 story noted that after the battle all was forgotten. When the general "bade farewell" to the Indiana Brigade, "he was especially complimentary to Col. Lane and his command." It was one of the few times in Jim Lane's life that he and his opponent abandoned a dispute.

The Third Regiment's term of service was only a year. When it expired Lane was allowed to reorganize it for further service in the field. It was mustered again into the U.S. Army as the Fifth Regiment Indiana Volunteers and returned to Mexico. It marched with Gen. Winfield Scott to Mexico City but appears to have taken no part in the major military actions. According to Leverett Spring, the Fifth did win some honor by "capturing Santa Anna's wooden leg."

Though his men saw little of the fighting, according to William Connelley, as noted in Wendell Stephenson's biography of Lane, the Indiana colonel was appointed provost marshal of Mexico City. He carried out his duties well enough that the people of Mexico City presented him with a banner. Lane was also rewarded by Indiana for his service in the war. The men of his regiment raised money for a sword that was presented to him during a state Democratic meeting in January 1849.

More than a year later, in the fall of 1850, an Indiana newspaper tried to claim that Lane had ordered the sword himself. A response came in the *Indiana Register,* which by then was being edited by Lane's brother. When the facts came to light, another newspaper in Lane's hometown reported that the first newspaper had retracted its claim. It wasn't the last time newspaper accounts would differ concerning events in the life of James H. Lane.

Before going off to war, James Lane became a married man. In 1842 he married Mary E. Baldridge, whom, Connelley wrote, was a "a granddaughter of General Arthur St. Clair," a Revolutionary War commander. Milton Reynolds, a man who knew Lane and whose article on Lane was published in Connelley's 1899 book, said that Mrs. Mary Lane was "a very remarkable woman as well as a very accomplished lady" and added that she was "a born politician."

A hint of Lane's feelings toward his wife can be seen in a letter he wrote to her from Mexico in June 1848. Lane was due to journey home from the war in a few days' time and promised Mary that if he were "spared" to rejoin his family, "my ramblings [are] over." He explained his service with "I had you know some reputation as a fighting man," and had he remained at home during the war it "would have ruined me forever." He wrote that he hoped she was proud of him and upon his return would "welcome your devoted husband," "receive him with open arms," and greet him "with the saying of well done."

It seems that during his return to Mexico, Lane was sick for some period of time. In referring to that illness, Lane told his wife, "I would have given worlds if you could have been with me even for a day" so that he could have "laid my head on your bosom" and told her how "deeply devotedly I love you." If "I had died your name would have been on dying lips." "[You] know I love you & the longer I live the stronger that love is getting." He requested of Mary, "kiss Ellen & J. H. a thousand times for me," and in closing the letter told her, "reciprocate my love & this world will almost be a heaven."

According to Milton Reynolds, the Lanes would have four children live to adulthood: two sons, James Jr. and Thomas, and two daughters, Ellen (or Ella) and Anna. There may have been at least one other child born to the Lanes, a girl who died sometime after the family came to Kansas.

Their father returned from the Mexican War a hero, and James Lane resumed his political career. Back in 1845 he had been nominated for lieutenant governor of Indiana and had lost by a single vote. The Democratic Party nominated him again in 1849 and that time, according to Connelley, Lane won the post by "a large majority." He served as an at-large elector during the presidential election of 1852 and cast his vote for Franklin Pierce. That same year Lane was elected to the U.S. House of Representatives to serve the Fourth Congressional District of Indiana.

It was while serving in the lower house that James Lane began to enter the national spotlight. Not long after his election, Congress returned to the issue of slavery. The country was split between the states where blacks were held as slaves, largely in the South, and the states where slavery was outlawed, mainly in the North. Questions over the morality and desirability of slavery in the United States had dogged the republic since it had declared its independence from Britain. This time the matter appeared in legislation opening two new territories to American settlers. One of those territories was known as Nebraska. The other, and the place that Lane would become intimately tied to for the rest of his life, was Kansas.

II.

Opening Kansas Territory

The territory that would become known as Kansas was due west of the Slave State of Missouri. For centuries it had been home to indigenous tribes, but Kansas was claimed by several nations once whites began to settle the Americas. Spain was first to declare ownership of Kansas, followed by France, then the United States and Mexico.

The first significant white encroachment into Kansas came in the early 1820s because of the creation of a commercial trade route, the Santa Fe Trail, between the Mexican settlement of Santa Fe and American towns in northwestern Missouri. In the 1820s the American government removed Indian tribes living east of the Mississippi River westward. What would become the states of Nebraska, Kansas, and Oklahoma were turned into a "permanent Indian frontier." The relocated tribes, along with those already residing in the region, were supposed to be "Christianized" and taught "civilization" by missionaries and Indian agents.

That process didn't last very long. Trade along the Santa Fe Trail steadily increased, and a movement to settle Oregon Territory on the northwest Pacific Coast swept the country in the 1840s, followed by the California gold rush of 1849. That brought increasing numbers of settlers through Kansas, and the U.S. Army built forts in the area to protect travelers from attacks by Indians angry at white incursions and treaty violations.

As the policy of a permanent Indian frontier broke down, Americans who traveled through Kansas began to reevaluate the collective view of the land. What had been thought of as the Great American Desert was seen as having fertile soil and the potential for settlement. By the early 1850s the notion of organizing Nebraska Territory (of which Kansas was a part) and opening it to white American settlers had taken hold in states such as Missouri, Iowa, and Illinois.

On December 4, 1853, Sen. A. C. Dodge of Iowa presented a bill in the Senate to organize Nebraska Territory. Sen. Stephen A. Douglas of Illinois, chairman of the Senate Committee on Territories, took control of the measure, added helpful amendments, and pushed it through to the full Senate on January 4, 1854. Stephen Douglas was born in Vermont and raised in New York, but since the age of nineteen he had been a Westerner. Only five feet, four inches tall, he was one of the most powerful men in the national Democratic Party. He was known everywhere as "the Little Giant."

The reasons Douglas took an interest in this Kansas-Nebraska bill can be seen in a letter discovered by Kansas historian and author James Malin. The letter, dated December 17, 1853, was sent by Douglas to a Nebraska delegate convention set to meet in St. Joseph, Missouri, in January 1854. Douglas wrote the letter in response to an invitation to attend the convention. He declined their invitation but felt strongly enough about what they planned to do that he wrote to express his support.

He began by telling the delegates that he was the "warm and zealous advocate" of the settlement of Nebraska Territory. Ten years before, when he had first entered the House of Representatives, he had introduced a bill to do just that, adding that as far as he knew it was "the first proposition ever made" to create a territory on the Plains. He continued, "From that day I have never ceased my efforts on any occasion" to organize the territory. Douglas even took credit for coining the name "Nebraska."

Douglas went on to say that he wanted this known to the delegates because a Missouri newspaper claimed he was hostile to the pending legislation. He was not, he wrote, and had long been opposed to the policy of a permanent Indian frontier. With the annexation of Texas, the admission of California, and the acquisition of the New Mexico territories from Mexico, Douglas told the

Sen. Stephen Douglas was the main force behind the Kansas-Nebraska Act. Supposedly Douglas sent Lane to Kansas to start an antislavery Democratic Party. *Photograph courtesy the Kansas State Historical Society.*

delegates that the "Indian Barrier" policy "has been suspended, if not entirely abandoned."

Senator Douglas told the delegates that if the nation were to "protect our immense interests and possessions on the Pacific," Nebraska Territory had to be organized and settled. Railroads and telegraph lines had to be built through to maintain this hold on the west coast region. "The tide of emigration and civilization must be permitted to roll onward until it rushes through the passes of the mountains, and spreads over the plains, and mingles with the waters of the Pacific," he wrote. Americans should have complete access to the lands west of the Mississippi.

Toward the end of his letter, he touched on the question of slavery in the new territory. Douglas wrote that "so far as the slavery question is concerned," the politicians in Washington ought to be willing "to sanction and affirm" the Compromise of 1850. He viewed the organizing of Nebraska as too important to be sidetracked by division over slavery.

The issue of slavery, however, turned out to be more important. The Compromise of 1820, which had admitted Missouri as a Slave State, was an agreement that states admitted north of Missouri's southern border not legalize slavery. A concession to the Slave States was made in the Compromise of 1850. Though accepting California to the union as a Free State, the compromise allowed the territories of Utah and New Mexico to decide for themselves whether or not they would sanction slavery.

This idea would become known as "popular sovereignty." Senator Douglas supported popular sovereignty, but not because he thought it would deal with the issue of slavery, as historian Robert Johannsen discovered in the 1950s. Douglas was a Westerner, and settlers to the territories on the Western frontier had long resented their lack of power in governing themselves. The territorial governments were under complete federal control, with the president appointing all elected officials. Congress sometimes dictated territorial law, leaving residents frustrated and bitter that they had no voice in how the territory was governed.

It was this perspective that shaped Douglas's approach to slavery in the Kansas-Nebraska bill. He wanted to give territorial residents the power to decide such an important issue themselves. He also believed, naively as it turned out, that popular sovereignty would lead to a more peaceful resolution over the slavery issue. Douglas himself thought the two territories were likely to become Free States anyway, so any concerns on the matter were irrelevant to him.

A senator from Kentucky put forward an amendment to the bill, challenging the Missouri Compromise. Douglas responded to the amendment by saying, "The repeal, if we can effect it, will produce much stir in the free states of the Union for a season. Every opprobrious epithet will be applied to me." However, Douglas decided to concede the point. The bill was revised to create two territories: a southern part, due west of Missouri, to be called Kansas; and the majority, west of Iowa and north to Canada, to be Nebraska. The bill, now known as the Kansas-Nebraska Act, would grant the residents of those territories the right to decide whether they would become Free or Slave States.

Southern politicians were, of course, pleased and enthused about the chance to roll back the 1820 compromise. They viewed the Kansas-Nebraska Act as important to the defense and survival of their peculiar institution. They believed that Congress did not have the power to exclude slavery from the territories and therefore should not, unless the people living there desired it excluded. Left unstated in their argument was the certainty that slave-owning settlers would be the ones to bring Kansas into the United States. After all, Kansas was next door to Missouri and thus more likely than Nebraska to support a slave economy.

Opposition to the Kansas-Nebraska Act in Congress came mainly from Northerners opposed to allowing frontier settlers to resolve legislative issues for themselves. Many of those opponents predicted that if the Missouri Compromise were killed off for good, nothing would prevent slavery from entering Nebraska. Nor, for that matter, would anything stop slavery from entering the states north of Missouri, and if that were so, from any other Free State, upsetting the delicate balance of Slave and Free States that the compromise had ensured. One of the opponents, Sen. Salmon P. Chase, said that passage of the act "will light up a fire in the country, which may consume those who kindled it." "We are on the eve of a great national transaction," said another, Sen. William H.

Seward, "a transaction that will close a cycle in the history of our country."

Missouri itself was also divided on the issue. While Sen. David Atchison was strongly in favor of the new bill, the state's other senator, Thomas Hart Benton, was opposed to it, reflecting the severity of the divisions in the rest of Congress. The session that began in 1853 saw the House of Representatives with 159 Democrats, 71 members from the Whig Party, and 4 from the new Republican Party. The Senate had 38 Democrats, 22 Whigs, and 2 Republicans.

Among the Democrats in the House was Congressman James Lane of Indiana. Congressman Lane appears to have spoken out on the issue in an unnamed and undated speech found in the Lane Papers at the University of Kansas. Few of the pages of the speech are numbered, so it is difficult to determine where his discussion of the issue starts, but on two pages Lane shows that he backs passage of the bill and made at least two points on the issue of popular sovereignty to support his position.

In the first point, Lane claimed that the Compromise of 1850 "directly asserted" the right of territorial settlers "to legislate upon all needful subjects, including the question of slavery." This was his definition of popular sovereignty, and in his view that principle and the ability of settlers to decide the slavery issue on their own were linked. Lane's second point was to wonder what opponents of the bill would say if it had included organizing the territory "west of Arkansas which is now slave Territory." Lane seems to have believed that Northern politicians would have had a hard time opposing the bill because of that concession to local preference on the Free State-Slave State admission question.

In spite of the division of Congress and the dire warnings from Northerners, there was not enough momentum in Congress to stop passage of the Kansas-Nebraska Act. It was approved in the Senate 37 to 14 on March 14, 1854, and in the House 113 to 100 on May 22. Two days after House passage, the Senate reconciled its version of the bill with the House's, and it passed 35 to 13. Pres. Franklin Pierce signed the bill into law on May 30. Kansas and Nebraska were now officially open to white settlement.

In the Northern states, a tide of outrage rose against passage of the act. As Leverett Spring put it, "Conventions, town-meetings,

[and] state legislatures denounced the repeal of the Missouri Compromise. Clergymen in great numbers and of all denominations swelled the chorus of protest, a spectacle that caused much unfriendly comment in conservative quarters." Senator Douglas remarked, "I could then travel from Boston to Chicago by the light of my own effigies."

Douglas's party fared badly in the election held in the fall of 1854. Just 7 of the 42 Northern Democrats who voted for the Kansas-Nebraska Act were returned to their seats in the House. The party went from having almost 160 members in the House to having 75. The Republicans seized control of the House of Representatives and went from being a fringe party to being a national party almost overnight. Among the Democrats on the outs in the November balloting was James Lane.

In Missouri, taking the lead in the effort to make Kansas a Slave State was Sen. David R. Atchison. Atchison was part of a clique known as the "F Street Mess," named for the street on which the senators' boarding house was located. These senators were perhaps the most ardent defenders of slavery in the Senate. Atchison himself was president pro tem of the Senate, and as Franklin Pierce had no vice-president, Atchison was, in the famous phrase, "a heartbeat from the Presidency." Atchison was just over six feet tall, often coarse, a drinker, and determined to extend slavery into Kansas.

Atchison's home state was typical of the frontier in that among its population were, as Leverett Spring put it rather prudishly, "thoughtless, passionate, whiskey-guzzling, guffawing unconventional men." Yet alongside this "rabble" were well-to-do plantation owners and their fifty thousand slaves. The majority of both classes viewed it essential to their economic, political, and social welfare that slavery be extended westward. Or, as attendees of a proslavery convention in Lexington, Missouri, in July 1855 stated, "restriction [of slavery] in the settlement of Kansas" would be "virtually the abolition of slavery in Missouri."

Once President Pierce signed the Kansas-Nebraska Act into law, Missourians dashed into Kansas Territory to obtain the best lands. At the time laws on territorial settlement required that residences be built on claimed land and that settlers reside on their claims for certain periods of time. However, in the race to win Kansas for slavery many merely cut notches on trees or placed fence rails on the ground.

There was one problem that the slavery side, especially those from Missouri, faced in their effort to make Kansas a Slave State. Missouri's population density was just two people per square mile. By contrast, Massachusetts had a density of 126 people per square mile. Missourians would need help from the rest of the South in settling the territory before Northerners if Kansas was to become friendly to slavery.

In New England, efforts began to combat the spread of slavery into Kansas Territory. The most well known was started by Eli Thayer, of Worcester, Massachusetts. Thayer set up the Massachusetts Emigrant Aid Company and was able to get his state legislature to charter the company. Eventually renamed the New England Emigrant Aid Company, it assembled groups of abolitionists to form colonies to settle Kansas. By the autumn of 1854 some five groups with a total of about 750 people had been sent to Kansas by the company.

The most important representative of the company in Kansas was Dr. Charles Robinson, of Fitchburg, Massachusetts. Robinson had been born in 1818, and as an adult, after contracting an inflammation of the eye, he became a doctor. He married in 1843, but by 1846 his wife and their two children were dead. Robinson suffered some sort of physical illness or breakdown following these tragedies. To recover his health, and to search for gold, he went west to California. His actions in California would to some degree foreshadow his career in Kansas Territory.

When California was governed by Mexico, land was distributed through titles granted by government authorities. Americans were used to moving onto unclaimed land, squatting on it, and using residency to prove their claim to the land. When California was admitted into the United States, the emigrant squatters came into conflict with the titled landowners. Charles Robinson allied himself with the squatters.

Robinson advocated fighting land disputes in court, rather than using violence against efforts to expel squatters, but in the summer of 1850 one such court case went against the squatters. To ease rising conflict between the two sides, Robinson met with the mayor of Sacramento. He asked the mayor not to make more arrests until the case reached the state supreme court. Robinson believed that the mayor had agreed to terms, but two days later more squatters were arrested, and on August 14 town authorities tried to break up a meeting at a disputed town lot. The squatters refused to be arrested, a battle broke out, three men were killed, and Robinson was seriously wounded. Robinson was threatened with legal charges, but they were dropped within a few months. He was later elected to the California House of Representatives.

In 1851, Robinson returned to Massachusetts. He married Sara T. D. Lawrence, the daughter of an important lawyer and a relative of Amos Lawrence, one of the major stockholders of the New England Emigrant Aid Company. When the company was formed in 1854, Robinson and another man were hired to go to Kansas and report on possible settlement sites. Eventually Robinson settled with the group that founded the town of Lawrence. His position as an agent for the company made him an almost instant leader of the antislavery movement in Kansas.

Thomas Gladstone, a British journalist who was in Kansas in 1856, described Robinson as having "cool self-possession, caution, and [a] soundness of judgment" that made him a leader. Leverett Spring, a friend and ally of Charles Robinson in his later years, claimed that Robinson was "the only free-state man of prominence in the territory who avowed himself an abolitionist." However, editor of the *Prairie City Freemen's Champion,* S. S. Prouty, speaking to the Kansas State Historical Society on January 27, 1881, called Robinson "a conservative man" who was considered "too business-like and practical by the idealists" of the antislavery movement.

Author and correspondent Albert Richardson came through Kansas in 1857 and 1858 and spent considerable time in the contest between the proslavery and antislavery factions in the territory. In his view the proslavery Missourians were "honest" but "ignorant" and "inflamed" by demagogues claiming that "abolitionists meant to establish a free state beside them, and 'steal' their negroes." He noted that only a few of the antislavery men in Kansas were abolitionists from New England.

The initial jockeying over slavery in Kansas in part stemmed from a lack of clarity in the Kansas-Nebraska Act itself. Nothing in the law specified a time frame for citizens to decide the issue. Douglas and, it seems, many antislavery settlers assumed that this decision could be made when the territorial legislature was formed. Southerners, too, believed that nothing could be decided until a state government was established. Thus they were not opposed on principles and on strategy.

Meanwhile, the president began to install the men who would administer the new territory, beginning with the appointment of a territorial governor. The man chosen for the job was Andrew H. Reeder of Pennsylvania. Reeder was born in 1807, was a lawyer and a loyal Democrat, but had never served in any elected office. His selection was a way for Pierce to improve Democratic fortunes in Reeder's home state. Reeder was sworn in on July 7, 1854, in Washington.

When Reeder arrived at Fort Leavenworth on October 7, he went to a reception held by proslavery men. Reeder called the reception "a foreshadowing of kindness and confidence," then denounced the early stirring of violence between the factions and pledged to "crush it out or sacrifice myself in the effort." Reeder then embarked on a tour of the territory, which annoyed the proslavery partisans, who had hoped to be his only source of information. After the tour he had the territory divided into districts and set an election for a delegate to Congress for November 29, 1854.

That election would be the first in a series of territorial elections marred by fraud and violence. This was also the first time men from Missouri entered Kansas in large numbers to cast ballots. They seemed to have been motivated by rumors that New England abolitionists were forming "military colonies" to invade Missouri in order to prevent slavery's expansion.

As it happened, the leading contender for the seat was the proslavery candidate and Indian agent J. W. Whitfield. Despite the fact that antislavery voters in Kansas were not inclined to vote against him, Missourians entered Kansas Territory in large numbers on November 29. They not only took part in the voting, but also took command of the entire process. Daniel Wilder's *Annals*

Andrew Reeder was the first governor of Kansas Territory. Although he arrived a Democrat, he was quickly driven from the party in Kansas by proslavery activists. Like the third governor, John Geary, Reeder would become an opponent of the national Democratic Party. *Image courtesy the Kansas State Historical Society.*

of Kansas showed that in one polling place, "H. Sherman's," the 442 voters there cast only 82 votes. On the other hand, at "110," probably 110-Mile Station along the Santa Fe Trail, the 53 voters there cast over 600 votes. Whitfield was declared the delegate on December 5.

Following the November election came another set for March 30, 1855, to put a territorial legislature in place. Kansas was invaded again. Election judges were compelled to receive the ballots handed them, or they were removed, replaced by "judges" more pliant to the proslavery faction. It is alleged that 6,307 votes were cast on March 30. This was used as ammunition by abolitionists, who cited a February census that found a population of about 8,600 residents and just under 3,000 eligible voters. The result of the election was an overwhelmingly proslavery territorial legislature.

Governor Reeder did hear some protests on April 5, but he was besieged by partisans on both sides. The Free State men demanded that the election results be set aside and another, more secure, election held. The proslavery men countered that the governor did not have power to overturn the results, only to validate them. Reeder tried to steer a middle course, ruling that eight candidates would not be allowed to take seats in the legislature, but the rest of the results would stand. At this point the Free State men repudiated both Reeder and the territorial legislature.

The legislature assembled for the first time on July 2, 1855. They met in the village of Pawnee, along the Kansas River, close to Fort Riley. Reeder asked the members "to lay aside all selfish and equivocal motives" to take care of the territory's business. After just four days of work, with reports of cholera in Pawnee, the legislature adjourned to Shawnee Mission and resumed work on July 16.

In the meantime, the new elections ordered by Reeder had been held on May 22. The proslavery candidates refused to take part, so the Free Soil faction got its first victory, leading to a territorial legislature with twenty-eight proslavery members and eleven antislavery members. However, the Free Soil Party wished to deny the legislation legitimacy, and pressure from both sides was levied against the Free-Soilers to keep them from taking their seats.

The proslavery members were successful at ousting the Free Soil delegates. Nine were immediately unseated, their places filled by the men Reeder had denied entry. S. D. Houston remained as the lone holdout until July 22, when he resigned. As he did, he said that "to retain a seat in such circumstances" was "a condescension too inglorious for the spirit of an American freeman."

By this time Reeder had broken his ties to the legislature and the proslavery faction. In part this was due to their actions, but this was also a result of the fact that Reeder had a financial interest in Pawnee. The legislature stayed there for four days, just long enough to move the territorial capital to the Shawnee Indian Mission southwest of Kansas City, Missouri. Reeder objected to the move and retaliated by vetoing the bills they passed. One of the legislators, Benjamin Stringfellow, became so enraged that he attacked Reeder. Other legislators petitioned President Pierce for Reeder's removal. Pierce obliged on August 15, citing Reeder's land speculation at Pawnee.

With the troublesome Reeder gone, the territorial legislature at Shawnee Mission insured that slavery would not be undermined. Anyone who aided in the escape of a slave would get the death penalty. Questioning the right to hold slaves in Kansas was a felony. A voter would be disenfranchised if he declined to take an oath to support the Fugitive Slave Law. Benjamin Stringfellow wrote to an Alabama newspaper that these laws "silenced the Abolitionists" because "they know they will be enforced to the very letter and with the utmost vigor."

However, the Free State faction was not about to give in to such bullying. They held another meeting in Lawrence on June 8. There were resolutions against the illegal voting of the Border Ruffians from Missouri and for Kansas to become a Free State. They also passed a resolution stating, "That in reply to the threats of war so frequently made in our neighboring State, our answer is, We Are Ready." By this, they clearly meant that they were now arming themselves to defend their rights.

To that end Charles Robinson wrote to Eli Thayer on April 2. He told Thayer of how the Missourians had invaded Kansas and kept antislavery voters from the polls. He reported that in response they had "formed themselves into four military companies" and planned to "drill till they have perfected themselves in the art."

"It looks very much like war & I am ready for it & so are our people," Robinson wrote. "If they give us occasion to settle the question of slavery in this country with the bayonet let us improve it." To that end Robinson asked Thayer to find out if "your Secret Society" could send two hundred rifles and "a couple of field pieces."

Shortly after sending that letter Robinson sent his friend George W. Dietzler to New England for guns for the Free State men to protect themselves during the May 22 election. Money was raised from individuals and sympathetic churches. Some of the money came from congregants of Henry Ward Beecher's church. As Beecher had recently said that guns were as important in Kansas as Bibles, the weapons purchased with the donated money became known as "Beecher's Bibles."

The shipments of Beecher's Bibles were a clear sign that both sides were preparing for an escalation of the conflict over slavery in Kansas Territory. Neither side seemed willing to consider any compromise or accommodation. This then was the charged atmosphere that former congressman James Lane strode into when he arrived in the territory in the first half of 1855.

III.

A Democratic Gamble

Aside from his vote on the Kansas-Nebraska Act, Congressman James Lane was not a very visible politician. In fact, while the debates over the act were taking place, Lane had written a letter back home expressing his support of land grants to veterans of the War of 1812 and then returned to the practice of law in Indiana with a partner, John F. Detweiler.

Then in October he got into a dispute that turned violent. One Saturday night Lane walked up to John B. Vail and began to strike him with his cane. Lane then walked across the street to a barroom in the McCormick House. Vail went after him, demanding to know why Lane had struck him. Lane told Vail to "go away" and that "he would give him no explanation" for the attack, apparently hinting that Vail in fact knew its source. Lane raised his cane again, Vail drew a poker, and the two struggled. Lane backed Vail outside and onto the street, where Vail pulled out a pistol and shot Lane, giving him a superficial wound. The newspaper account contains no suggestion of what was at the heart of the argument.

Later in 1854 Lane was sued by one or more individuals. He apparently lost, for in January and February 1855 the local sheriff seized his property and sold it for payment of the suit. This matter apparently carried on for over a year, for in a local newspaper dated January 11, 1856, it was reported that Lane's "household property" was taken to be sold for additional payment for the suit.

This legal matter may have figured into Lane's decision to move west. Coupled with the Kansas-Nebraska Act's lack of popularity,

Lane may have felt his political fortunes in his home state were too low to carry him farther. Whatever his reasons, Jim Lane left Indiana for the new territory of Kansas in the spring of 1855.

Leverett Spring, although no Lane supporter, provided an interesting account of Lane's appearance in the territory in his piece on Lane's political career. Spring writes that Lane entered Lawrence on April 22, 1855, "alone and unannounced," riding "in a primitive, rickety buggy, drawn by an old, moccasin-colored horse, which, it is to be hoped, had seen better days." Lane was "lank, almost haggard in figure, and dressed in overalls," and someone looking at him "would have taken him for an itinerant day-laborer." He stopped his buggy in front of the office of the *Kansas Free State.*

He went inside and began asking about the village of Tecumseh, some twenty miles to the west. Almost immediately, Spring said, the men in the office began to wonder about their visitor. "The easy, assured manner of the stranger, his quick penetrating glance, the fluency and originality of his talk, soon dissipated any unfavorable conclusions which his country jeans and generally disreputable appearance may have suggested."

"Who are you anyway?" someone asked.

"My name is Lane," was the reply, "and I hail from Indiana."

Someone else in the office that day was also from Indiana and had heard of Lane. The man knew he was "far from being an itinerant day-laborer" but was "a man of considerable political and military prominence," a "stump-orator, presidential elector, lieutenant-governor, member of the lower house of Congress and colonel of two regiments of volunteers that won distinction in the Mexican war." The man may have known enough to understand Lane's explanation of his appearance.

"My route to the territory," Lane said, "lay through Missouri. I should have fared badly if I had been recognized. So I adopted this disguise of overalls and a round-about."

Apparently assured, the men in the office asked him why he should bother continuing on to Tecumseh, as "that town was still in the experimental stage and might come to nothing," Spring wrote. "Lawrence, on the contrary, had an assured future." Lane looked around the town, talked to several people, then made up his mind to stay. The next day he "published a card announcing the fact" that Lawrence would be his hometown.

A writer more favorable to Lane, William Cutler, provided his own explanation of why Lane had come to Kansas. In Indiana he had been "an ardent supporter of the Douglas bill and the doctrines of squatter sovereignty." But the uproar over his support of the Kansas-Nebraska Act caused him to decide "to leave his State and cast his lot with the new Territory he had helped to create."

Today it is generally accepted that Lane came to Kansas to organize the Democratic Party in the territory. Since his arrival, however, the questions of what sort of Democratic Party and who was propelling Lane's attempt have dogged authors and historians.

Sidney Clarke, one-time congressman from Kansas who knew Lane personally, speculated about just these questions when writing about Lane for a Kansas City newspaper in 1879. According to Clarke, one view was that Lane had arrived in Kansas under the general direction of national leaders of the Democrat Party. They had taken a beating since passage of the Kansas-Nebraska Act and sent Lane in a bid to recover "the fortunes of that party." This suggests that Lane's mission was to create a local organization that would adhere to the will of party leaders and not act on its own, as the Missourians had apparently done. Specifically, Clarke noted that Lane's arrival in Kansas was said to be at the behest of Stephen Douglas. Douglas was interested in running for president, and he wanted Democratic Party organizations that would be loyal to his bid.

This theory has long been the popular view of Lane's initial political efforts in Kansas. William Cutler suggested as much in his state history. Leverett Spring wrote that shortly after Lane appeared in Kansas, "the report got abroad that he had come at the instance of Senator Douglas and the administration to attempt the formation of a new, Anti-Southern Democratic party on the platform of 1852."

Interestingly enough, Lane biographer Wendell Stephenson would not go so far. He believed that Lane did relocate to Kansas to form a Northern-allied Democratic Party, but Stephenson thought Lane's only motive was to obtain "political preferment at its hands." He was unsure if Lane had come to Kansas at anyone's behest or if he arrived on his own initiative. He did admit that while there was no evidence of Lane's ties to Senator Douglas or President Pierce, Lane did make such claims and therefore "it is difficult to see how he would assume such a position without any authority, when it would imperil the cause he was advocating from its inception."

The most detailed account of this story occurs in the 1885 book *The Grim Chieftain of Kansas*. It is now certain it was written by Reeder M. Fish, one of Lane's friends. Among the incidents of the territorial period recalled by Fish is the alleged conversation that Senator Douglas had with Congressman Lane to persuade him to vote for the Kansas-Nebraska bill. Fish's narrative contains plenty of firsthand information—such as Lane telling Douglas that one of the Indiana Democratic Party leaders was nicknamed John Lard Oil because he had whiskey shipped to him in barrels marked "lard oil"—but it is presented as a drama between two characters, rather than as a conversation between two men.

Early on in the book, Douglas states that his purpose in meeting with Lane was to convince him to support the bill. Lane replies that "such is the opposition of my constituents to the repeal of the Missouri compromise that it would be nothing short of political suicide for me to support your bill." Douglas asks him if the opposition was from "abolitionists" and might be "ephemeral," to which Lane says that it comes from "nearly all the leading Democrats of my district." Douglas counters that if Lane were to vote against his bill, the congressman would be "a bolting candidate" against the national party and "a regular Democratic candidate" would go against him at the fall election. Lane responds to the threat by stating that he would not "sacrifice myself and all my prospects" for Douglas's bill so long as other Democrats in Washington oppose it and as long as the people of his district do so too.

It is at that point in the conversation that Douglas dangled the prospect of a Senate seat in front of Congressman Lane. The senator told Lane he was certain that within a year Kansas would be admitted to the union. He and other party leaders wanted "some first-class young man" to organize a Democratic Party in the new territory. Douglas told Lane he wanted him to do the job, promising "the support of the administration" if he took it on. Douglas even assured Lane that if he went he would be "dictator of the party" in Kansas, determining the other senator, controlling who took federal posts, and having a powerful national standing.

Lane appeared intrigued. Douglas added that if Lane accepted the task he would have to go to Kansas without an official position but as "a private citizen." He would have to issue a call for a Democratic convention himself and take charge of it. If he did so, Douglas promised, the "president will recognize your organization as the legitimate Democratic party of Kansas." But Lane would have to do so secretly. He had already made his position on the Kansas-Nebraska bill clear, and that would mark him as an enemy to Southern politicians. To counter that, Douglas told Lane to go so far as to attempt to buy slaves in Missouri. He did not have to go through with the purchase, so long as he made sure people knew of the attempt.

Perhaps to reassure Lane that there was no danger from those Southern Democrats, Douglas then expressed his view that his bill might make slavery "possible in Kansas" but "not at all probable." There would be more settlers going to Kansas from "the North and West" than from the South. The legal question of slavery in the territories, what would become known as the Dred Scott case, was not yet resolved, so it was "foolish" to bring slaves to Kansas until then. Douglas was certain that by that time Kansas would have become a Free State. He was supposedly so confident he even promised that Lane could run for president "after my second term."

Lane admitted that he was "very much impressed" with Douglas's careful planning. But there was still the problem of his stated opposition, which if he changed his stand now, "people would think and say I was bought." Douglas replied that he would have the president send word to party officials in Lane's district to give Lane new instructions favoring passage of the bill. Lane then agreed to Douglas's scheme, changed his vote when new orders from his district came, and went to Kansas with the support and encouragement of Senator Douglas.

Some backing for Fish's view on this matter comes from an 1866 piece on Lane that appeared in a Leavenworth newspaper. The article stated that Lane had been "inclined" to oppose the Kansas-Nebraska Act, but "yielding to the solicitation of party friends, the

rigor of party discipline, and a quasi instruction from his constituents," he supported it. In light of what Fish wrote, the latter of
those three reasons is quite interesting.

William Connelley, in his 1899 book about Lane, found an
undated article written by Milton Reynolds, a later associate of
Lane's. Among the aspects of Lane's life about which Reynolds
wrote was the story of Lane being sent to Kansas by Douglas. On
one hand, Reynolds said he believed any reports of this connection were "myths, fictions, and vain imaginings of those who would
further mystify" Lane's character. On the other hand, Reynolds
said that if the stories were true, Kansas history still would have
turned out much as it did.

Whatever the truth of this story, what is known is that Lane's
effort to get the Democratic Party under way took place in
Lawrence on July 27, 1855. The meeting was held in the office of
one Dr. J. N. O. P. Wood. Lane was elected president of the meeting. One attendee moved to create a committee to draft resolutions stating the views of the party. Here are some of those
resolutions, as published in Cutler's 1883 history of Kansas:

> Resolved, That in the opinion of this meeting, the best inter-
> ests of Kansas required an early organization of the Democratic
> party upon truly national ground, and that we pledge ourselves
> to use all honorable exertions to secure such a result. . . .
> Resolved, That we indorse the principles of the Kansas-
> Nebraska Bill, and claim the right, unmolested, of exercising all
> the powers granted to us under the provisions of that bill. . . .
> Resolved, That as true American citizens, we can appreciate
> the rights of the citizens of the different States of this Union,
> both of the North and South, and that by no act of ours will we
> trample upon those rights or interfere in anywise with their
> domestic institutions.
> Resolved, That, while we observe the rights of the citizens of
> the different States, we will expect them to reciprocate. That we
> feel we are fully capable of managing our own affairs, and kind-
> ly request the citizens of Northern, Southern, distant and adjoin-
> ing States to let us alone.
> Resolved, That while making this request, we wish it distinct-
> ly understood that we appreciate the right of suffrage as the
> most important privilege guaranteed to us by the founders of

our institutions, and that we regard the ballot-box as the palladium of our liberty, and will not, if in our power to prevent, permit the privilege to be wrested from us, or permit the ballot-box to be polluted by outsiders or illegal voting from any quarter.

The most obvious point missing from these resolutions is a statement on slavery itself. This silence allowed later writers to interpret the convention's views. Leverett Spring in his *Prelude to the War for the Union* wrote that the convention accepted "as a foregone conclusion that Kansas would become a slave state if its soil should prove to be adapted to servile labor." But William Cutler said that the convention's purpose was to prevent Free State Democrats from being drawn into the Free State movement, which clearly suggests Lane and the other attendees were opposed to slavery in Kansas.

Both Cutler and Milton Reynolds noted that Lane's convention largely failed to organize the Democratic Party as he had wanted. Cutler wrote that a local Democratic newspaper, "intensely proslavery," denounced the convention and warned its readers that Lane's effort was "calculated to divide and weaken the Pro-slavery forces." Reynolds noted that the effort was "ridiculed by the Democratic organs" in the area.

An Eastern newspaper clipping in the Thomas Webb Scrapbooks at the Kansas State Historical Society provides another view of the meeting's failure. This story said that the convention's organization—attributed to Mark Delahay of Illinois—was carried out by "Douglas men to organize a National Democratic party" in Kansas Territory. The meeting went nowhere because "Slavery or no Slavery" was the only "practicable" political issue in territorial politics. It added that "much to the surprise of many," Delahay and others had "suddenly united" with the Free State movement.

This view was similar to those expressed in the two major antislavery newspapers in the territory. In late June the *Herald of Freedom* in Lawrence expressed "regret" at news of plans for a Democratic organization coming to its attention. "Such a movement can result in no good to any one, but may do much damage," the editorial said, adding as the Eastern paper did that there was only one important issue in territorial politics. The *Kansas Free State* of Lawrence, reporting on the meeting in September, called the meeting a failure, wrote that "we meet with scarcely a man who acknowledges that he is a member of the National Democratic party," and noted that the factions were already divided along the lines of the slavery question.

Clearly Lane's gamble on forming a Democratic Party in Kansas that might align itself with Senator Douglas and the president while still being an antislavery organization failed to pay off. It would be up to him to decide whether he would remain with the Democrats or join the growing Free State movement.

Of Lane's views on the slavery issue at the time, Lloyd Lewis thought that Lane was "an Antislavery Democrat" in the mold of those who "on the hard and bony knees of Old Hickory [Andrew Jackson] had learned to hate the Secessionists of the Deep South." However, Leverett Spring wrote that Lane was "pro-slavery in sentiment, boasting that he would as readily buy a negro as a mule, [and] conceding the legality of the territorial legislature." Spring alleged elsewhere that Lane "was in the habit of denouncing" Free Staters as "the offscouring and scum of Northern society." William Cutler's history countered that view, for he wrote that Lane "took no prominent part in politics" when he first arrived in Kansas. Instead Lane bided his time, "taking no positive ground toward either faction beyond the point of safe retreat."

Author Jay Monaghan, writing in his book *Civil War on the Western Border*, quoted two sources about Lane's view of the issue. Someone from Lane's home state of Indiana said that Lane had "vowed" to make Kansas a Free State. The other retold the story about Lane coming to the territory at the behest of President Pierce and Senator Douglas to turn Kansas into a "free Democratic" state. But after noting that his first two sources were "hindsight recollections," Monaghan wrote that Lane had "announced publicly that he had come to look for a location to raise hemp, and that for working the soil he knew no difference between a Negro and a mule."

However, even biographers who at times argued for the truth of Lane's proslavery sentiments found evidence to the contrary. Leverett Spring in his article on Lane's Kansas career provided a counter to his own remarks on Lane's view of slavery. Spring recounted an incident in Nebraska in 1856 when Lane, addressing a crowd that included proslavery Missourians, told them that he was once a proponent of slavery. His view changed when he and a carpenter visited the owner of a sugar plantation looking for work. When told of the reason for their visit, the plantation owner explained that he had bought two carpenters the previous day. Lane then wondered to the crowd, "If such men are buying carpenters, machinists, engineers, how soon will they sell you and me in their marts of human merchandise!"

Spring also claimed that something else turned Lane against the proslavery party. "Five days after the convention," he wrote, Lane went to Pawnee because for "some whimsical reason he wished to obtain a divorce from his wife." Lane expected to be granted a divorce by the proslavery legislature, "but he was disappointed." Spring wrote that a member of the territorial legislature said "that the rebuff which Lane experienced at Pawnee was the turning-point in his Kansas career." Spring said that "the affair scarcely deserves any such prominence," and that it "must be considered merely as an incident." Yet the fact that he went into this "mere incident" suggests that Spring gave it some credence as to Lane's motivation.

So did Albert Richardson, who went so far as to state that Lane "came to make Kansas a slave state," but when his divorce was not granted he switched sides. The root of all these stories about the divorce may be John Stringfellow, if a story in an 1879 issue of the *Kansas Chief* of Troy can be believed. The *Chief* quoted a St. Joseph, Missouri, newspaper in which Stringfellow made the divorce accusation. The cautionary note to this source is that Stringfellow was the brother of proslavery partisan B. F. Stringfellow and was coeditor of a proslavery Atchison newspaper.

Wendell Stephenson, in researching his 1930 biography of Lane, could find no historical evidence that Lane had petitioned for a divorce to the territorial legislature. He also noted that the legislature during its session voted to refuse to grant any divorce petitions.

In fact it wasn't Jim Lane who petitioned for divorce but his wife, Mary. The petition was not filed until a year after the alleged refusal described above and was filed in Indiana. It was published in an August issue of one of the main proslavery newspapers in the territory, the *Lecompton Union*. In the petition Mrs. Lane accused her husband of abandonment of herself and their children. It is unclear whether he abandoned them in Kansas, in the Kansas City area, or in Indiana. What is clear is that Mary Lane changed her last name back to Baldridge, that Jim Lane was ordered to pay three hundred dollars in alimony, and that custody of their children was split.

To some degree these remarks concerning Lane's point of view in the summer of 1855 have to be taken with several grains of salt. Lane was a politician with ambitions to high office. It would not have helped his career for him to express negative views on slavery to an audience in proslavery Missouri. Naturally enough, rival politicians in search of mud to sling at Lane would have wanted to use such comments to question his sincerity and trustworthiness. It is a very old trick of adversarial politics to take out of context statements an opponent makes. It would be remarkable indeed if Lane's enemies never resorted to such tricks. Perhaps what is remarkable is that the authors and historians critical of Lane accepted these political tricks at face value.

Additionally, in Lane's native Indiana, as in most of the Western frontier north of the Ohio River, opposition to slavery was based on economic beliefs instead of moral principles. Westerners viewed slave labor as unfair competition to wage labor and plantations as a method of displacing individual farms. This ideology was also tinged with racism, namely that black slaves competed for farm jobs with white laborers and that free blacks competed with white men for urban employment. Lane had to have grown up with those beliefs, and even if he did not share them, the politician in him would not have allowed him to openly disagree with real or potential constituents who held those beliefs.

Furthermore, if Lane did indeed arrive in Kansas in disguise or under an assumed name, those precautions suggest he had something to hide while en route to the territory. If he really did think that Kansas could or should become a Slave State, then he ought to have gone through Missouri openly. However, since he went through the state quietly, keeping his name and place of origin secret, that would seem to indicate that he was not, as Missourians of the time would say, "all right on the hemp."

This appears to be how John Speer viewed his friend's early

thoughts on the slavery issue. When he asked in his 1896 book on Lane if he was "a pro-slavery man," Speer answered that while "ultra abolition" types might have thought so, that was in comparison to their own stance. Lane was "no more pro-slavery" than President Pierce or Senator Douglas, nor Henry Clay, a powerful politician of the era of Lane's father. Speer noted that Clay had once said that he "would rather be instrumental in relieving his country of the great stain of slavery than to be a conquering hero."

Speer believed that because Lane had the "odium" of having voted for the Kansas-Nebraska Act, many of slavery's foes in Kansas held that against him. "His democracy might have been forgiven," Speer wrote of Lane's party-line vote, "but the sin of breaking down the 'Missouri Compromise'" was harder to get past. Yet if "we had tabooed all the men holding the views of Lane," he added, "we would have neither statesmen, nor [an] army, nor [a] navy."

There is one interesting aspect of the matter that emerged in a letter John Brown, Jr., wrote for the twenty-fifth anniversary of Kansas statehood. In that letter Brown tells of a conversation he had with Lane early in 1856. Lane was a candidate for senator along with Andrew Reeder as part of a Free State movement to oppose the established territorial government. He wanted Brown's vote in his favor, but Brown was reluctant to give it.

Lane asked Brown if he had "anything against me that would deprive me of your vote?"

"Gen. Lane, I will frankly tell you that I have not, at least during a part of our acquaintance, had a good opinion of you."

"Why?"

"Well, do you remember the speech you made last summer in Lawrence, in which you said that, 'so far as the rights of property are concerned, I know of no difference between a negro and a mule.' I heard you say that."

"Well, Brown, I've felt like kicking myself ever since."

But at that point, perhaps because of Lane's actions since that speech, Brown told him that he had already decided to vote for him, suggesting that for at least one member of the Brown family, deeds counted far more than words. It also suggests indirectly that Lane's views on slavery were evolving, or that his remarks on the issue had been misinterpreted by friends and foes alike.

James Lane's views on slavery might be a puzzle. But the man's appearance was more distinctive and his abilities close to famous.

Richard J. Hinton, who served alongside Lane as a military aide in 1864, described Lane physically as "tall, spare and sinewy. His frame is muscular and nervous. . . . high cheekbones, square chin, . . . deep-set eyes of grey and hazel combined, they are full of magnetic fire." English reporter Thomas Gladstone described Lane in 1856 as a "young man, full of impetuosity and firey [sic] daring" who had "devoted himself with great spirit to" the effort to make Kansas a Free State.

Kansas author Noble Prentis, who knew well Lane's portrait, once wrote that Lane "does not look like any of the others" whose pictures were held by the Kansas State Historical Society. Prentis observed that Lane's hair "stands out in every direction" like a minstrel's wig. "The mouth suggests imprecations and nicotine, the eyes anything you like. There is a suggestion of recklessness about the visage."

Lloyd Lewis said his research uncovered a person who was "a strange, magnetic man in his middle forties, six feet tall, slender, wiry, nervous, tremendously alive. He burst with vitality—his voice was hypnotic. His hair was long and reckless, and above his ears black locks curled like horns." Lewis added that Lane could even impress "hostile audiences," able to "rise in front of a crowd where Western rivermen and horsemen stood fingering their revolvers and vowing to kill him, and within thirty minutes he would have them shouting 'yea' to a resolution endorsing him for President of the United States."

Albert Richardson provided an interesting personal portrait of Lane compiled from his own experiences as well as from talking to others. He described this new Kansas politician as being "zealous without convictions, pungent, firey [sic], [and] magnetic," with a "thin, wiry form." Richardson described one aspect of Lane's personality that he credited for his eventual success. Lane "had a sinister face, plain to ugliness," but "he could talk away his face in twenty minutes." He explained, "His personal magnetism was wonderful, and he manipulated men like wax."

This descriptions leads to what was most remarkable about Jim Lane: he was a powerful speaker. One man, T. W. Higginson, saw

Lane speak in Nebraska in 1856. Historian Leverett Spring quoted him as saying, "if eloquence consists in moving and swaying men at pleasure I never saw a more striking exhibition of it." Spring himself wrote,

> Lane's oratory faithfully reflected the character of the man, in which elements of chaos and lunacy were bound up with extraordinary astuteness and knowledge of human nature. It owed little to elocutionary grace. His manner was strained, angular, and dramatic, while his voice vibrated between shouts and blood-curdling whispers. Neither weight of thought, nor subtlety of logic, nor elevation of sentiment, nor exceptional range of vocabulary, appeared in his oratory.

Spring was no supporter of Lane, but even he conceded that Lane "had no equal" on the stump. "Types can do only scant justice to oratory that is essentially personal," Spring said many years later, "and hence his speeches lose in print." Lane had "sure tact in humoring the prejudices and firing the passions of an audience; unmeasured invective; an intensity of utterance that sometimes reached the verge of frenzy; grotesque, extravagant, ringing turns of phrase, and what, in the absence of a better word, is called magnetism."

Verres Smith, in the March 1870 issue of *Lippincott's Magazine,* provided direct quotes from some of Lane's speeches to illustrate his point that the man "was the most finished actor I ever saw." He would start by referring to himself in the third person, such as, "They say Jim Lane is illiterate." He would rebut the point, in that case by saying that "his mother was a Connecticut schoolmarm and a most devout Methodist, and from his youth up he was most carefully educated for the Christian ministry." Then came the kicker, sure to get a laugh from the crowd, "but his modesty, his insuperable modesty, kept him out of the pulpit!"

Noble Prentis spoke to those who knew him and reported that Lane would often punctuate phrases with a shriek of "Great God." Lane also "purposely mispronounced well-known names" as part of his oratorical bag of tricks. Prentis wrote that state supreme court justice Samuel Kingman once told him that Lane could "stand up before a crowd of five hundred men, two hundred and fifty of whom are all ready to hang him to the next tree, and, at the end of half an hour, have them all cheering for him." This assertion was supported by another man who knew Lane, J. M. Hubbard. Hubbard was quoted in a piece about Lawrence minister and author James Horton in 1904 and said that he had known of no one except Lane who could "soothe dissatisfaction, quell discontent and reconcile conflicting interests" among slavery's opponents in Kansas.

Sidney Clarke did know Lane as both a political ally and personal friend. Clarke believed that Lane was as much an actor as a public speaker. "If he had been educated for the stage he had all the natural qualifications to have taken the first rank among the great actors of modern times," he wrote. Hubbard witnessed a bit of that acting during a speech. At one point Lane cast off his coat while speaking. A short time later Lane tossed off his vest, and not long after that, the cravat around his neck, all seeming to punctuate his remarks. James Horton added that he saw such a performance by Lane on more than one occasion.

Lane followed a formulaic approach to speeches that was popular during his time, but it was his unique ability to captivate a crowd that made him such an influential leader. As Lloyd Lewis put it, the formula for stump speeches in Lane's time was: "Get up, say that somebody had said something about you, repeat it twice, and then say 'it ain't so.'" Verres Smith provided two examples in his 1870 piece. To the charge that he was a libertine, Lane replied, "Why, when he was twenty-one years old he had never smoked a cigar, sworn an oath or kissed a girl!" When accused of being a profane man, Lane said, "Great God! What! Jim Lane an irreligious man?" He then admitted that he swore just once, at the Battle of Buena Vista. When faced with "acres and acres of Mexicans," he told the men of his Indiana regiment, "Charge on 'em, God d—n 'em!"

Smith went on to list two more strengths of Lane's speaking skills. Smith wrote that it might "astonish" his readers to know "that scholarly men and men of travel would pronounce him the most pleasing person they ever met, though there was not a common thought between them." A paragraph later Smith said that Lane had a "marvelous" ability to adjust himself to fit his audience. "In Kansas he wore the fells of wild beasts," but in Boston, Lane wore "black broadcloth and white cravat, and whined through his nose" like a New England parson. Smith added that it was when Lane came to Kansas that he began to prefer "Jim Lane" to "James Lane," in part because of its "easy condescension," and to avoid confusion with a cousin named Henry S. Lane.

Lane lived in a time when it was far more important for a politician to be able to move a crowd than to address them eloquently. Only after his death, when newspapers were being published in every city and town and avidly read by the population, would it be more important to have good speeches written than to give a rousing address to a crowd.

But not everyone liked this man who could speak so powerfully and passionately. Hannah Ropes, a contemporary who wrote about the Kansas troubles as they were occuring, said of Lane, "If there is any good in him, I never, with all my industry in culling something pleasant from the most unpropitious characters, have been able to make the discovery."

John J. Ingalls was more ambivalent toward Lane's character. He once wrote that Lane's "oratory was voluble and incessant, without logic, learning, rhetoric, or grace; but the multitudes to whom he perpetually appealed hung upon his hoarse and harsh harangues with the rapture of devotees." Ingalls conceded that Lane had "an extraordinary assemblage of mental, moral, and physical traits," but was a "lean, haggard, and sinewy figure with a Mephistophelian leer" who in religious matters "partook of the sacrament as a political device."

While Lane left bad impressions with some, to others he was a great man. Lloyd Lewis described him this way:

> There was always the hint of Mephistopheles about him—or of Dionysus, the god of revelry, who loved the plain people and spent his life with them. His eyes baffled men who tried to describe them—they were deep-set and dull when he was quiet; black diamonds, reporters called them, when he was speaking. The touch of genius and its cousin, madness, always there somewhere behind the glaze or the flame.
>
> He had a wide, loose mouth, as mobile as that of a Shakespearian "ham" actor. He was, indeed, an actor, an artist— perhaps a great artist. Astute critics thought him the man of his time who could sway crowds most wholly to his will. A curious

mesmerism would flow out from his gestures, his voice, his thoughts, a magnetic overtone that held crowds laughing, weeping or gritting their teeth, just as he willed. His voice could be a bugle call, or a lullaby.

He had what all great artists have—the power to make the thing they imagine and conceive pass out from themselves and possess other minds.

Again and again is it recorded that Jim Lane's enemies feared to meet him lest they be charmed out of their principles. . . . For after you have heard all the topsy-turvy tales about Jim Lane, even believed all the half-affectionate, half-scornful anecdotes of his stormy career, even accepted all the stories of his riffraffish, scalawagism as partly true, you cannot laugh him off, or brush him aside. Always a figure of titanic accomplishment comes striding back through the fog. For when everything has been said and done, it was Jim Lane, more than any other man, who made Kansas free soil. He was the organizer of victory; he was the shrewd, scheming politician who knew what weakling to buy and what strong man to inspire.

Wrote Sidney Clarke in 1879, "He could speak in a peculiar whisper, which could be heard in the largest hall, or with a voice so electric and powerful that it seemed to his [listeners] as irresistible as a mighty torrent." That, in Clarke's view, made Lane the leader among all the qualified men in the Free State movement.

John Speer knew Lane better than anyone outside his family. In his biography of his friend, one of the first personal statements about Lane that he made was not about his speaking style or appearance, but his abstaining from alcohol. "So remarkable was this as a characteristic," Speer wrote, "that, in speaking of it to his daughter, she expressed surprise at the idea that he ever partook of liquor at all."

But if James Lane had no fondness for drink, Speer observed that he did like chewing tobacco. He recalled a story told to him by a Topeka lawyer. As a young man the lawyer attended a religious camp meeting at which Lane spoke. During the meeting Lane rose and once again spoke of his beloved mother and the prayers she had taught him. He moved the crowd with his testimonial, then sat down and allowed the minister running the meeting to continue his sermon. The minister turned to the subject of "all the vices that humanity is heir to," wrote Speer, and eventually turned to "the vice of tobacco." Lane was apparently so moved by the preaching that he pulled out "a foot of dog-leg tobacco" and passed it forward. The minister was ecstatic. "We will cast this vile weed to the four winds of Heaven!" the minister shouted, and he tossed the tobacco away. The young man and a friend tried to find the plug of tobacco afterward. "They searched all through the brush and weeds," Speer said, "but the weed of weeds was lost." The next day the man went to a Lane caucus, and lo and behold there was the man "chewing apparently the same dog-leg piece" he had tossed out the night before.

Perhaps the best summary of Jim Lane came from Samuel Reader. Reader was in 1856 a very young man who served with Lane at what would come to be called the Battle of Hickory Point. Writing later, Reader aptly noted, "General Lane's friends called him a clear-headed, heroic champion of our cause; his enemies the reverse. He was and still is, a puzzle." Though critical of Lane's actions at a skirmish in 1856, Reader admitted that he had been "swayed" by his "subtle influence," and that there was "a secret pleasure in the knowledge that I was one of 'Jim Lane's boys.'"

IV.

Lane, the Free-Soil Man

With the failure of his effort to create a Democratic Party, Jim Lane faced a choice. "Apparently he must either abandon the territory or make terms with the antislavery people," Spring wrote succinctly.

Antislavery forces throughout Kansas were engaged in efforts to organize during the summer of 1855. Between June 8 and August 15, seven Free State conventions were held in Lawrence. According to contemporary historian R. G. Elliott, on July 17 several Free Staters met at the office of the *Kansas Free State* newspaper in Lawrence to discuss plans for their antislavery movement. So many of them showed up that the office could not hold them all, so they decided to go to the banks of the Kansas River at the end of New Hampshire Street. Because of that move the meeting became known as the "Sand Bank Convention."

Elliott was present at the meeting and later wrote that Lane was there as well. Lane, said Elliott, didn't want his presence at the meeting published, perhaps because he was still trying to organize an antislavery Democratic Party. The general sentiment of the meeting was that the various antislavery political groups in the territory ought to form a unified political party. Not everyone present supported the notion, most especially John Speer, but he changed his mind by mid-August.

Perhaps the most important of these Free State meetings occurred on July 11. There were unanimous statements about "the illegality of the Legislature" and repudiation of its work. But this time Charles Robinson and others began to call for the drafting of a state constitution. The gathering decided to call a Free State meeting for August 14 to consider the notion of establishing a Free State government. It would be at that meeting that Jim Lane would leave the Democratic Party behind and cast his lot with the Free State political movement.

According to William Cutler, the convention began at ten o'clock on the morning of August 14. Philip C. Schuller, of Council Grove, was elected president of the convention. Several vice-presidents were elected, including George W. Smith and Martin F. Conway, and George W. Brown and John Speer became the secretaries. The rest of the morning was dominated by the formation of a "Committee on Resolutions" and the reading of a letter from Samuel D. Houston, the Free State legislator who had resigned. The afternoon session was taken up mainly with speeches that were, in Cutler's words, "strong and uncompromising in their Free-state utterances."

On the heels of those speeches came Jim Lane, who in his own speech, said, "It requires wisdom, it requires manhood to restrain passion. I say it as a citizen of Kansas, I wish we had wisdom to-day. There is the existence of a union hanging upon the action of the citizens of Kansas. Moderation, moderation, moderation, gentlemen!" Later he said, "I desire Kansas to be a free State. I desire to act with my brethren, but not in a manner to arouse the passions of the people of the other States. I would not repudiate the Legislature, but the acts of that Legislature which contravene the rights of popular sovereignty."

"The speech of Col. Lane was not received with full favor by the members of the convention," Cutler wrote, "who, from his previous record, his late attempts to organize the Democratic party, and from the guarded, cautious and somewhat ambiguous terms of his speech, were inclined to distrust the sincerity of his motives."

There were more speeches until Charles Robinson came up with a series of resolutions for the convention to approve. The resolutions began by asserting that the Kansas-Nebraska Act had given "the lawful inhabitants" of Kansas Territory the power "to make such laws and establish such institutions as would be most suitable to themselves." However, "the Territory was invaded and the inhabitants overwhelmed by large and numerous bands of armed men from a foreign State, who violently took possession of nearly all" the polling places, "ruthlessly abolished the legally established mode of conducting" the election, and with "utter disregard of the act of Congress" carried out the election. The territorial legislature chosen was "now in session on the borders of the State of Missouri, making laws for the governance of the inhabitants and citizens of Kansas."

There followed six points on which the delegates had to vote as part of the resolution. The first denounced the March 30 election and the legislature chosen by it. The second and third repudiated the legislature's legitimacy. The fourth called for unity among antislavery residents in word and deed. The fifth point was the most dramatic step, as it called for "the people of the Territory" to "elect delegates to a convention to form a State constitution." The last point lauded Governor Reeder "for the firmness, ability and integrity shown in the discharge of his duty as Executive officer of this Territory."

The only dissension on these points came from a minority who had objections to the call for a Free State constitutional convention. William Cutler, in his account of this convention, said that the minority was not concerned about "the advisability of the movement so much as to the primary source from which the call should emanate." This dissent could be explained, wrote Cutler, because at the convention were "Free-state Democrats, Free-state Whigs, straight Abolitionists, moderate Free-soilers," and "many Pro-slavery settlers who, in the interest of law and order, condemned the outrages and despised the assumed authority of the Legislature."

The convention, upon hearing the resolutions, began to vote on each. The first was approved without trouble, but on the second "an animated discussion ensued, interspersed with motions from" Lane and Cyrus K. Holliday "to refer back to the committee or a new committee." At that point the convention adjourned for the day.

During the night tensions were eased, as Holliday brought forth a plan to "remedy all defects" in the resolutions. Lane still opposed the resolutions; according to Cutler, "he desired to oppose the acts of the Legislature in a legal way." But his objections were overcome and Lane even made a motion to adopt the fifth resolution. Once the resolutions were approved, John Speer put forward a motion for a delegate meeting to be held in Big Springs on September 5 to attempt to create a Free State political party.

That night, August 15, a "Ratification Convention" was held in the public hall in Lawrence. Cutler wrote that the meeting "was a regular 'love feast'" and "a general ratification of all that had been done by everybody during the past two days."

The meetings in Lawrence and the planned convention were part of an attempt by the opponents of slavery to decide how best to resist their foes politically. Historian and author James Malin found that a division amongst the factions developed over whether to form a political party to challenge territorial elections or to form a statehood movement. The purpose of these meetings was for leaders to gauge public sentiment and come to some agreement concerning their political approach. With the groundwork laid, slavery opponents from around Kansas headed for Big Springs in early September to establish a single political party.

The territorial legislature, as noted previously, also stepped up to the task of putting pressure on the Free Staters. These measures might have sustained the enthusiasm of the proslavery movement, but they would also prove a propaganda boon to the Free State cause. Nevertheless, as the summer of 1855 came to a close, slavery's supporters in the territory were in charge. They found further assistance, although perhaps inadvertent, from the next governor of Kansas territory.

Daniel Woodson had served as the acting governor until a replacement for Andrew Reeder had been appointed. The post was first offered to Pennsylvanian John Dawson on July 31 but he declined, so it was then offered to Wilson Shannon, who accepted on August 10. Wilson Shannon had been born in Ohio in 1802, was a lawyer, had been governor of Ohio and a minister to Mexico, and served one term in Congress alongside James Lane. Leverett Spring called Shannon "a lawyer of good repute," but while Shannon's "sympathies and instincts" leaned "toward whatever is just and honorable," he was "a tenacious, unwavering Democrat of the old school."

Shannon's first appearance in the region was on September 1, when he arrived in Westport. He gave a speech to a largely proslavery crowd, offering support to the territorial legislature and, according to William Cutler, "avowed himself as in favor of 'slavery in Kansas.'" Shortly thereafter Shannon "publicly denied the utterances as reported," but his speech may have created the impression among the Free State faction that the new governor sympathized with their opponents. This in turn may have caused them to assume that the whole territorial government was against them.

The convention got under way on September 5 in what, at the time, was a small settlement along the Oregon Trail in northwest Douglas County. The village later was described by one author as "a place of four or five shake-cabins and log-huts." Delegates from all over, including proslavery bastions such as Lecompton, attended the convention. Everyone was armed, to the point that when one, while "at the rude country hotel" in the village, asked the landlady for his coat, she told him to get it himself, replying that she "'would not touch that armory for all the property in the room.'"

The convention convened at eleven o'clock. The morning session was dominated by the creation of two committees, one on credentials and one on a permanent organization. In the afternoon came the report from the credentials committee, which listed James H. Lane among the delegates from the First District. After a reading of the list of delegates, G. W. Smith was elected president of the convention. Once the president and the other officers officially took their seats, a series of committees was appointed, among them the Committee on Platform. The chairman was James Lane.

Lane critic Leverett Spring said that he had "intrigued himself" into the position. R. G. Elliott, who was present at the convention, later wrote that this was a "misapprehension of the character" of the sentiment at the time. The convention's purpose was to harmonize the "diverse elements" of the antislavery movement, mainly the progressive abolitionists with the conservative Westerners. What's more, Elliott believed that the Westerners' view was the majority view there and in the territory. Who else ought to lead the committee but a Westerner, and who else but the most experienced politician among them?

The next day the convention began at nine with a reading of the minutes and a minor discussion about the rules, in which Lane took part. Then came Lane's report on the platform his committee had drafted. It began by stating that as the opponents of slavery in Kansas were "about to originate an organization for concert of political action in electing our officers and molding our institutions," it was "expedient and necessary that a platform of principles be adopted." Since "the great and overshadowing question whether Kansas shall become a free or a slave State must inevitably absorb all other issues except those inseparably connected with it," the platform was to hold to that issue and no other.

The platform contained seven resolutions. The first urged Free State unity. The second called for resistance to further invasions. The third stated that Kansas's "true interests" required that Kansas "should be a free State," that "slave labor is a curse to the master and the community, if not the slave," "that our country is unsuited to it," and that party members should "devote our energies" toward excluding slavery. The fourth resolution was a slight concession, promising "fair and reasonable provision in regard to the slaves already in the Territory."

It would be the fifth, sixth, and seventh resolutions that would become controversial. The fifth stated that "the best interests of Kansas required a population of free white men" and expressed support for "stringent laws excluding all negroes, bond and free, from the Territory." The sixth pledged to "discountenance and denounce" any attempts at full-blown abolitionism and to support federal laws calling for the return of escaped slaves. The seventh and final resolution declared that "the stale and ridiculous charge of abolitionism, so industriously imputed to the Free-state party, and so pertinaciously adhered to in spite of all the evidence to the contrary, is without a shadow of truth to support it."

William Cutler wrote that Lane's committee report "was adopted unanimously with enthusiastic cheers." Alice Nichols wrote that the sixth resolution was approved by a vote of ninety-nine to one. That resolution was an expression of what was called "black law" and it would be the subject of much debate in later years, especially when it came to Lane's support of it. Typical of the anti-Lane authors was Leverett Spring, who claimed the provision's adoption was due to "Lane's negropbobia" and that thanks to Lane the convention's "anti-slaveryism was of a diluted milk-and-water type."

A later author who generally took Spring at his word, Alice Nichols, did not entirely buy this view of Lane and the black law. She conceded that most of the delegates were farmers working "single handed" and were unwilling "to compete with large holdings using slave labor." Historian and author James Malin wrote that the platform "reflected dominant western sentiment" at Big Springs, that the platform committee was "dominated by westerners," and that therefore "whatever influence Lane exerted" conformed to the majority's expectations. These views were echoed by author Albert Richardson, who noted that most of the Free Staters were not "against slavery in the abstract" but opposed "only to slavery in Kansas." They were in "deadly terror of being termed 'abolitionists'" and afraid of "negro equality" but saw "unpaid labor [as] prejudicial to the interests of their forming State."

Those Western men were largely emigrants from the states north of the Ohio River and west of the Appalachians. Their newspaper was the *Kansas Free State*. To its readers slavery was not a moral issue but an economic one. Opposition to slavery should be based on the "facts" that slavery "paralyzes the hand of industry," "drives all energy and enterprise from its presence, and substitutes idleness." Slavery would make Kansas a backward place with cheap property, no public schools, and diminished upward economic mobility. Added to that view was the belief that the New England abolitionists, "the people of Eastern cities," were trying to teach morals to "an inferior order of people, unfit for social intercourse," namely Westerners.

The contrasts between the two factions of the Free State movement can be seen in how the two Lawrence newspapers interpreted the black-law provisions. The *Herald of Freedom* of September 3 stated that it was opposed to black laws because its editors opposed "every form of tyranny." The *Free State* editorialized on September 10 that the Big Springs platform was "such as every Free State man [could] stand upon" and was satisfactory to all except "those who desire division in our ranks."

John Speer noted as much in his 1896 book about Lane, stating that he had heard some Westerners say that if there were to be "negroes among them," they "wanted them slaves." Indeed, Speer himself opposed black-law provisions, and he initially withheld his support from Lane at Big Springs on that ground. Speer wrote that when Lane met him on the road between the delegate election and the Big Springs convention, he asked Speer why he opposed him. Speer replied that it was due to Lane's support of the "barbaric black laws."

Lane replied by asking if Speer believed that a majority of the people supported such laws. Speer conceded the point, but observed that if the Free State constitution held such laws, Kansas would not be admitted as a Free State because that would cost the cause the backing of powerful Republicans in Congress. Lane and Speer discussed the matter, and Lane offered a compromise. "If he could get into the Constitutional Convention" slated to occur after Big Springs, "he would use all his powers to get a [black-law] clause in as a separate question, distinct from the constitution," to be voted on separately and then only as "instructions to the first legislature." "We shook hands on that," wrote Speer, "and agreed cordially to be friends."

At the September convention, after the platform was approved came the report of the committee on the legislature. That report called the territorial legislature "a foreign body, representing only the lawless invaders who elected them." The committee recommended the convention's delegates "disown and disavow" the legislature, for they had "no allegiance or obedience to the tyrannical enactments of this spurious Legislature," and called for a pledge to "resist them primarily by every peaceable and legal means within our power, until we can elect our own Representatives, and sweep them from the Statute-book." One of the resulting resolutions urged the antislavery faction to "resist them to a bloody issue as soon as we ascertain that peaceable remedies shall fail."

The resolutions were approved almost unanimously, with Lane making one minor objection to language that impeached the territorial court. Interestingly, in the late 1870s Charles Robinson claimed that Lane "desired to soften down the language" of the resolutions as well. He wanted to substitute "bloody issue" with the

Charles Robinson, who would become the first governor of Kansas, worked with Jim Lane for a short time in the second half of 1855. Afterward Robinson and Lane became bitter enemies. Robinson's enmity toward Lane continued for almost three decades after Lane's death. *Photograph courtesy the Kansas State Historical Society.*

words "sanguinary issue." What's remarkable about this is that from the time of the convention until his death Robinson would charge Lane with being the most violent of the Free State radicals.

The vote on the resolutions was followed by a report from the Committee on State Organization, which decided that a move to frame a state constitution would be "untimely and inexpedient." That report was, wrote William Cutler, "the first really discordant element in the convention." Most of the delegates were in favor of such an effort, and Lane took part in the discussion that followed. Indeed, R. G. Elliott, who was chairman of that committee, later claimed that it was Lane who persuaded many of the delegates to change their minds on the issue by tapping into popular sentiment for it and by invoking the ideal of popular sovereignty. The delegates decided to call for a convention in Topeka to be held on September 19 "to consider the propriety of the formation of a State Constitution."

An article from an Eastern newspaper in the Thomas Webb Scrapbooks puts an interesting spin on this discussion. The newspaper seems to be very abolitionist in its sentiments, for it accused Lane of being a "timid counsellor." As "a friend of Senator Douglas," Lane "tried to cool the ardor of the other delegates by suggesting doubts and difficulties." He did so by following Douglas's lead and urging them to "form a state constitution and apply for immediate admission into the Union." This was because Douglas wanted the "Kansas question" quieted to aid his bid for president. However, according to the article, the "convention wisely dismissed this project." It is not clear if this was a misinterpretation of events at Big Springs, but the story does provide a window on how some abolitionists viewed the convention and its goals.

The report on state organization was followed by the one drafted by the committee on electing a territorial delegate to Congress. That committee called for an election "on the second Tuesday of October next" "for the purpose of electing a Delegate to represent this Territory in the Thirty-fourth Congress of the United States." This was going to be different from the proslavery legislature's stated election day, and the committee explained that they had chosen another day for their election because to "vote upon the same day at the same polls would be an acknowledgment of the right of the late Legislature to call an election." Even should they set the election for that day, "experience tells us that we shall by force be prevented from exercising that right." This report was also approved.

Logically, this report would have been followed by the nomination of candidates. Instead came the report of the Committee on Miscellaneous Business. It brought up resolutions denouncing Andrew Reeder's ouster. Lane was opposed to those resolutions, wrote William Cutler, "on the common sense ground that he had not the slightest knowledge of the facts recited in the resolutions, was unwilling to express an opinion thereon, or to enter into a quarrel between Reeder and the Administration." However, the "resolutions were adopted, nevertheless."

Then came the nominations, in which Martin Conway suggested Reeder. His was the only name put forward, and the nomination "was received with an outburst of applause." Reeder accepted the nomination, urged "peaceful resistance" to "the tyrannical and unjust laws of the spurious Legislature," and called for an appeal to Congress. Force should "be depreciated so long as a single hope of peaceable redress remains," but "should all peaceful efforts fail," then "there still remains to us the steady eye and the strong arm."

There were two last pieces of business. Lane, along with Samuel C. Pomeroy and George W. Brown, were assigned the task of relating to Governor Shannon the results of the convention. The other was the creation of the Kansas Free State Executive Committee. Charles Robinson was put in charge of that committee, and among its members was John Brown, Jr.

The intent of the Big Springs convention had been to form a Free State political party. Such a party now existed, but the meeting that organized it found critics as well as supporters.

Leverett Spring was one such critic. In his book on the period he wrote that the convention "exposed itself to damaging criticism" thanks to "Lane's 'black-law' platform and Reeder's heated declamation." The words "bloody issue" were pounced on by the administration and its friends, including Stephen Douglas, who decried "the daring and defiant revolutionists in Kansas."

The negative assessments were disputed by R. G. Elliott in 1904.

He claimed that the convention was the second of five significant events that eventually led to statehood for Kansas. The Free State factions coalesced into a single movement at Big Springs, Elliott believed, and from then on were able to organize an effective opposition to the proslavery elements in the territory.

The call at Big Springs for another convention at Topeka was to lay the foundation for a movement toward statehood by the Free State faction. In some ways this would be a pursuit of a two-track strategy by the Free Staters. The party formed at Big Springs would compete with proslavery politicians for control of the territorial government. Meanwhile, the Topeka effort would draft a state constitution for the admission of Kansas without slavery.

The latter effort, known to history as the "Topeka movement," was a radical step. One Free Stater, H. Miles Moore, conceded that it was "a desperat[e] and strong" action, while another, Edward Fitch, admitted to his father that such a convention was "a State Prison offense." Still, there was historical precedent for territories moving quickly to statehood. Some asserted that because of this precedent their actions conformed to the ideal of popular sovereignty.

Naturally, Leverett Spring credited the statehood effort to Charles Robinson. He wrote that it was Robinson who was behind the policy repudiating "the territorial legislature as an illegal, usurping, 'bogus' concern" and organizing a state government "independent of the territorial government" and "aiming to effect its overthrow." R. G. Elliott, on the other hand, attributed the move toward statehood to Lane. He said that Lane had mentioned the idea to him "on the day of his arrival in Lawrence" and claimed that Democrats in Washington supported it.

The convention met in Topeka on September 19 as planned. It began at eleven in the morning with the choosing of two temporary officers and the creation of two committees. The first action was a report from the committee on delegates, which stated that Lane was again one of the representatives of the First District. After that a slate of permanent officers was chosen and parliamentary rules were adopted for the convention. A Business Committee composed of fifteen delegates was appointed, and that was the end of the first day.

The second day began with Lane moving to recommit a report by the Business Committee. Lane then offered a motion to create a committee of eighteen members, with one member from each district. William Cutler wrote that Lane urged that the convention give the committee "full powers to write, print and circulate an address to the people of this Territory and to the civilized world, setting forth our grievances and the policy we have been compelled to adopt, and which we have determined at all hazards to carry out." This Committee on Address motion was approved, and Lane was appointed its chairman. The convention broke for lunch, reassembling at two in the afternoon.

The afternoon session began with the report of the Committee on Business. Their report called for an election on the second Tuesday of October to choose individuals to write a constitution. These representatives would meet in convention in Topeka exactly one week later. There would also be "a committee of seven" appointed by the convention chairman to record the proceedings and "have a general superintendence of the affairs of the Territory so far as regards the organization of a State Government." The committee would be called the Executive Committee of Kansas Territory. The executive committee would publicize the election and proclaim the list of elected delegates.

As to who would be allowed to vote in the October election, the report said that "all white male inhabitants, citizens of the United States, above the age of twenty-one years, who have had a bona fide residence in the Territory of Kansas for the space of thirty days immediately preceding the day of said election, shall be entitled to vote." Delegates had to have lived in the territory three months in order to be qualified to serve at the convention.

Once a constitution was adopted, authenticated copies would be sent to the president, the president pro tem of the Senate, the speaker of the House of Representatives, each member of Congress, and the governor of each state in order to secure Kansas's admission to the nation. The long report was adopted, and Lane was appointed as one of the members of the Territorial Committee. With that accomplished, the convention adjourned.

Lane was elected chairman of the executive committee and was therefore catapulted to the leadership of the Free State movement in Kansas Territory. He would be in a strong position to exert his influence on events in Kansas. He would be able to stump for candidates and was certain to have a voice in the constitutional convention that would shape state law. Lane would also, as chairman of the committee, have his name on every document issued by the committee. This would make his name one of the most familiar in Kansas and could only increase his power in territorial affairs.

On October 1 there was a territorial election held for the post of delegate to Congress. This time the Free State party urged its members not to bother even to take part. Even so there was another invasion of Missourians and more illegal balloting. Again J. W. Whitfield won the position. The Free State faction voted on October 9, electing Andrew Reeder as their own delegate. This was to be one more mess for authorities in Washington to sort out.

A short time later members of the proslavery faction met in Leavenworth. They called on the "lovers of law and order" to obey the laws passed by the legislature and stated that it was "treason" to resist them. The Executive Committee of Kansas Territory ignored the threat and announced the names of the delegates elected to the Topeka constitutional convention on October 16. Among them were Jim Lane and Charles Robinson, both chosen as part of the delegation from the Second Representative District.

The Topeka constitutional convention met on October 23, 1855. According to Robinson, the convention membership consisted of eighteen Democrats, six Whigs, four Republicans, two Free-Soilers, one Free State man, and one independent. James Redpath assembled a statistical list of the members of the convention. The statistics for James Lane stated that he was a lawyer, thirty-three, and had been born in Kentucky. The first statement was probably true; the second was off by more than a decade; and the third continues to be up for debate. It is unclear why Lane's age would have been recorded so erroneously, although considering how young most settlers were at the time, Lane might have misstated it in an attempt to connect with them. It also has to be said that any inaccuracies may lie with Redpath alone.

The first day of the constitutional convention proved to be a bust. Only twenty-one members were present, less than a quorum, so it adjourned until the next day. Nine more members appeared the next day, meeting the quorum, and business proceeded. Mark Delahay nominated Lane as president. Though Charles Robinson alleged that Lane's run was to enhance his reputation, which had supposedly been tarnished by a scandal, Leverett Spring conceded somewhat that Lane was qualified to lead the convention. He admitted that Lane "was not without experience in parliamentary affairs," and the convention "needed a chairman who appreciated the anomalous conditions under which it convened and the serious perils to which it was exposed." Lane was elected, and according to William Cutler, "made a short and characteristic speech on taking the chair."

That speech was published in Kansas in a now-obscure Topeka newspaper, the *Daily Kansas Freeman,* and nationally in the *New York Daily Times.* In his speech Lane shows himself as more the statesman than the rabble-rouser. He began by declaring, "You have met, gentlemen, on no ordinary occasion—to accomplish no ordinary purpose. You are the first legal representatives the real settlers of Kansas have ever had." Later he added, "Your work is to give birth to a Government—your labor is to add another State to our Union." From there Lane went in some surprising directions. He told the delegates that Kansas would soon be home to "industrious" farmers, that factories, colleges, and cities were soon to spring up, and that the "Arts and Sciences will be cultivated, and this will be the center of civilization." He talked of the importance of laws for schools and agriculture and of limiting the powers of the new state government.

Then he turned to matters of greater immediate interest to those particular men gathered in Topeka. Reminding them that "the ballot-box has been used as a mere instrument of oppression," Lane urged them to first "guard the ballot-box" to "prevent a repetition" of the "greatest crime that can be perpetrated in a representative government like ours." On the matter of slavery, Lane said that none of the supporters of the Kansas-Nebraska Act initially thought that Kansas could become a Slave State. But now it was being forced into Kansas, and that while the people who elected those delegates wanted it forced out, they also expected the "final settlement" of the issue would be on "a fair and liberal course" toward both sides of the question.

Lane concluded his speech by saying, "I trust the object of our coming together may be successfully accomplished, and that upon your return to your constituents you may be met with the salutation of 'Well done good and faithful servants.'"

The work of the Topeka convention lasted until November 11. The convention members framed a constitution and set December 15 for it to be voted on. There would also be submission of two other questions, a banking law and the black law, apparently just as Lane and John Speer had discussed weeks before. Finally, if the constitution was ratified, an election of state officers would be held.

The constitution created at this convention was largely similar to those that already existed in other Free States. As to slavery, there were two relevant sections on the matter under a bill of rights. One stated, "There shall be no slavery in this State, nor involuntary servitude, except for crime." The other read, "No indenture of any negro or mulatto, made and executed out of the bounds of the State, shall be valid within the State." The constitution defined qualified voters as "every white male person, and every civilized male Indian who has adopted the habits of the white man."

Once the constitution was approved, an election was to be held "on the third Tuesday of January, 1856, for Governor, Lieutenant Governor, Secretary of State, Treasurer, Auditor, Judges of Supreme Court," for a variety of other state offices, for "Members of the General Assembly," and a congressman. The executive committee would be responsible for handling the election and for putting this government in place on March 4, 1856.

Leverett Spring believed that Lane contributed very little to the convention's work. He claimed that Lane only gave a "brief inaugural speech," made "occasional remarks more or less pertinent during the debates," and of course promoted "the 'black law' scheme." Most of what Spring wrote about Lane and the convention covered a duel that almost broke out between Lane and another delegate. The other man "happened to repeat certain damaging stories, which were current, in regard to Lane's private morals."

> The truth of the stories nobody denied, but as they were proving harmful to [Lane's] political aspirations, something must be done to counteract their effect. His election as president of the convention had been a useful testimonial of confidence. What

would be more likely to emphasize and re-enforce this testimonial than a challenge, especially if it should be declined? Contrary to all expectations the troublesome delegate sent a prompt acceptance. As Lane neither wished nor intended to fight, the situation was awkward and his friends had difficulty in extricating him from it. Indeed they found no easier way of escape than to withdraw the challenge and to make satisfactory apologies.

Spring often favored Charles Robinson's version of events, but in this case he seems to have avoided it. This makes sense, for when Robinson spoke of the duel in 1877, his account confused rather than clarified the matter. According to Robinson it was G. P. Lowrey, Andrew Reeder's private secretary, and not a convention delegate who repeated the tale of Lane's Lawrence scandal during the convention. This so enraged Lane that he challenged Lowrey to a duel. Lane asked Robinson to act as his second in the duel.

The issue at the heart of this scandal remains obscure. According to Indiana reporter Bob Markwalter, Lane's wife was having an affair. Kendall Bailes wrote in 1962 that a Mrs. Lindsley of Lawrence accused Lane of "attempting to seduce her," a charge Lane "emphatically denied." A clipping in the Webb Scrapbooks claimed that Lowrey said Lane was "making himself disagreeable to married women who had no sort of affinity for him." All these tales suggest that whatever Lowrey said, it had something to do with Lane's relations with women and was false enough or salacious enough to anger Lane to the point of considering a duel.

When Lane approached him to be his second in the planned duel, Robinson replied that he was opposed to dueling and later claimed that he "soundly reproved" him for considering it. Robinson added that killing Lowrey would neither end talk of the scandal nor enhance Lane's reputation. Indeed, Lowrey's second, Marcus J. Parrott, reported that Lowrey wanted a meeting instead of a duel. Lane was insistent on the matter. The battle was set for eight in the morning, but Lane managed to postpone it until eleven.

That day the convention began business as it had the day before. At ten Lane made what Robinson called "a characteristic speech" that lasted almost an hour. When he was done, Lane "gathered up his coat and hat" and walked out. One of the delegates then announced that "a hostile meeting" was about to take place involving some of the members and put forward an expulsion resolution against the participants. The reason for such a resolution seems confusing, for according to Robinson it was offered by one of Lane's allies. Robinson alleged that the resolution was a way for Lane to back out of the duel without giving in to Lowrey.

At that point, as the fight was about to begin, Robinson resigned as Lane's second in favor of Southerner James F. Legate. Legate told Lane that there would have to be a fight or Lane would have to withdraw his challenge. The tale becomes further confused because, according to Robinson, Lowrey, whom the night before had not wanted a duel, now insisted upon one. Lane then backed down and withdrew his challenge.

According to Kendall Bailes, the duel ended when Lane and Lowrey agreed to an "equivocal document" in which Lowrey said that his comments were intended as confidentially spoken to Parrott, "without pretending to vouch for their truth, or to injure Col. Lane." Parrott and Legate accepted that statement as "satisfactory," and everyone was to "consider the affair honorably and finally settled." That story seems to be backed by two clippings in the Webb Scrapbooks.

The scandal was not a big enough story to prevent the convention from carrying on its work and did not interrupt preparations for the December constitutional election. William Cutler reported on the results of the election of December 15, 1855. Despite the Leavenworth poll book being destroyed by a mob, "For the Constitution" garnered 1,731 votes, and "Against the Constitution" just 46; "For a General Banking Law," 1,120, and 564 against; "exclusion of negroes and mulattoes from the State," 1,287 in favor, and 453 against exclusion.

On December 22 a meeting was held in Lawrence to nominate a Free State ticket. Listed among the candidates were: for governor, Charles Robinson; for lieutenant governor, W. Y. Roberts; and for representative to Congress, Mark W. Delahay. During that Lawrence meeting some of the attendees tried to "bolt" the new party, claiming that abolitionists had too much power. They wanted to substitute Robinson with W. Y. Roberts for governor and replace several other candidates. Not only did Roberts not go along with the bolters, neither did Lane, who had said several times he was no abolitionist.

By this time the two factions in the struggle over slavery in Kansas had almost come to blows at Lawrence. Events there would not only shape the direction of the conflict, but would also lead to an elevation in the stature of Jim Lane among the followers of the Free State movement. However, it appears that what happened in Lawrence in December 1855 also inaugurated a political rivalry within the movement that would carry on for decades.

V.

The Wakarusa War

One of the men who would play an important part in the events of early December 1855 was Samuel J. Jones, the sheriff of Douglas County. Jones had been appointed by the territorial legislature. He was a Democratic officeholder and had served as postmaster of Westport. William Cutler, author of an 1883 history of Kansas and a Free State man, wrote that Jones "had no interest in Kansas beyond that of other border ruffians who were attempting to force slavery into the Territory." Sheriff Jones and Sen. David Atchison became the most high-profile opponents of the Free State movement.

As that proslavery movement gathered steam, Governor Shannon chose to ally with it, Atchison, and Jones. He made this choice with the view that the officials of this government represented law and order. He also may have had little choice at first. Daniel Woodson, the secretary of the territory, was not only an ardent proslavery man, but was the man the faction wanted as governor instead of Shannon. Woodson was thus both Shannon's rival and the governor's only source of information.

Shannon had agreed to preside at a "Law and order" convention in Leavenworth on November 14. The true colors of the convention were shown when its members declared the Free Staters' actions as "practical nullification, rebellion, and treason" and said the Topeka convention "would have been a farce if its purposes had not been treasonable." Shannon was accused later of having spoken to the crowd and during his address saying loudly, "The president is behind you, the president is behind you."

Wilson Shannon became the second governor of Kansas Territory. Easily manipulated by both factions in the territory, he managed to defuse the Wakarusa War, but in the end he left the territory a failed governor. *Image courtesy the Kansas State Historical Society.*

In the meantime, the Free State executive committee believed the situation was improving for them. At a November meeting Lane moved that a proclamation be issued setting December 25 as a day of thanksgiving. The motion was approved and a proclamation drafted. "While insult, outrage, and death has been inflicted upon many of our unoffending citizens," it read, and "while the attempt is being made to inflict upon us the most galling and debasing slavery, our lives have been spared, and a way pointed out which, without imbuing our hands in blood, we can secure the blessings of Liberty and Good Government." The proclamation was issued on November 27, 1855. And while there would be things to be thankful for on that Christmas Day, the Free State movement would have to endure more outrage first.

On November 21 a proslavery man, Franklin Coleman, killed Free State proponent Charles W. Dow at the village of Hickory Point in Douglas County, ten miles south of Lawrence. According to most accounts, Coleman had been provoking Dow for some time. Then, while Dow was returning from a local blacksmith shop, Coleman confronted Dow in front of the Coleman home and killed him.

Historian Dale Watts, in an article on political murders during the territorial period, found evidence that the slavery issue was not the cause of Dow's killing. The cause, Watts said, was mainly due to Dow's trying to get "valuable timber land." He had marked off the lines of his property on what Coleman believed was his own land. Tensions between the two claimants grew until Coleman finally shot Dow.

Whatever the actual cause of the Dow murder, it did have an effect on the larger conflict. The next day a group of men, including many Free Staters, met at Hickory Point to investigate the murder. Blame immediately fell on Coleman. Coleman surrendered to Governor Shannon in Shawnee Mission, but not before swearing out a warrant against Jacob Branson. Dow had resided with Branson, and Branson was believed to have attended the Hickory Point meeting.

That night Sheriff Jones arrested Branson, and he and a posse attempted to take their prisoner to Lecompton. Free State men in southern Douglas County were alarmed, fearing that Jones and his men might murder Branson. Several of them assembled, and on the road to Lecompton they met Jones and his posse. The Free Staters urged Branson to stop complying with Jones and go with them. Branson agreed, and soon word spread of his "rescue."

By this time the Missourians were, to quote Leverett Spring, "eager to try more vigorous and summary measures in the treatment of territorial abolitionism than had thus far been prescribed," and instead of "legislating the Yankees out," they chose "the policy of wiping them out." In their minds, Lawrence was now seen as "the headquarters of sedition." They believed that Lawrence would have to be destroyed if they were to have the peace they desired. The Branson episode gave the proslavery partisans the excuse they needed to march on Lawrence.

The rescue party may have sensed as much, for they immediately went to Charles Robinson's house atop Mount Oread in Lawrence. Robinson called a town meeting, at which he said the people of Lawrence should deny any responsibility in the rescue of Branson, send the rescue party out of town, and prepare the town's defenses. Meanwhile, Sheriff Jones sent word to Missouri of what had happened to him. He then demanded Governor Shannon give him three thousand men to put down the "rebellion" in Lawrence. Shannon, without bothering to get corroboration for Jones' report, obliged. Soon the armed supporters of slavery in Kansas were converging on Lawrence with the view of settling matters once and for all.

In turn the citizens of Lawrence organized their own militia to defend the town. Robinson was put in charge of the volunteers, and Lane was made second in command. This order of command would seem, on the face of it, somewhat strange. Robinson had never been in battle, while Lane was a veteran of the Mexican War who had not only served with gallantry, but had served as colonel of a regiment. So why was Lane put under Robinson's command?

Leverett Spring believed that at that "grave and critical juncture" the people of Lawrence "did not dare to risk a frothy, pictorial, unballasted leadership." Spring conceded that Lane's "military reputation" had grown quickly since he came to Kansas, and that people on both sides of the dispute thought him to be "a powerful fighter." However, Spring wrote in an article on Lane's career, "something had happened in the past six months which disturbed their confidence in the veteran of the Mexican War." Yet what that something was, Spring never said.

Interestingly Robinson himself said nothing about this in his book on the period, *The Kansas Conflict*. He wrote only that he was told the Committee for Safety had been formed. He even failed to include that he had been chosen to lead it. Considering the differences between himself and Lane at the time and later, his silence is puzzling.

John Speer was not so quiet on this question. When he wrote of Robinson's being ranked above Lane, he said there was "a prejudice in the minds of many New England men against Western men." The New Englanders apparently did not think the Westerners were sound enough on the slavery issue to be trusted. Speer seemed to imply that their joint command was a concession to the divide within the movement. If that was so, then Robinson's elevation over Lane was probably a grant to the less numerous but more influential New England side.

There may have been another reason for Free Staters to lack trust in Lane. In a controversial movement, Lane had met with one of the proslavery militia generals, a man named Richardson. While Lane was at Topeka at the end of November, Speer wrote, he invited Richardson to dine with him. Although the invitation seemed friendly, Lane's letter criticized Sheriff Jones and hinted that he knew the proslavery mob had orders that Lawrence was "to be demolished without delay." Nevertheless, the dinner was certainly suspicious in the eyes of the abolitionists, though Speer thought Lane and Richardson only swapped "lies," with Lane giving out false information to hamper "the enemy."

Whatever the reason for the choice of command, Lane and Robinson went to work preparing the town. Rifle pits were dug, impromptu fortifications were erected, and drilling of the Free State militia began. Sara Robinson, observing the drills from her home, wrote of the scene: "There is young manhood in the ranks, and some who have not yet counted their score of years; but the mantle of discretion and prudence has fallen upon them. The blood of '76 runs in their veins, and the fires of its unquenched love of liberty sparkle in their eyes."

Wilson Shannon did not see the situation in those terms. He grew alarmed at the news of the resistance to law and order being carried out by the people of Lawrence. Governor Shannon asked President Pierce for the authority to order Col. E. V. Sumner at Fort Leavenworth to send soldiers to protect Jones. Shannon told Sumner of his request, to which Sumner advised Shannon to "countermand any orders" given to the territorial militia "until you receive the answer" to the request to Pierce.

However, that militia was already acting on its own. By December 4 reports were reaching Lawrence of the numbers they faced. There seemed to be a combined "force eight hundred strong for the destruction, the annihilation of Lawrence," Mrs. Robinson wrote.

There was one death during the "siege" of Lawrence, that of Free Stater Thomas W. Barber. Barber and his wife lived eight miles southwest of Lawrence, but he had been staying in the city as one of its defenders. On December 6, Barber decided to return home and see his wife; two other men went with him. Three miles south of Lawrence they met about a dozen horsemen coming from Lecompton. Two of the horsemen ordered the three to turn back, and when the three men refused, a short gunfight ensued. Barber was shot in the side and died.

Barber's body was brought to the Free State Hotel in Lawrence. The murder and the appearance of the widow inflamed the residents of Lawrence. Hannah Ropes wrote that it was Lane who stirred them up, "detailing to eager listeners the most painful circumstances of poor Barbour's [sic] death, and, with wonderful ingeniousness, keeping up the wicked spirit of vengeance among those over whom he exercised any power." However, William Cutler wrote that but for "the constant watchfulness, cool counsel and determined orders of Robinson, Lane, and others in command," Barber's "infuriated friends bent on vengeance" would have launched "a wild sortie" against the proslavery forces.

During the siege, noted Jay Monaghan, the weather turned cold and the defenders of Lawrence started grumbling about the situation. Lane observed this dissatisfaction while inspecting the defenses. He came down off his horse, stepped up on the nearest embankment, and spoke to the men. It seems that at this hour Lane first engaged in what a later author called his "striptease oratory." While addressing the defenders Lane first took off his military cloak, then his hat, and next his coat. Soon his necktie was cast to the ground, and then Lane unbuttoned his shirt "down the front." As he did, there were "shouts and cheers of applause" from his audience.

It was a cold day, so one wonders why Lane resorted to such a spectacle. One reason could have been that he was throwing off clothes to punctuate angry statements. The actions also might have been a display of strength. What better way to discourage grumbling about the cold than to remove some of your clothes while telling others it's not so bad?

Part of the problem in classifying Lane's actions comes from the lack of clarity about what Lane said on that day. Jay Monaghan himself was not sure. "Did Lane merely want to keep the men from deserting," he wondered, "or did he try to precipitate an immediate attack on the entrenched enemy?" The author conceded that supporters of Lane would later insist the former and his enemies the latter. Considering that Lane took part in later negotiations to end the standoff, and the anger expressed at the resolution by a certain now-famous abolitionist fighter, it would seem more likely that Lane was advocating a strong defense than encouraging an attack.

Despite holding a strong position, or perhaps because of the uncertainty of the will and patience of their "soldiers," the leaders of Lawrence decided to send a party to open negotiations with Governor Shannon on December 6. The governor was in a poor mood, claiming that Free Staters had driven out "politically obnoxious" settlers and were "displaying a startling spirit of insubordination and rebellion." The party replied by saying that Shannon had been lied to. "Lawrence was no more responsible for the rescue of Branson than for the precession of the equinoxes," they commented. Shannon pledged to go to Lawrence, but to demand obedience to the law and a surrender of their guns. The negotiators told Shannon that no one in Lawrence would readily give up their guns, but he was welcome to speak to their leaders.

According to Douglas Brewerton, Shannon may have already had a change in view toward the situation. On December 5,

Colonel Sumner received permission from President Pierce to intervene in the matter. When he informed Shannon, the governor informed the colonel that he wanted Sumner's men "stationed in Lawrence" to "prevent an attack." On December 6, Shannon went from Shawnee Mission to the militia camp on the Wakarusa River. He told Brewerton he was disturbed to find "a strong disposition" in the camp that was "almost universal" in favor of an attack on Lawrence. The next day, December 7, one of the militia leaders told Shannon that some of the others had decided to start intercepting his correspondence to Sumner so they could "make the assault" on Lawrence before any mediation could occur.

In was in this tenuous condition that Shannon, along with Nathan Boone, a descendant of the famed frontiersman Daniel Boone, met with the Free State leaders in Lawrence. Boone and Shannon spoke at length with Lane and Robinson. Shannon asked them to surrender their arms to the commander of the territorial militia, but Lane and Robinson replied that the people of Lawrence would not comply with such terms. However, Lane and Robinson did indicate to Shannon that there was some willingness to obey the territorial authorities, provided they could test them in court. Shannon offered a compromise in which the citizens of Lawrence would yield to Jones' warrants in exchange for a dispersal of the men outside of town. Shannon returned to Lawrence on December 8, again met with Robinson and Lane, and agreed to the terms they had discussed the day before.

This "treaty," recorded in full by John Gihon, began by stating that there had been a "misunderstanding between the people of Kansas" and the governor that had arisen from the Hickory Point affair. Since "both Governor Shannon and the citizens of Lawrence" wanted "to avoid a calamity so disastrous to the interests of the territory," both sides would come to an agreement. The people of Lawrence would formally state that the rescue of Branson "was made without our knowledge or consent." If anyone in town was found to have "engaged in said rescue," the people pledged "to aid in the execution of any legal process against them."

For his part, Governor Shannon agreed "to use his influence to secure to the citizens of Kansas Territory remuneration for any damage suffered in any unlawful depredations, if any such have been committed by the sheriff's posse in Douglas county." Finally, Shannon had to say that he had not called on "residents of any other states to aid in the execution of the laws; that such as are here are here of their own choice, and that he does not consider that he has any authority to do so, and that he will not call upon any citizens of any other state who may be here." The agreement was signed by Shannon, Robinson, and Lane and dated December 8, 1855.

Sara Robinson wrote that Shannon then asked Robinson and Lane to accompany him to Franklin, the Missourians' headquarters, "to meet the officers in the invading army" to help him in persuading them to disperse. According to Leverett Spring, both Shannon and Lane failed to mollify the Missourians. It was only when Robinson pointed out that the Free Staters had a constitutional right to bear arms and that "Lawrence was not a party to the assault upon Jones" did they back down. On the other hand, a clipping from the *St. Louis Republican* in the Thomas Webb Scrapbooks claims that it was Shannon who brought the Free Staters to terms and suggests that his reasoning won over the Missourians.

No matter who was responsible for easing the tensions, many of the Missourians were angry with Shannon's treaty, among them Sheriff Jones. Senator Atchison, however, considered the Free Staters' position "impregnable," and said that if they attacked Lawrence "as a mob," the result would be "the election of an abolition president and the ruin of the Democratic party."

Clearly the treaty failed to bring about a spirit of good will between the two sides. Sara Robinson alleged that Lane and Robinson were promised an escort back to Lawrence, but when they left "only one was provided to go with them." After a mere hundred yards or so, the man abandoned them "in the enemy's country, without escort to pass the picket-guard." Worse, a winter sleet storm then came up. The two men "trusted to their horses to keep their way homeward." Robinson's horse did slip, but neither was injured, and the two men made it back to Lawrence safely. But, wrote Mrs. Robinson, that was only because "a party of the ruffians" who had "left Franklin with the design of assassinating Generals Robinson and Lane" got lost in the winter weather.

If there were proslavery fighters unhappy with the treaty, there were also radicals in Lawrence equally upset at the onset of peace. Perhaps no one was angrier than John Brown. Brown had been born in Connecticut in 1800 and grew up in Ohio. A devout Protestant, he devoted his life to the destruction of slavery in America. He moved to Massachusetts in 1846 and came into contact with many prominent abolitionists. They were not militant enough to suit Brown, so he set about his mission his own way. First he tried to establish a black colony of freedmen in upstate New York. He also lent aid to the local Underground Railroad. After six of his sons moved to Kansas in 1855, Brown followed them, but with the goal of fighting the establishment of slavery in the territory. When Lawrence came under threat, Brown and his sons joined the Liberty Guards from Osawatomie in Miami County and marched to defend the town.

At first Brown was welcomed by Lane and Robinson, but almost immediately he became troublesome for the two leaders. Brown refused to take orders and began to call for an attack on the proslavery encampment. Lane and Robinson, along with the other Lawrence leaders, were able to keep a rein on John Brown until the treaty with Shannon was signed.

According to Brown biographer Oswald Villard, Brown wrote to a friend that the treaty had come about because of "a good deal of trickery on the one side and the cowardice, folly, & drunkenness on the other." On December 8, Shannon, Lane, and Robinson addressed a crowd in Lawrence to explain the situation. Shannon said he had misunderstood the Lawrence citizens, Lane vowed to stay in town until the Missourians left, and Robinson said he and Lane "had taken an honorable position." Brown, "boiling over with anger," then stepped before the crowd.

"He declared that Lawrence had been betrayed," Villard wrote, and called for a night assault on the proslavery camp. "I am Abolitionist, dyed in the wool," Brown said. He volunteered to be one of the men in the attack. Villard believed that Lane was sympathetic to Brown's demand, but yielded to the wishes of the majority when Brown was removed and Robinson told the assembly that the treaty was "a triumph of diplomacy."

After the Lawrence crisis ended, Lane's executive committee

John Brown was eager to use violence to end slavery. Although he was an abolitionist like Charles Robinson, Robinson and his allies tried to tie him to Jim Lane. *Photograph courtesy the Kansas State Historical Society.*

busied itself supporting the Free Staters' efforts to defend themselves against another incursion. On December 23 the committee
got a letter from Eli Thayer proposing to equip the Free State militia with one thousand stand of "improved arms," to be paid for
with state "certificates of indebtedness." That motion was
approved, along with another on January 16, 1856, appointing
general agents to travel the United States and ask for weapons. If
a clipping in the Webb Scrapbooks from a Connecticut newspaper
can be believed, Lane received a letter from the governor of
Indiana that "500 men with money and ammunition" were ready
to march to Kansas "should war again be menaced."

In spite of these preparations, the situation grew calmer. Calm
was enforced not by the government but by the weather. William
Cutler wrote that the winter of 1855-56 "was colder than had been
known in Kansas before." A storm blew into the state on December
22 and the snow fell until Christmas Eve. The temperature on
Christmas Day was believed in one place to have reached 30
degrees below zero. The winter weather remained harsh until the
last week of February 1856.

Though hostile actions on both sides were interrupted by the
cold, emotions were still high. In late January, Lane's executive
committee sent a letter to Pres. Franklin Pierce calling for U.S.
Army troops to protect Free State citizens and to stop the
Missourians from entering Kansas. This call probably stemmed
from the death of another Free State man earlier in the month.

Tensions were further increased on the proslavery side by the
Free State election of January 15. Cutler wrote that the proslavery
press "immediately charged" the election "as a direct violation of
the Shannon treaty." On that day Sheriff Jones sent a letter to Lane
and Robinson asking, "Did you or did you not pledge yourselves,
at a council held in Franklin on the — day of December, to assist
me, as Sheriff, in the arrest of any person in Lawrence against
whom I might have a writ, and to furnish me with a posse to enable
me to do so?"

Instead of simply referring back to the treaty, Lane and
Robinson replied, "In reference to your note of yesterday, we state
that at the time and place mentioned, we may have said we would
assist any proper officer in the service of any legal process in this

city, and also no further resistance to the arrest by you of one of the rescuers of Branson would be made, as we desire to test the validity of the enactments of the body that met at the Mission, calling themselves the Kansas Legislature, by an appeal to the Supreme court of the United States." Jones decided to interpret the reply as meaning that the truce was over. So did Sen. David Atchison, according to Cutler, "who, by the somewhat fussy and nervous manner in which he had sought to patch up a compromise during the late Wakarusa war, had laid himself liable to the imputation of cowardice among his followers." The stage appeared to be set for a renewal of the conflict between the sides.

Interestingly enough, it was during this time that Charles Robinson received advice on Free State strategy from abolitionist and politician Amos Lawrence. In January 1856, Lawrence sent a letter to Robinson urging him "not under any circumstances" to resist "any legal representative" of the federal government, and not to allow antislavery leaders to do so either. The policy Robinson "must adopt," said Lawrence, was to show "the greatest forbearance" and to call for the "total discouragement of all aggression" in order to "gain time and strength."

The advice sounds very much like what Robinson did in California, fighting for squatters' rights through legal and political means instead of resorting to violence. Yet it should have been obvious to Robinson the problem with such a strategy: it was unlikely to work against a ruthless opponent. And like the squatters, the Free Staters faced an opponent who was willing to do anything to secure victory.

Furthermore, Robinson seems not to have considered any alternatives to either fighting or waiting in early 1856. He had to have been aware of the writings of Henry David Thoreau and Thoreau's idea of civil disobedience. Why then didn't he speak out about the concept? Robinson could have put forward a series of actions that might have resisted proslavery authorities without resorting to open warfare, such as a peaceful march on Lecompton or the carrying of antislavery signs in Leavenworth. There would have been enough action in such protests to keep the more radical elements of the Free State movement quietly satisfied, but not so much that authorities could have gotten away with using violence to suppress them.

Robinson's 1892 memoir is worth examining for the general inconsistency in the way he later interpreted events. When he wrote of the early shipments of guns to antislavery settlers, he said that they were "needed in self-defense against ruffians, and not for offensive war against the Federal government." Later in the book he would insist that Lane and John Brown engaged in "general war against the Federal Government." Yet Robinson did not mention the letter from Lawrence in his book nor his and Lawrence's Fabian policy.

Robinson came to hate Jim Lane with a passion that seemed to border on a mania. It may have been that toward the end of his life he realized the strategy of waiting in the spring of 1856 had been a failure. At this crucial time Robinson and those following his lead had surrendered the initiative to the proslavery faction, but his intense aversion to Lane, who had favored action, prevented him from openly admitting the mistake. Therefore, he claimed instead that he supported defensive fighting and tried to accuse "radicals" like Lane and Brown of engaging in open rebellion, despite the evidence to the contrary. Whatever Robinson's motives or views were at the time or later, his choice to give up the initiative would prove to be a mistake that the Free State faction almost failed to recover from.

The January 19, 1856, issue of the *Herald of Freedom* carried news that a local Republican Party organization had come into existence a few days earlier. Among the supporters of this new Republican platform were "Col. Lane, Mr. [G. P.] Lowrey, Mr. [Martin] Conway, Mr. [James] Legate," and another man, "all National Democrats." The newspaper noted this turning point, paying special attention to Jim Lane. He had come to Kansas with "squatterphobia" and was "now beginning to give evidences of a speedy recovery." "If Col. Lane adopts the Republican creed, he will be a valuable accession to the party."

Not long after this piece, on February 6, 1856, Lane's territorial executive committee announced that Charles Robinson had been elected the Free State governor of Kansas at the January 15 election. The next day Robinson was chosen as the first major general and commander in chief of the Kansas militia. Lane was appointed the second major general; he could now be called General Lane by friends and foes alike. Filling out the Free State militia hierarchy, Cyrus Holliday was appointed brigadier general, and Gaius Jenkins and Milton Dickey were appointed colonels.

On March 4, 1856, Lane called to order the first session of the Free State legislative assembly. After they chose several officers, Charles Robinson was sworn in as Free State governor. Sara Robinson noted that there was one serious problem the members of this assembly faced: the question of swearing an oath of office. One of the members, she wrote, "expressed strong desires" against taking the oath, "as such an act would be considered treasonable, and they would be immediately arrested." On the other hand, by failing to take the oath "the present free-state constitution would be of no account." The question was settled, and despite rumors of impending arrests, all was quiet in Topeka. The ceremony marked the official end of the Executive Committee of Kansas Territory. The committee issued a final report, and the new government adjourned. It took no action to undermine the territorial government.

In spite of the adjournment, Douglas Brewerton did not think all would remain quiet. He wrote in early 1856 that he felt "confident" Governor Shannon would not tolerate this shadow legislature. He believed Shannon would have the new officers arrested for their actions. The Free Staters would not be charged with treason, but they could be imprisoned under a territorial law barring anyone from taking up an office "without being duly elected."

In the first days of the legislative session Jim Lane had been given the task of acting as an agent for the committee. His job was to travel the states and elicit support for the cause. Lane was also elected by the Free State senate as a senator, representing the territory in Washington. He would be charged with the task of taking a memorial stating their position to the nation's capital and presenting it to Congress. These were the only real actions the body took, aside from issuing bonds and making speeches.

On March 24 the *Kansas Free State* made note of Lane's trip. It wrote that he had left a week ago "to lay our constitution before Congress" and to "labor for our admission into the Union." But while the editorial expressed confidence in Lane's abilities as a "superior canvasser," it also expressed "fear that the pro-slavery democracy of the north" would be "too far gone in corruption to admit of redemption." It was an ominous note for a mission that would be less than successful.

When Jim Lane arrived in Washington with the Free State memorial, he found the House of Representatives controlled by a majority that supported the Free State movement in Kansas. The Senate was another matter, and according to Jay Monaghan, Lane went to Sen. Lewis Cass for assistance. Cass had first set forth the idea of squatter sovereignty, and as sentiment in Kansas was leaning Free State, he agreed to introduce a bill in the Senate for Kansas's admission under the Topeka constitution.

However, according to Leverett Spring, one of the senators who received Lane's memorial said "that he felt humiliated because he could not rise in his seat" and "answer the sneering question, 'Who is James H. Lane?'" The senator "proceeded to give a pretty full sketch of the apparently forgotten politician who stumped Indiana for every Democratic presidential candidate from Martin Van Buren in 1840 to Franklin Pierce in 1852." Spring added that even Stephen Douglas denounced the memorial, asking "whether here is not evidence of the most glaring fraud ever attempted to be perpetrated upon a legislative body." "The campaign in Washington was disastrous," Spring wrote. "It could not have succeeded in any event, but poor generalship converted what might have been an orderly retreat into a rout."

This is not quite how Monaghan viewed the matter. He wrote that Douglas spoke out "to defend the administration and make one more attempt to hold the Democratic Party together." To that end Douglas denounced the bill, saying that Kansas lacked enough residents and that Southern emigrant aid groups ought to work as hard as the New England companies had before anyone should assert what the residents of Kansas wanted. Only then did Douglas go further and accuse Lane of bringing to the Senate a "partially forged document." When the bill failed, Lane tried to challenge Douglas to a duel. Monaghan wrote that Douglas declined the challenge "as coming from one of inferior station."

Kendall Bailes put yet another spin on Lane's Washington visit.

He wrote that Lane was "careless in his presentation of the memorial," and that allowed Douglas and other Democrats to attack it as a forgery. Lane then wrote "a half hostile, half friendly letter to Douglas" that the senator "was at a loss to interpret." Bailes added that Lane's challenge was actually a rumor sweeping the city, and when Lane finally left it was "much to the relief of everybody."

On April 16, 1856, the *New York Times* devoted a story to the then-ongoing debate over the Kansas memorial. The story reported on the proceedings in the Senate two days earlier, about a week since Senator Cass had presented the memorial and Senator Douglas had attacked it. On that day, April 14, another senator presented Lane's statement addressing the claims of forgery. According to the *Times,* Lane argued among other things that "no one thought of doubting the authenticity of the Bible because he did not read it in the original parchment sheets."

After Lane's statement was read there appears to have been a debate about it. At length, yet another senator rose and told his fellows that Lane had provided "a full, free, and candid explanation of the facts" surrounding the memorial. The contents of the document were supposed to be up for examination by the Senate, not charges about the paper's authenticity. Then Douglas shifted matters to the Topeka constitution and the fact that in his view it had not been approved by a legal vote of territorial settlers. From there the debate seems to have denigrated into a series of insults, culminating in Douglas making the comment that "the people of Illinois are a white race opposed to amalgamation" and implying that "Abolition agitators" were attempting to do what his constituents opposed.

Two May issues of the *Kansas Free State* also provide some interesting views of Lane's failed mission. On May 5 it reported that Lane was angry with Douglas, asked why "the Colonel was sent to Washington with revolver in hand to demand our admission into the Union," and commented that Lane was "as belligerent as ever." Two weeks later, however, it published Lane's letter to Senator Douglas and Lane's commentary on the letter, neither of which are quite so belligerent.

Lane's letter began with the question of the forged memorial. Lane wrote that after it had been "the subject of severe criticism," he spoke in the Senate with Douglas present, giving a "full" and "frank" explanation of what happened. After that Douglas had repeated the "charges of the most grave character" against Lane that he first had voiced in criticizing the memorial. Lane wrote that Douglas had given him no opportunity "to speak in my own defense" despite "the friendship, personal as well as political, which has heretofore existed between us."

Lane's follow-up letter to the newspaper is very long and difficult to read. Essentially, Lane claimed that Douglas had used language against him that a senator ought not to have used, that the senator had refused to explain why he spoke against him so harshly, and that Douglas had treated a former friend and ally like a pariah. In the tone of this letter Lane sounds more hurt than angry, more of a man betrayed for politics' sake than a man looking to fight any opponent of his views.

It is not easy to untangle the tale of Jim Lane's ill-fated mission to Washington in the spring of 1856. It does seem, though, that the mission was probably doomed from the start. The president and his Democratic allies, including Douglas, were not about to support a Free State government strongly tinged with Republicans. Perhaps the peculiar circumstances in which Lane delivered the memorial to Congress gave those Democrats an opportunity not just to attack it, but the Free State movement in general. Considering how administration Democrats stood before Lane began his trip, it seems unlikely that, even had Lane brought pristine documents with him, those documents would have found much acceptance in Washington.

This incident may have been a turning point in Lane's political career. Until then Lane seemed to be a Free State Democrat. In the months after Washington, Lane would apologize for his Democratic roots and stump for Republican candidates. Sometime in April 1856, Lane crossed his own personal Rubicon; he changed political parties. Not everyone would accept Jim Lane the Republican, but they would have to deal with his zealous conversion one way or the other.

While Jim Lane was in the nation's capital, Congress did take some action on the situation in Kansas. On March 19 the House created a committee "to inquire into and collect evidence" on the

Kansas problem. The committee was composed of three men, Republicans William Howard of Michigan and John Sherman of Ohio and Democrat Mordecai Oliver of Missouri. Eventually the committee headed to Kansas to obtain testimony from both sides in the conflict.

In April 1856 the Branson affair rose up again to create tension between the factions. On April 19, Sheriff Samuel Jones returned to Lawrence, this time to arrest Samuel N. Wood for aiding in "liberating" Branson from custody. Wood refused to go along with Jones, saying he did not recognize Jones' authority. Jones was rebuffed, but he returned the next day. He failed to find Wood but tried to apprehend another man. He grabbed the man so hard that, as Sara Robinson put it, the man "thought it was his intention to knock him down." The man struck Jones, "whereupon the bold sheriff, with his comrades, left for Lecompton, muttering, however, 'he would bring in the troops, and the arrests should be made.'"

That's just what he did, although making sure to twist the facts his way. He sent word on April 20 to the U.S. marshal in the territory that he had arrested Wood the day before but that "he was rescued from my hands by a mob." Jones returned to Lawrence on April 23 with American soldiers in tow. Instead of arresting Wood, Jones arrested several other men. These men went with Jones, but on the night of April 23 a shot was fired at the sheriff. Jones' shooting was denounced in Lawrence the next day, but that didn't prevent anger from stirring the proslavery side.

The situation continued to deteriorate when the Douglas County grand jury, a proslavery body meeting in Lecompton, began to issue indictments. They were encouraged by Judge Samuel D. Lecompte, chief justice of the territory and the man for whom Lecompton was named. On May 5 the jury declared the two Free State newspapers in Lawrence, the *Herald of Freedom* and the *Kansas Free State*, "nuisances" that had to be abated, along with the Free State Hotel in Lawrence. On May 7 the jury summoned former governor Andrew Reeder to appear before them. Reeder refused, was cited with contempt of court, and forced to flee the territory. The grand jury moved on to the members of the Free

State shadow government. Charges of treason stemmed from the accusation that they had been part of an illegal effort to undermine the legitimate territorial government.

Before Charles Robinson was indicted he gave his testimony to the congressional committee. Once that was done he planned to head out of the region to rally support for the Free State cause. Sara Robinson noted that she and her husband left Kansas City by boat around May 9. When the boat reached Lexington it was forced to stop. Charles Robinson was detained in Lexington until May 20, when he was returned to Kansas.

As May proceeded, others were caught up in Sheriff Jones' net, including John Brown, Jr., and Josiah Miller, editor of the *Free State*. Miller was actually put on trial for treason but was acquitted by the men who arrested him. The people of Lawrence tried repeatedly to call on Governor Shannon for aid against the proslavery posses riding into town and hauling off men, but Shannon believed the authorities were legitimate and refused to do anything to stop them.

On May 19 another shooting took place, and another Free State man was dead. Two days later, on May 21, "hordes of men, armed with United States muskets," appeared in Lawrence. They were, wrote Mrs. Robinson, a "mongrel crew of Carolinians, Alabamians, and Missourians." United States Deputy Marshal W. P. Fain went to the Eldridge Hotel to arrest two men. He then commandeered the Robinson house and dismissed "his monster posse of two hundred and fifty horsemen, and five hundred infantry." Sheriff Jones appeared, told the men of "his attempted assassination," and asked for their help in enforcing "certain writs in his hands." Jones demanded Samuel Pomeroy surrender the town's cannon and Sharps rifles. After a few minutes Pomeroy told Jones that the cannon would be given up, "but the rifles are private property, and will be retained."

By this point there were between five hundred and eight hundred proslavery men in town, according to Sara Robinson. At the place where they were gathering appeared Senator Atchison, who spoke to them in an incendiary address. "Boys," he said, "this day I am a Kickapoo Ranger, by G-d. This day we have entered Lawrence with Southern Rights inscribed upon our banner, and not one d——d abolitionist dared to fire a gun." With that, the mob descended on the Eldridge Hotel and the offices of the *Herald of Freedom* and *Free State* newspapers. The hotel was looted and seriously damaged, the printing presses of both newspapers were destroyed, and many houses were plundered of almost everything of value.

Around seven in the evening the mob left Lawrence. Thousands of dollars of property were destroyed, many people had been robbed of their possessions, and one of the finest hotels on the frontier was in ruins. Men like Jones and Atchison had finally achieved their goal of punishing the abolitionists. But this was not the end of the struggle over Kansas. Indeed, events were coming together to turn the struggle in very different, and very violent, directions.

In Washington, Congress was deadlocked over bills admitting Kansas as a state. The Republicans, who were in control of the House, wanted Kansas brought into the union under the Topeka constitution. The Democrats, holding a majority in the Senate, called for a constitution drafted by delegates chosen from the proslavery territorial legislature. Neither side's bill could get through Congress and tensions were high.

Into this volatile mix stepped Sen. Charles Sumner of Massachusetts. Senator Sumner supported the Free State cause, and like many Northerners he was increasingly angry at the news and rumors from Kansas. "My soul is wrung by this outrage," he told a colleague late in May, and "I shall pour it forth." He did so over two days, May 19 and 20, on the floor of the Senate in a speech he called "The Crime Against Kansas." His speech was full of emotion, bitterness, and hate. "Murderous robbers from Missouri, hirelings picked from the drunken spew and vomit of an uneasy civilization," were committing the "rape of a virgin territory, compelling it to the hateful embrace of slavery," Sumner said. He attacked powerful Southern senators, including Atchison and Andrew P. Butler of South Carolina. Sumner went so far as to claim that Butler was a Don Quixote whose "mistress" was "the harlot, Slavery." Democrats were incensed by the speech, and even some Republicans were uncomfortable.

Congressman Preston Brooks, one of Butler's cousins, confronted Sumner on the Senate floor. After telling Sumner that his speech was "a libel," he began to beat Sumner with a cane. Sumner was seriously injured, and although he remained in the Senate, he was largely ineffective. Brooks was fined a mere three hundred dollars; a vote to expel him failed to gain a two-thirds majority.

The assault became a sensation. Brooks was sent canes from all over the South. It seemed to many opponents of slavery that the South would do anything to preserve its views on the issue: voter fraud, intimidation, beatings, murder. Some abolitionists suggested going beyond the strategy of peaceful political resistance to slavery and its supporters, "to strike back" against "the rod of the slave." That next step was about to be carried out in Kansas in one of the most famous and notorious incidents of "Bleeding Kansas."

John Brown was part of a larger group of men from the Osawatomie area who, when informed that Lawrence might be under threat of attack, had rallied to march to aid the city. Long before they reached Lawrence they found out about the sacking of the town and the arrests of several Free State leaders. The men decided to continue on to the city to determine what they could, but at some point Brown and a smaller group of men broke away from the rest.

Brown had decided to take matters into his own hands. Initially, he may have wanted to kill all the proslavery settlers along Pottawatomie Creek, near where he and his sons lived. Either he reconsidered or was persuaded to concentrate on the most prominent proslavery men in that area. With him were four of his sons and three other men. They killed James Doyle, two of his sons, Allen Wilkinson, and Henry Sherman. All five men were hacked to death.

At first few believed the murders had actually taken place. The *New York Times,* which had published its account from a story in the proslavery *St. Louis Republican,* said that the story from St. Louis was "quite as improbable as many others that have appeared in that journal." Sara Robinson dismissed the accounts she heard.

Ever since the news of the murders on Pottawatomie Creek got out, there has been debate over what John Brown had in mind when he and his followers committed them. Brown's supporters likened them to a preemptory raid. His critics decried them as a cold-blooded massacre of peripheral proslavery men. Certainly the murders caused an escalation of the conflict between the proslavery and Free State sides in Kansas. The also proved to be another propaganda blow to the Free State movement.

On June 23 one of Brown's sons, John Brown, Jr., was arrested along with another man as a result of treason indictments. Sara Robinson wrote that Brown "had a rope tied around his arms so tightly, and drawn behind him, that he will for years bear the marks of the ropes, where they wore into his flesh." The younger Brown "was then obliged to hold one end of a rope, the other end being carried by one of the dragoons; and for eight miles, in a burning sun, he was driven before them, compelled to go fast enough to keep from being trampled on by the horses." Brown and the other man were taken to Lecompton to be held with other Free State prisoners. The torture he endured is believed to have driven the younger Brown insane.

The Brown arrest was followed by one positive bit of news for the movement. The House committee dispatched to Kansas to investigate the situation presented its report on July 1. The report stated that "organized invasions" from Missouri had indeed taken over territorial elections. The territorial legislature was an "illegally constituted body," the Topeka constitution embodied "the will of a majority" of residents, and "a fair election" could not take place "without a new census, the selection of impartial Judges," and U.S. soldiers "at every place of election."

The situation turned negative again when Governor Shannon gave orders to Col. E. V. Sumner to disperse the Free State legislature when it assembled. When Sumner's men arrived in Topeka around July 3, it had, according to Leverett Spring, "a discouraging and unbracing influence upon" the legislature. Some of the attendees wanted the legislature to proceed, while "others denounced further resistance to the territorial laws as a blunder, and counseled immediate submission." No one could agree on anything and everyone waited.

As soon as Sumner arrived in Topeka, he contacted the Free State leaders in that city and asked them not to meet. The Free

Staters refused his request, but they did agree to compromise. The legislature would come together and start a formal session but would "quietly disperse" when Sumner came forward with the troops. At noon on July 4, the session began. A few minutes later Sumner appeared. A call of the roll began, but found there was no quorum present. Sumner stood up and gave the order for the legislature to disperse, which, according to Spring, he said was "the most painful [duy] of his whole life."

All might have seemed hopeless for the Free Staters, but appearances can be deceptive. The day before the Topeka legislature was dispersed, Colonel Sumner spoke to one of the Free State men in Topeka, Samuel Walker. He told Walker that he had heard that Jim Lane was on the other side of the Missouri River "and means to fight." "There isn't a word of truth in the story," Walker replied. "Lane is not in the territory. He is somewhere in the East making speeches."

Indeed he was. While the fortunes of the Free State movement in Kansas seemed to be at their lowest depth, Lane was telling the North of how Kansas was suffering under the lash of slavery. His speeches would become a sensation, and within two months of the dispersal of the legislature, the tide would turn. Lane would be at the center of it all.

VI.

Captain Cook on a White Horse

May 31, 1856, was a Saturday and therefore ideal for a mass meeting in Chicago. As Lloyd Lewis put it, "the workingmen would be free, and the sailors in from the lakes and the longshoremen up from the docks, and the farmers across from the fields" would all be able to attend. The subject of that meeting would be Kansas. The featured speaker, Jim Lane. This meeting, although hundreds of miles from the area in question, was important to both the territory and the man. It was an opportunity to win nationwide sympathy for the floundering Free State movement and national fame if the man rose to the occasion.

"Something like delirium—and revolution—was in the air," Lewis wrote. Not only had news arrived of the "Sack of Lawrence," but also of the beating of Senator Sumner. Just before the meeting got under way the crowd sang the "Marseillaise." The mood of the audience was against the "Slave Power" and passions were running high. No record was made of exactly all that was said on that Saturday night. William Cutler, whose account is quite detailed, had to rely on the memory of an eyewitness some twenty-five years later. But from that we can look back on that Saturday night.

The meeting began with a speech by one Norman Judd, who was followed by Francis Hoffman. J. C. Vaughn spoke next, offering a series of resolutions. One resolution assured "That the people of Illinois will aid the Freedom of Kansas," another called for sending "a colony of 500 actual settlers," and another, "That these settlers will invade no man's rights, but will maintain their own."

Following Vaughn was W. B. Egan, "one of the most eloquent Irish orators of the city," who further roused the crowd.

Then the man in charge of the meeting introduced Lane. "As he rose up and came forward," wrote Cutler, "he was greeted with an outburst of applause from the crowd that continued for some minutes, during which time he stood statue-like, with mouth firm set, gazing with those wondrous eyes down into the very heart of the excited throng." For the next hour or so Lane had complete sway of the crowd, controlling "its every emotion—moving to tears, to anger, to laughter, to scorn, to the wildest enthusiasm, at his will." The audience "saw the contending factions in the Territory through his glasses. The Pro-slavery party appeared like demons and assassins; the Free-State party like heroes and martyrs."

> I have been sent by the people of Kansas to plead their cause before the people of the North [Lane began]. Most persons have a very erroneous idea of the people of Kansas. They think they are mostly from Massachusetts. They are really more than nine-tenths from the Northwestern States. There are more men from Ohio, Illinois and Indiana, than from all New England and New York combined. . . .
>
> The Missourians poured over the border in thousands, with bowie knives in their boots, their belts bristling with revolvers, their guns upon their shoulders, and three gallons of whisky per vote in their wagons. When asked where they came from, their reply was, "From Missouri;" when asked, "What are you here for?" their reply was, "Come to vote." If any one should go there and attempt to deny these things, or apologize for them, the Missourians would spit upon him. They claim to own Kansas, to have a right to vote there and to make its laws, and to say what its institutions shall be. . . .
>
> The Legislature first passed acts virtually repealing the larger portion of the Constitution of the United States, and then repealed, as coolly as one would take a chew of tobacco, provisions of the Kansas-Nebraska Bill. Of this bill I have a right to speak—God forgive me for so enormous and dreadful a political sin—I voted for the bill. I thought the people were to have the right to form their own institutions, and went to Kansas to organize the Democratic party there, and make the State Democratic, but the Missouri invaders poured in—the ballot

boxes were desecrated—the bogus Legislature was elected by armed mobs—you know the rest. . . .

The Pro-slavery fragment of the Democratic party also delights in the term "nigger worshipper," to designate Free-State men. I will show you that these Pro-slavery men are of all nigger worshippers the most abject. According to the Kansas code, if a person kidnapped a white child, the utmost penalty is six months in jail—if a nigger baby, the penalty is death. Who worships niggers, and slave nigger babies at that? To kidnap a white child into slavery—six months in jail—to kidnap a nigger into freedom—Death!

Is there an Illinoisan who says enforce these monstrous iniquities called laws?—show me the man. The people of Kansas never will obey them. They are being butchered, and one and all will die first! As for myself, I am going back to Kansas, where there is an indictment pending against me for high treason. Were the rope about my neck, I would say that as to the Kansas code it shall not be enforced—never!—NEVER!

Lane finished his address with accounts of the attacks on the Free State settlers. He said he knew of "fourteen cases of tar and feathering," "the most awful and humiliating outrage ever inflicted on man." Charles Dow had been "shot dead while holding up his hands as a sign of his defenselessness." Thomas Barber was "unarmed, shot on the highway, brought dead to Lawrence, where his frantic wife, a childless widow, amid shrieks of anguish, kissed the pallid lips that of her were silent evermore."

In conclusion I have only this to say: The people of Kansas have undying faith in the justice of their cause—in the eternal life of the truths maintained—and they ask the people of Illinois to do for them that which seems to them just.

The *Chicago Tribune* reported on the mass meeting on June 2 with headlines reading, "Illinois Alive and Awake!" "$10,000 Freemen in Council!" "2,000 Old Hunkers on Hand!" "$15,000 Subscribed for Kansas!!!" Below are excerpts from the story as printed by William Cutler in 1883:

We regret we can only give a meager outline of the eloquent and telling effort of Col. Lane. He was listened to with the deepest interest and attention by the vast throng, and as he detailed the series of infamous outrages inflicted upon the freemen of Kansas, the people were breathless with mortification and anger, and wild with enthusiasm to avenge those wrongs. During Col. Lane's address, he was often interrupted by the wildest applause, or by deep groans for Pierce, Douglas, Atchison, and the dough-faces and ruffians who had oppressed Kansas, and by cheers for Sumner, Robinson, and other noble men who have dared and suffered for liberty. . . .

Take it with its attending circumstances—the shortness of the notice, the character of the assembled multitude, and the work which was accomplished—it was the most remarkable meeting ever held in the State. We believe it will inaugurate a new era in Illinois. We believe it is the precursor of the liberation of Kansas from the hand of the oppressor, and of an all-pervading political revolution at home.

The newspaper then printed details of the contributions of the donors whose names they knew. "An editor and a lawyer, four Sharpe's rifles and themselves," read one. Among the other contributions were "six rifles, three with double barrels, sure as each pop," "one sixteen-shooter," "one six-shooter, and ten pounds of balls," "one can of dry powder," along with rifles, pistols, and "one horse."

Lloyd Lewis described the effect of Lane's speech more succinctly. "Lane had let loose havoc and the dogs of war," he said, adding that "women wept, men wept, the people milled around the platform singing, shouting. They were the Commune that night, and Jim Lane was Danton, and it was all very well for our record as a safe and sane nation that the American Tuileries were 800 miles away." Even Leverett Spring had to admit, "It was at Chicago that Lane won his greatest triumph."

The result of that meeting was, as William Cutler stated, "the first great outburst of enthusiasm." That enthusiasm was as "the 'little cloud no larger than a man's hand' which forthwith spread over the whole heavens, and out of it came money, and arms, and ammunition, and a ceaseless tide of emigrants and troops of armed men—all setting Kansas-ward."

It should not be assumed that it was Jim Lane's passion alone that stirred his audience in Chicago. He did have powerful points to make, and they may have made as much impact as his speaking style. One of those points is worth examining both for its sake and because of what it would have communicated to the Chicago crowd.

Lane had said that a man kidnapping a white child would get six months in jail, while a man who took a slave child would be executed. Lane's oratorical point addressed the Westerner's view that slavery was a threat to the rights of white citizens. Lane had provided evidence that slavery's supporters were so willing to protect their institution that they would put it above the safety of white children.

Yet this oratorical point also hints that Lane was a bridge-builder. New England abolitionists, if they could overcome Lane's language, would have seen in that argument further proof of their view that slavery was immoral and unchristian. Lane's Chicago speech does suggest that he could present arguments that could appeal to both groups and therefore bring them together.

Jim Lane had been on his speaking tour of the North for some time before his powerful Chicago address. On April 5 he had been in Harrisburg, Pennsylvania. Two clippings in the Webb Scrapbooks illustrate how polarized the country was becoming over the issues of Kansas and slavery. The *New York Tribune* reported on the speech favorably and claimed that Lane's appearance had "evidently done good here." Yet the Democratic *Commercial Journal* in Pittsburgh lambasted locals for giving "this treasonable Lane" a chance to speak and labeled a follow-up resolution in support of him as "aid and comfort to the enemy." Another clipping shows that later in April, Lane was in Indiana to give another speech. The story reported that the "officious leaders" of the local Democrats "were not at all desirous to have Lane make a speech," but when Lane appeared "there was a fair proportion of that party composing his intelligent audience."

After his appearance in Chicago, Lane continued to speak across the North. Toward the latter part of June he appeared in Cleveland. Although a newspaper reported that his "voice was almost gone," he went ahead with his remarks. He told his audience that he "had been reared in the belief that two things were essential—to attend to the 'stated preaching' of the Gospel, and to vote an unscratched Democratic Ticket." But now the "leaders and supporters" of that party "were traitors, and not Democrats."

That point was followed by Lane's assertion that the "laboring white man could not live in a Slave State." Slavery had created the following classes: first, "the slaveholder"; second, "the slave"; third, "the free negro"; and "last and lowest, the laboring white man." This stated hierarchy also spoke to the views of many Westerners of the time. Slavery, they believed, was more of a threat to the freedom of whites than it was to slaves. Slave owners would not only become tyrants to their slaves but would tyrannize anyone who disagreed with slavery. One had only to look at the "bogus Legislature" and its proslavery laws to see evidence of that fact.

In the wake of speeches by Lane, Andrew Reeder, and other Free State men from Kansas, an aid movement sprung up to assist their cause. This led to a meeting in Buffalo, New York, on July 1, which created the National Kansas Committee "to receive, forward and distribute the contributions of the people, whether provisions, arms or clothing, to the needy in Kansas." The members of the committee were comprised of one representative from each Northern state, except Illinois, which had three, and Massachusetts, which had a separate organization. The head of the committee was New Yorker Thaddeus Hyatt, and the organization was headquartered in Chicago.

For the next several months the committee distributed nearly $120,000 in cash aid to Kansans and settlers bound for Kansas. The committee also gave out weapons, clothing, and other provisions. The total value of the Kansas aid amounted to approximately $200,000. However, perhaps only half of that made it to Kansas; the rest, according to William Cutler, "was intercepted and destroyed or appropriated by the numerous bands of Pro-slavery regulators who infested all the landings on the Upper Missouri." Meanwhile, a Boston Relief Committee collected about $20,000 for Kansas by June 1, 1856. This group remained in operation until the spring of 1858 and ended up donating some $80,000 in clothing and cash.

No doubt these large donations alarmed the proslavery faction in Kansas. "The Pro-slavery party had believed it an easy task . . . to force and intimidate into submission" their opponents, wrote Cutler. But the "unexpected outbreak of aggressive retaliation which immediately followed the sack of Lawrence . . . gave evidence that the work of subjugation, instead of being accomplished, was but just begun."

Not only that, said Lloyd Lewis, but Lane's speaking tour energized the new Republican Party. "Every speech made for Free-Soil Kansas was a Republican speech," he said. Lane's "most sensational speeches" across the North "were one of the most vital factors in the national financing of the Republican party." "Without Lane's inflammatory speeches in the midlands, would this money-raising device have been so effective? Probably not."

Jim Lane was able not only to put his rhetorical devices to use when moving supporters of his own cause, but he also proved effective in assuaging even the staunchest slavery advocates. According to Leverett Spring, before his successful speaking tour Jim Lane got caught up in a challenge from proslavery sympathizers. It came from "two aged men" who told Lane "to name two or ten of his followers" who would arm themselves "and meet an equal number of pro-slavery men at short range on the field of honor." Spring alleged that Lane did not like these "bloody instructions" and proposed an alternative. He would meet with Senator Atchison, each man "supported by one hundred picked men" to "arbitrate the fate of Kansas by wager of battle in the presence of twelve United States senators and twelve members of the House of Representatives." No one "saw fit to accept the revised challenge."

It sounds ludicrous, the idea of a staged battle to decide whether or not Kansas would become a Slave State or a Free State. Giving the notion some thought, though, might reveal a bit of Lane's clever thinking. The proslavery faction had long regarded their opponents as soft and cowardly. Yet when those "soft" abolitionists rallied at Lawrence the previous winter, it was the proslavery side that backed down. Viewed in that light, Lane's counterchallenge seems to suggest it would be the proslavery men who would be beaten and humiliated before respectable witnesses. Afterward it would be hard to cover up the truth of who was brave and who was not.

On a more basic level, Lane's counterproposal also seems like a smart way to dismiss those "two aged men." Their initial challenge to him was a traditional duel, and duels were largely about personal honor. Instead of accepting or rejecting the challenge, Lane returned with the outrageous suggestion of a staged battle. Nowhere in that suggestion does Lane refer to the matter of honor, much less accept that his honor was in question. In fact, the suggestion might contain this jab: "Instead of holding a meaningless duel, why don't we conduct a battle to decide the essential issue? Would you rather fight for honor or for what really matters?" His wild proposal therefore allowed Lane to refuse a duel without conceding anything.

Jay Monaghan, in writing about the incident, noted that after Lane made the counterproposal there were "many guffaws" and the "trial by combat ended in a farce." In his 1896 book about Jim Lane, John Speer claimed that while the idea for the counterproposal had been Lane's, it was Speer who had phrased the challenge in writing. Although he took the matter seriously, Speer admitted to Lane's intentions and wrote that when Lane put forward his suggestion, the "challenges stopped."

Another interesting display of Lane's rhetorical skill occurred in Nebraska City, Nebraska, during the summer when Lane and his "Army of the North" were about to enter the territory. According to Leverett Spring, the local newspaper "made a sharp attack upon Lane," and some of the men with him called for a retaliatory attack on the newspaper's office. Lane supposedly had "considerable difficulty" stopping them, and the mess "caused so much excitement" that Lane decided to hold a "conciliatory meeting." As it happened, at that meeting—in addition to the locals and the Lane men—were "many armed Missourians."

"Lane's oratory was equal to the emergency," Spring conceded. Lane started his remarks "by congratulating himself on the fact that so large a portion of Missouri had responded to his call for a conference." Lane then revealed that he had "once believed in slavery" but had experienced a change of heart. He launched into his story of visiting a sugar plantation while seeking carpentry work years before. When he told the plantation owner why he and a fellow young carpenter had come to see him, the man "laid himself back with his thumbs in the armholes of his vest and replied, 'I bought two carpenters yesterday.'" "Great God!" Lane shouted. "If such men are buying carpenters, machinists, engineers, how soon will they sell you and me in their marts of human merchandise!" Wrote Spring, "When Lane concluded his speech the Missourians, who had intended to use their knives and revolvers before the meeting was over, applauded him no less enthusiastically than his own men."

After Lane's Northern speaking engagements, he planned to return to Kansas but recognized that his movements would best be undertaken in some secrecy. He was well aware of the obstacles between him and the Kansas border, for prior to his Chicago speech a group of Illinois settlers had been prevented from entering Kansas by proslavery Missourians. Their plight was taken up by the National Kansas Committee, which formed an "armed company" to remove "the obstructions to the peaceful emigration" of Northerners to Kansas. Lane realized that whoever came with him back to the territory would not be welcomed in Missouri. They would have to bypass the state entirely if they were to avoid trouble. Lane probably also recognized that by avoiding Missouri, his movements would not be firmly known by the proslavery authorities. If the armed company promised by the National Kansas Committee did not materialize, or if it was smaller than he had hoped, he would still be able to use it to his advantage if it moved to Kansas undetected by Missouri authorities. Indeed, such a secret trail would further enhance his reputation as a leader to both his friends and his enemies.

On July 4, 1856, circulars appeared announcing what would become known as the "Lane Trail" into Kansas. The route was fairly straightforward: Chicago to Iowa City, Iowa, then west and southwest to Nebraska City, Nebraska Territory, and south and southwest into Kansas. The route was published throughout the North so that the various Kansas Committees could enter the territory with Lane.

Lloyd Lewis believed that the publicity was all Lane's doing. It was an effort "to spread terror among the Border Ruffians." Lane let it be known that he had an army coming to relieve the Free State movement. Kansans were told, "Look for Captain Cook on a white horse," and everyone recognized that Cook would be Jim

Lane. It was all "amazing propaganda" to "cow the Pro-slave bands."

When Lane arrived in Nebraska, it was at the head of a group of only six hundred or so. This group was no army, but settlers wanting to move to Kansas. Of course these settlers were Free Staters, which was excuse enough for slavery's supporters to be concerned. Although unimpressive on its face, Lane's "Army of the North" had achieved its objective. Lane had raised his profile once again.

Even the Lane Trail would prove useful to Lane as time wore on. The following year it would be used as part of the Underground Railroad for funneling freed slaves out of the region. John Brown would use the route as his path out of Kansas Territory after that. And a month after Lane's "army" marched the trail, a young Preston B. Plumb led ten men in Lane's footsteps bearing Sharps rifles, Colt pistols, Bowie knives, ammunition, and a brass twelve-pound cannon.

The material did not reach Kansas in time for Lane's next move against the proslavery faction, which was probably just as well. Tensions were about to rise again as the two sides in the territory's "civil war" faced off. Only this time, unlike in the Wakarusa War, there had already been acts of violence. Another confrontation could very easily lead to armed conflict and open warfare.

Meanwhile, back in Kansas the other leaders of the Free State movement were still under arrest for treason. The situation in Lecompton was not all bad for the men confined there or all good for the residents. One of the captives wrote in a letter dated July 31 that the townspeople were "frightened to death" and keeping a guard "around their town every night for fear of an attack." The prisoners, on the other hand, had had visitors who brought them corn, apples, grapes, beets, and cucumbers. The captive also wrote that while they "could escape," they did not want to because they had a "kind captain" watching over them and "we do not want to get him into trouble."

Charles Robinson also wrote from Lecompton. On August 16 in a message to "Messrs Allen, Blood, Hutchinson & others" he said, "While this excitement continues we think that not more than 4 or 5 persons should visit our camp in a day" so as not to harm the prisoners' "keepers." In that same letter Robinson noted that the prisoners were aware of the increasing hostilities between the two factions. Robinson, of course, urged negotiation, "provided the other party is willing." Yet he closed with, "With pride for the heroism of our 'boys' & thanksgiving for your success we remain for life or death, victory or defeat."

Robinson also sent a message to another Free State man, Samuel Walker, asking him to visit him in Lecompton. Once Walker arrived, Robinson told him of Lane's coming and that five hundred Missourians were supposed to be on their way to intercept the Free State leader. Robinson told Walker to lead fifteen men north to meet Lane at Nebraska City and gave him two hundred dollars for expenses and a horse. Walker went to Lawrence, picked out the men who would join him, and set out to meet Lane.

Walker first went to Topeka, then outside present-day Marysville, the party ran into John Brown and twelve others. Walker chose to chase down reports of Missourians in the area while his and Brown's men continued north. Shortly reuniting, the group arrived in Nebraska City a day later, and Walker gave Lane a letter from Robinson.

Lane may have interpreted Robinson's message as instructing him not to return to Kansas. According to Jay Monaghan, this message came at the same time that Lane was being discouraged by leaders of the Kansas relief committees from helping emigrants to enter Kansas, as they feared he was part of the "lawless element" defying the U.S. Army. After Lane read Robinson's letter, Walker said his head was "bowed" and tears were "running down his cheeks." "Walker," Lane said, "if you say the people of Kansas don't want me, it's all right, and I'll blow my brains out." "General," Walker replied, "the people of Kansas would rather have you than all the party at Nebraska City." Walker promised to get Lane a good disguise and escort him back to Kansas. Lane agreed, leading to one of the epic events in his life.

Lane started out from Nebraska City with Walker and John Brown and their respective parties, some thirty men in all. Lawrence was 150 miles south. The group set out daybreak at a hard pace. One by one the members of the escort had to stop in order to rest themselves or their horses. But Lane pressed forward. When the party reached the Kansas River near Topeka, there were only six men left, including Lane. Walker's horse made it across the river, Lane and another man swam, and the rest got stuck trying to cross. The men then ate their first meal since leaving Nebraska.

Lane and the man who had swum the river with him got new horses, and they and Walker turned east for Lawrence despite the fact that it was now raining. Walker later noted that he fell off his horse three times due to "hunger and fatigue," and each time Lane helped him back up into his saddle. Walker stopped at his house near Lawrence, too tired to continue. The other man rode two more miles before he gave up the ride. "Lane went into Lawrence alone," Walker later said, "reaching there at three o'clock in the morning." Then, said Albert Richardson, who also wrote an account of the incident, "after three or four hours' rest [Lane] was attending to his ordinary business."

In thirty hours Jim Lane had ridden almost nonstop from Nebraska City to Lawrence via Topeka. The men riding with him, who were supposed to be protecting him, found they lacked the strength to keep up with him. Even John Brown failed to keep pace. It would be a story that Lane's friends would tell long after he had died, a reminder of the man's will and stamina.

Less well-remembered, except perhaps by Charles Robinson, was a tale from that time claiming Lane wanted to move on Lecompton once he returned to Kansas Territory. Ostensibly it was to liberate the Free State prisoners, but Robinson would later hint that it was for "their destruction by the army." Robinson wrote openly in his memoir that as Gaius Jenkins was one of the prisoners, and since Lane and Jenkins were engaged in a land dispute, Lane might have wanted Jenkins killed during the rescue. Although he did not articulate it, Robinson seems to have wanted his readers to think that Lane wanted Robinson killed as well.

This tale is brought into question by two letters given to the Kansas State Historical Society by the widow of Richard Hinton and quoted in an article about James Horton in 1904. The first letter is from Lane to Robinson, Jenkins, John Brown, Jr., George Smith, George Dietzler, G. W. Brown, and Elisha Williams. It was dated August 11, 1856, and sent from Topeka. Lane's letter begins with him stating that he had returned to Kansas "with a sufficient force" and was "ready to rescue you." He explained that it would be "best if you can escape to do so, and let me meet you with my defending force just outside of your prison-house." Prompt action was important, as "the bloodhounds" were seeking him and his men. If they could not escape, "I can and will attack your guard," Lane wrote, but he added, "although it were the best policy, if blood is to flow, that it be shed in your defense than in your rescue." If the letter is accurate, then it speaks for itself.

The second letter is from Robinson to Lane and was written later that same day. Robinson reported that the prisoners had been told their prosecutions were about to be dropped or that their trials would be held in a Northern state such as Pennsylvania. "I have no doubt that something will be done, and to anticipate any such assistance would be prejudicial to our cause," Robinson said. He continued, "It would afford us a great pleasure to see you, and perhaps we may. . . . Guerilla operations are rife now, and they should be attended to," he advised. "The Missourians are stridently intending an attack, but we can *sweeten them now*. The officers here are willing that our people should put an end to these invaders without troubling them."

Added to these is the letter that John Brown, Jr., wrote to his father, dated August 16, 1856. In that letter the younger Brown said, "The prospect now appears so favorable for us, that it does seem as though I had not better try to meet you just now. The prospect is that there will be either a writ of Habeus Corpus [*sic*] issued or a change of venue which will in either case take us into the States for trial." Later the son advised, "In view of present prospects the prisoners think best that no attempt should be made at present to release them."

It seems clear from both Brown's and Robinson's letters that the prisoners were certain they were in no danger. They had enough liberty to send confidential correspondence and not worry about them being intercepted. Lane's own letter seems to suggest that he would not try any rescue unless asked or ordered to do so. It is probable that Robinson's later charge was another attempt to diminish Lane, who although not at the head of the expected "army," led men willing to fight the proslavery faction not at the polls or in debates, but with firearms and cannon.

On August 12, wrote William Cutler, "a party of twenty-five horsemen and fifty-six footmen left Lawrence, for the purpose of attacking Franklin, recapturing the cannon, then in possession of the enemy at the place, and breaking up the marauding gang that had their headquarters there." Quoting Thomas Bickerton, Cutler said that the main reason for the attack was to capture the cannon so they could use it against another proslavery outpost.

Bickerton had met with a man named William Hutchinson when he arrived in Lawrence the day before, August 11. Hutchinson told Bickerton "he would show me a man from the States named 'Cook,'" who was in fact Jim Lane. Later, when the force approached Franklin, "who should come along but this 'Joe Cook,' on horseback, and make himself known to the boys. They were very much elated with seeing Lane, and seemed now to think that everything would go right."

In Franklin, after several hours of indecisive firing, Bickerton made a suggestion to one of the other leaders of the force. "I proposed getting some hay and setting fire to them," he said. They found a wagon, loaded it with hay, and set the hay on fire. They dragged the wagon to the post office, where most of their opponents were seeking shelter. The building started to catch fire, the men inside asked for quarter, and the shooting stopped.

Another account of the action at Franklin comes from A. J. Hoole, a South Carolinian who had come to the territory in April. Hoole, writing to his sister on August 27, claimed that between 250 and 300 "Abolitionists" attacked a mere 14 men. The abolitionists were repulsed in their attack twice, and all 14 men escaped once the building was set on fire. On the abolitionist side, "32 were killed and wounded, 7 or 8 killed."

These conflicting accounts of the events at Franklin show the problem that anyone writing about this era today faces: accuracy. As Dale Watts' study of political violence in the territorial period demonstrated, accounts often came from "highly biased sources" writing "for propagandistic purposes." The reasons for this bias varied: some accounts were to elicit support; some to diminish opponents; and some were assumptions based on rumors. The only death at Franklin that Watts found was of an unknown Free State man.

The Franklin fight was followed by news of another murder along the Wakarusa. Around August 12 a Free State man named Hoyt was asked to persuade some Georgians in a so-called fort on Washington Creek to leave area settlers alone. The men there claimed their camp was "a peaceable one," so Hoyt felt safe in approaching them to talk. Upon arrival Hoyt was shot and killed.

The murder of Hoyt enraged the Free Staters in the area. They decided to retaliate against his killers, whose camp was also known as Fort Saunders. Lane, still in his disguise as Captain Cook, was reluctant to attack, but the anger of the men changed his mind. The day after the murder they marched on Fort Saunders, found it abandoned, and burned it to the ground.

After destroying Fort Saunders, Lane's men started back to Lawrence, but en route they were told that men under Henry Titus were attacking Free State residents near Lecompton. Lane and his men changed course and headed for Fort Titus, a few miles south of Lecompton. Along the way some of Titus's men ran into Lane's force. A skirmish broke out, leading to the wounding of two of Titus's men and the capture of another.

On the morning of August 16 a group of horsemen under Capt. Henry Shombre approached the fort in hopes of surprising the men there and capturing them. Having arrived at the fort, they charged a group of tents nearby, causing the men in them to flee toward the Titus home. The attackers came too close to the fort, the men inside fired a volley, and four of the Free State fighters were wounded, Shombre mortally.

Lane and the rest of his force arrived a little later with the cannon taken at Franklin in tow. "On the first shot being fired the Lawrence boys shouted that it was a new issue of the *Herald of Freedom*," wrote William Cutler. After the cannon had been fired about half a dozen more times "the white flag appeared" and the men defending the fort surrendered. Seventeen men were taken prisoner, including Titus, who was himself wounded, and weapons and provisions were claimed by the Free Staters. Two men were killed on the proslavery side and another mortally wounded.

The bombardment of Fort Titus could be heard in Lecompton, and not just by the townspeople. Army soldiers under the command of Maj. John Sedgwick also heard the cannon fire. Sedgwick sent some of his men into Lecompton with orders to report to Governor Shannon. They found the townsfolk "in a high state of trepidation," fearing an attack by Lane's men, and territorial officials had "left the town or [were] hidden from sight." William Cutler wrote that "Shannon was reported to have been found on the river bank in the act of embarking on a scow, to cross the river."

The battle at Fort Titus brought Shannon back into the fray as a mediator. He, along with an officer and a Lecompton doctor, traveled to Lawrence to arrange another truce. Sara Robinson claimed that Shannon and the doctor "were ready to make terms," for while in Lawrence they "trembled like aspen leaves for fear." As part of the terms, Shannon arranged for the men arrested after the fight at Franklin to be exchanged for Titus and his men. Shannon told the people of Lawrence that "he wished to set himself right" with them. He "desired peace and harmony for the few days of his continuance in office" and pledged that the agreement would be carried out.

Yet blood continued to be shed. On August 19 a man named Hoppe was killed by Charles Fuget near Leavenworth. Fuget had vowed to kill the first Free State man he met, and that man was Hoppe, whom Fuget shot and scalped. When a German in Leavenworth spoke out against Fuget's crime, Fuget killed him as well. Fuget was put on trial for Hoppe's murder but acquitted, probably by a proslavery jury.

At the end of August a band of proslavery fighters marched on Osawatomie. On August 30 two of them came across Frederick Brown, one of John Brown's sons, and shot him. Within two hours some three hundred men were encroaching upon the town. John Brown had less than three dozen men with which to oppose them so decided to retreat to the Pottawatomie River. A battle ensued and lasted for some time. Once Brown's men ran out of ammunition they left the area, and the town was sacked.

Historian Dale Watts found that not only Frederick Brown but also another man were killed before the attack on Osawatomie. During the battle two proslavery men were killed, one Free State man was killed during and a second after, and a third was killed nearby on September 1. More violence occurred that first day in September when a group of proslavery men led by Frederick Emory tried to drive William Phillips out of Leavenworth. A gunfight ensued in which Phillips killed two of his attackers before Emory killed Phillips.

By now Wilson Shannon was no longer the territorial governor of Kansas. His replacement had not yet arrived, so on August 21, Daniel Woodson, the proslavery secretary of the territory, became acting governor. It was Woodson who called out the territorial militia, members of which had attacked Osawatomie.

Woodson tried to order Col. Phillip St. George Cooke, in overall military command in Kansas, to march on Topeka, "disarm the insurrectionists," and prevent the Free State forces from interfering in the actions of the territorial militia and their Missouri allies. Cooke responded by telling Woodson that he "had transcended his instructions in the orders he had given." Cooke added that he would refuse to obey orders unless they came directly from Washington.

Around that time, Lane led some three hundred men against Atchison's camp along Bull Creek near Osawatomie. Before a battle could occur Atchison and his men returned to Missouri, and with that Lane took his command back to Lawrence. On September 4, Lane did march on Lecompton and, according to John Gihon, "before any intimation was received by the citizens, his cannon were frowning upon their houses." Sara Robinson wrote that from Lecompton came pleas to Fort Leavenworth for troops, as "one thousand men" were about to attack.

But Lane had other ideas. He sent two men into the town to ask whoever was in charge to release the Free State prisoners. Mrs. Robinson wrote that when the pair asked for the man in command, they were told he was a "General Richardson." Richardson appeared a moment later, and they asked whether he was in command. "Well, I don't know as I am." When asked if he remained in charge, he said, "No, I suppose not; I resigned this morning."

Another man stepped forward, a General Marshall, and told the two men that he was "ready to receive any proposition." One of the two told Marshall, "I am directed by General Lane, commander of the free-state forces of Kansas, to demand of you the unconditional and immediate release of all the free-state prisoners now in Lecompton."

"We wish to make no compromises with General Lane," said Marshall, "only that he shall treat our prisoners as kindly and courteously as we treat his."

"Do I understand you to refuse to surrender the prisoners demanded?"

Marshall answered that was so, and the two men prepared to leave. Marshall then stopped them, asking them "to wait a few minutes," and stepped away. When Marshall returned he told them that "all the prisoners demanded had been released that morning, and that provision had been made to obtain an escort of United States dragoons to attend them to Lawrence the next day." Marshall asked them to tell Lane to release his prisoners.

At that same moment Col. Phillip St. George Cooke was meeting with Lane. Colonel Cooke told Lane and his staff, "Gentlemen, you have made a great mistake in coming here to-day. The territorial militia was dismissed this morning; some of them have left, some are leaving now, and the rest will leave and go to their homes as soon as they can."

One of Lane's men said to Cooke, "When we send a man, or two men, or a dozen men, to speak with the territorial authorities, they are arrested and held like felons. How, then, are we to know what is going on in Lecompton? Why, we have to come here with an army to find out what is going on. How else could we know?"

"To this," wrote Mrs. Robinson, "Col. Cooke made no reply."

As it was, the Free State prisoners entered Lane's camp that evening and the next day were escorted to Lawrence. But the situation remained tense. On the day of Lane's march on Lecompton three men were supposedly attacked by ruffians between Leavenworth and Lawrence, with two of the three killed.

In mid-September the new territorial governor, John W. Geary, arrived to restore calm to Kansas. Geary had been born in Pennsylvania, the same state that former governor Andrew Reeder was from. Geary was a Mexican War veteran who had served as the postmaster of San Francisco, a judge, then the first mayor of the city after its incorporation. He had returned to his home state in 1853 and lived privately until he accepted the post of territorial governor of Kansas.

Geary had been appointed governor late in July and spent August in consultation with the president and administration officials about the policy he would pursue in Kansas. Much was riding on Geary's performance. If he could quiet the disorder in Kansas, he might save the Democrats from defeat in the upcoming fall election.

Geary's appointment was not received well by the proslavery side. Senator Atchison put his name to a letter that denounced Geary because, according to one of Geary's friends, the new governor "was determined not to affiliate with either of the opposing factions."

Geary's personal secretary, John Gihon, wrote a book in 1857 about his and Geary's experience in Kansas. Gihon's account of their journey from Fort Leavenworth to Lecompton shows just how difficult Geary's task was going to be, if the Atchison letter hadn't made it clear enough.

They left the fort on September 10 along with "three friends" and a military escort. Passing the town of Leavenworth, Gihon noticed that the town was "barricaded by a line of heavy transportation wagons" along its western side. "These were intended as a protection against an expected assault from Lane," he wrote; "but to a military eye, it was evident that a barricade of pipe-stems would have answered a far more useful purpose. The wagons would have proved more serviceable to the attacking than to the repelling forces."

Around noon the party reached a village called Alexandria, about thirteen miles west of Leavenworth. Alexandria was comprised of just two homes that served as a local post office and as stores. Geary was told that an hour earlier the stores had been robbed, with one of the young men on the scene claiming that "the attack was made by about one hundred and fifty of Lane's men."

Governor Geary was an experienced frontiersman. He examined the "moccasin tracks" of the robbers and other clues on the scene. He told the officer in charge of the military escort that the young man's story was false and that "certainly not over a dozen horsemen" had carried out the attack. Eventually Geary's party caught up with the riders. At the first house they claimed to be Free State men, but a sergeant with Geary recognized them as proslavery men he had seen in Leavenworth that morning.

The man who was initially blamed on the Alexandria raid, Jim Lane, by now already had a fearsome reputation. Gihon noted that it had not taken Geary long to learn that the "very name of Lane was a terror, and it was only necessary to get up a rumor that he was within a hundred miles, to produce a universal consternation." If a report came that Lane was "actually approaching a pro-slavery town," panic ensued. "Vaporing generals, colonels, captains and privates, suddenly stopped in the midst of their stories of valiant deeds, and remembering that they had forgotten their needed arms or ammunition, or that the women and children must be carried to a place of safety, off they ran for shelter in the woods or elsewhere, creeks and rivers furnishing no obstacles to their flight." Of course, said Gihon, once the "danger" was past these would get together "over . . . bad whiskey" and tell of "what terrible deeds he would have accomplished, had the cowardly abolitionist dared to make his appearance."

A. J. Hoole, the Southerner who claimed that forty Free State men were killed at Franklin, inadvertently also reflected these attitudes in his letters home. In one written after Shannon's resignation, he described Lane's followers as an overwhelming force of "from 1500 to 2500 men," while in another, dated April 12, 1857, Hoole claimed that when Lane rode within a hundred yards or so of a house, the Southern women inside showed no fear of him and even "talked about killing him."

A Kansas City newspaper in its August 30, 1856, issue expressed the general panic Lane's presence incited in the proslavery faction. It claimed that Lane "with over one thousand men has cut off all communications" with proslavery friends in Kansas. "He has seized all the crossings of the Kansas and Wakarusa Rivers." It added, "the roads will have to be opened by force," their side was "in a state of siege," and the "Government of the Territory is subverted and the Revolution complete."

Geary's own understanding of the crisis in Kansas can be seen in a letter he wrote to his superiors the day before he left Fort Leavenworth. On September 9 he said, "It is no exaggeration to say that the existing difficulties are of a far more complicated character than I had anticipated." Not only did he have to deal with "bands of armed ruffians and brigands," but he had to cope with "the influence of men who have been placed in authority, and have employed all the destructive agents around them to promote their own personal interests, at the sacrifice of every just, honorable and lawful consideration."

Among the "actual pro-slavery settlers" were "well-disposed persons," and "among the free-soil residents are many peaceable and useful citizens." But in both camps there were "a few troublesome agitators." On the Free State side, the "chief of these" was Jim Lane, "encamped and fortified at Lawrence with a force, it is said, of fifteen hundred men."

Lane certainly did not have that many men at his command. Had he, the proslavery forces would already have been driven from the territory. But Geary's assessment was true that Lane was taking an active role in the Free State resistance.

As Geary and his associates arrived in the territory, Lane was in the Topeka area leading a small group toward Holton. En route he was met by men from Ozawkie who told him that Border Ruffians were in the area. They said they had already burned Grasshopper Falls (now Valley Falls) and were threatening to attack other Free State towns nearby. Lane was told that the proslavery forces under Capt. H. A. Lowe were at Hickory Point, a tiny village about five and a half miles north of present-day Oskaloosa in Jefferson County. The surrounding area had a mix of proslavery and abolitionist settlers. Back in June two proslavery men were driven from the area, and on September 8, Border Ruffians attacked the village and looted one of the stores.

Very early on the morning of September 11, some of Lane's men surprised a proslavery camp and took prisoners and arms. In the meantime Lane raided Ozawkie, burning a store and a few houses, driving out the proslavery men there, and raising his own numbers. Two days later the abolitionists arrived at Hickory Point, discovering a force of some one hundred men ensconced among the three cabins, store, small hotel, and blacksmith shop that comprised the village.

Samuel Reader, at the time a teenager, was one of the men who followed Lane to Hickory Point. He later wrote down his experience, giving us an interesting view of both Lane and the Battle of

Hickory Point. Reader's story began with him, his uncle, and some other men going in search of a horse taken by some Free Staters, the horse "having been mistaken for a proslavery horse." When they came to the Kansas River they saw "a body of mounted men." Reader's uncle pointed to one of them and shouted, "There is Lane!" Reader then joined Lane's party on the march north.

Later in the day the force came to a house. Inside, wrote Reader, a young woman spoke to Lane, saying that she was a teacher. Lane "promptly" offered his assistance in finding her a school at which to teach. She did not recognize Lane and asked him his name. Lane looked to one of the Free State leaders with him, who with a laugh encouraged him to tell her. "General Lane turned to the young woman, and said very quietly and impressively, 'My name is Lane.' 'What?' she asked. 'You are James H. Lane?' Lane bowed. 'Well,' she continued after a slight pause, 'as I am not personally acquainted with General Lane you must excuse me for doubting your identity.'" The men around Lane laughed, and Reader said that "Lane looked very sheepish."

Lane's men arrived at Hickory Point on the morning of September 13. Lane tried to convince the proslavery men to surrender, telling them in a message that he had fifteen hundred men. The messenger Lane sent came back and said to him, "The leader of the gang read your summons and returned it with these words, 'Take this dirty paper back . . . and tell him we will fight him and all the hireling cutthroats and assassins he can bring against us.'" The battle then got underway.

Lane's men fired first, putting up a ragged barrage against their opponents. Reader thought their shooting "was very deliberate" but "seemed better" than the firing his fellows were receiving. "None of us were hit," he wrote, saying that the proslavery men's "bullets generally passed over our heads." Eventually the indecisive shooting petered out.

Lane understood that without stronger firepower his force was unable to make any headway against the foes. "We can drive them out, but we should lose too many men," Reader said he heard Lane tell the "officers" with him. "We must wait another day and get artillery." Lane decided to pull his men back to Ozawkie.

Lane sent word to James Harvey in Lawrence to bring up a cannon.

In the meantime Governor Geary issued a proclamation ordering all armed groups to disperse. Lane tried to intercept Harvey but, in taking a different road, missed him. Harvey and his men arrived at Hickory Point the next day. After an indecisive bombardment and exchange of small-arms fire, Harvey decided that sending a hay wagon against the blacksmith shop then setting it ablaze might drive out his foes. He gave the order, and although the men moving it took fire, they were able to torch the wagon. The proslavery force raised a white flag, both sides agreed to disperse, and the Battle of Hickory Point was over.

The day before the action at Hickory Point started, Governor Geary referred to his disbandment order in a letter to the secretary of state. "I have determined to dismiss the present organized militia," he wrote, for several reasons: "[that] they were not enrolled in accordance with the laws; that many of them were not citizens of the territory; that some of them were committing outrages under the pretense of serving the public; and that they were unquestionably perpetuating, rather than diminishing, the troubles with which the territory agitated."

When news reached Geary of Hickory Point, he dispatched Col. Phillip St. George Cooke to intercept and arrest the Free State raiders. Cooke intercepted Harvey on September 14 and brought Harvey's men to Lecompton the next day. According to John Gihon, initially Harvey's men "denied having been guilty of any overt act," but when they were "taunted by some prominent proslavery men" nearby, they admitted to having taken part in the fighting at Hickory Point. When asked if they had read the governor's proclamation, "one of the leaders readily and wittily replied, 'Oh, yes, and before we commenced our fire upon the border-ruffians, we read the proclamation to them, and commanded them to surrender in the name of the governor.'"

According to William Cutler, Lane's actions after the first day at Hickory Point became "the subject of severe criticism on the part of his opponents, who attributed to him cowardice, selfishness, and the baser motive of treachery in thus, without notice, abandoning his friend." The explanation for Lane not meeting up with Harvey was simple enough. Lane's message had called for Harvey to come from Lawrence "by way of the Topeka road." When Lane heard of Geary's proclamation he pulled back along the route he expected Harvey to take, but Harvey took another route.

Geary did not seem to hold this against the Free State side, for around this time he went to Lawrence. He told the leaders there, including Robinson, that the town would be protected. Not long after that meeting he went to a camp of proslavery militia that had gathered on the Wakarusa. He ordered them to disband, as he had their opponents. He even confronted David Atchison. "When I saw you last," he told the senator, "you were acting as vice-president of the nation and president of the most dignified body of men in the world, the Senate of the United States. It is with sorrow and pain that I see you now, leading on to a civil and disastrous war an army of men, with uncontrollable passions and determined upon whole-sale slaughter and destruction."

The political struggle in Kansas carried on after the fighting had ended. On October 6 there was another election held in Kansas. On the ballot were the seats in the legislature, the delegate to Congress, and a call for a constitutional convention. The Free State faction decided not to take part, feeling that to do so would give the process legitimacy. In spite of this there was still more ille-gal voting, and again there would be a proslavery territorial legis-lature and congressional delegate.

That same month the Free Staters captured after Hickory Point were put on trial. Most were acquitted or had their trial post-poned, but several were convicted of manslaughter. Sheriff Jones wrote to Geary asking for balls and chains for those convicted. On November 21, Geary coolly replied that Fort Leavenworth had "no balls and chains for the purpose indicated in your request, nor is it deemed advisable to procure any while the trial of the remain-der of the Hickory Point prisoners remains unfinished." The next day Geary took the prisoners out of Jones' custody and eventually released them.

The year 1856 was a presidential election year, and Kansas figured prominently in the contest. The Republican Party held their first national convention, in Philadelphia. Formed only a few years earli-er with opposition to slavery's extension as their main platform, the party chose John C. Frémont as their candidate for president.

Frémont was a famous explorer, was married to the daughter of Sen. Thomas Hart Benton, and had no voting record that the rival campaigns could exploit to undermine his positions. The Democratic Party convention flirted with renominating Franklin Pierce and nominating Stephen Douglas before settling on James Buchanan. Buchanan had been a congressman, a senator, a diplomat, and secretary of state. He had been an ambassador to Britain the past few years, so like Frémont he had no ties to the Kansas situation. A third political party, the North American Party, strongly associated with the anti-immigrant Know Nothing movement, nominated former president Millard Fillmore as their candidate.

Because of the deepening divisions between North and South over slavery, in the North the competition was between Buchanan and Frémont, while in the South it was between Buchanan and Fillmore. Southerners threatened disunion if Frémont were elected, which divided members of the old Whig Party and became fuel for the Democrats. Republicans, fearful of being tainted with the notion of "racial equality," hedged under the assault, which left some Republicans uncertain about backing their party and candidate.

Frémont's campaign was energized by a powerful slogan: "Free Soil, Free Speech, Free Men, Frémont!" However, Frémont was an inexperienced politician, and his campaign suffered due to that and to the various divisions of the party and the nation. It perhaps didn't help that by the time the election occurred, the fighting in Kansas had come to a temporary end. Frémont did win eleven states and received 114 electoral votes. Fillmore won only the state of Maryland. Buchanan won the rest of the Southern states, five Northern states, and garnered 174 electoral votes. James Buchanan became the new president of the United States. He now inherited responsibility for resolving the situation in Kansas, and dealing with men like Jim Lane.

VII.

The Lecompton Constitution

January 6, 1857, was the day set for the next session of the Topeka legislature. However, only a few members showed up, and among the missing were Gov. Charles Robinson and his lieutenant governor. The session was adjourned until the next day, when enough members had appeared to form a quorum. After organizing a committee to draft a memorial to Congress, a deputy marshal appeared and arrested some of the members, most likely for treason. The arrests were made without any resistance, and the following day the remaining members voted to recess until June 9.

Robinson's absence at this time was a cause for concern. Some even believed he had abandoned the movement. Later Robinson explained that he was in Washington trying to shepherd the Topeka constitution through Congress. He also revealed that, as he believed Geary to be a fair man, he had decided to resign. He gave his letter of resignation to the lieutenant governor to present to the Topeka legislature.

In the meantime, on January 12 the proslavery faction held a convention at Lecompton. The Law and Order political party renamed itself the National Democracy of Kansas. That same day at Lecompton the new territorial legislature began their session. The members vowed to overturn any veto of the governor, starting with a bill to allow district court judges to grant bail for any crime. Geary vetoed the bill and his veto was overturned as promised.

On February 19 the legislature passed an act to take a census for an election of delegates to draft a state constitution. The election would be held on the third Monday in June, and the delegates would assemble in Lecompton on the first Monday in September. Before it could be passed, Geary met with the two important members of the body. He pointed out to them that while the act limited the ability of new residents to the territory to vote, it did nothing to stop Missourians from registering and voting. They ignored his objections and passed the bill, he vetoed it, and they again overturned his veto.

Geary's next crisis in Kansas came when Samuel Jones resigned after the Topeka arrests in January. A Douglas County board appointed a William T. Sherrard to replace Jones as sheriff. Sherrard was, in the words of William Cutler, "a man totally unfit for the position, illiterate, debauched, and otherwise incompetent. His only recommendation to offset his many disqualifications was that he was a blatant bully of the most brutal Pro-slavery type." Geary held off on granting Sherrard a commission, and Sherrard "insolently demanded it with oaths and threats." In short order he began threatening Geary's life. On February 18, Sherrard got into a gun battle at a Lecompton meeting with another man and Geary's secretary, and Sherrard was killed.

By then Geary seemed to have had all he could take. He sent word to the new president, James Buchanan, that he would resign. He told Daniel Woodson on March 10 that this decision was due to ill health, but clearly he felt he could no longer do his job properly and if he continued to do so his life would remain in danger. He left Kansas in secret, just as Shannon and Reeder had done.

On April 10, 1857, Robert J. Walker was appointed governor of Kansas Territory. Walker was a Pennsylvanian like Geary and Reeder but had perhaps the most enviable credentials of any of the territorial governors. He graduated first in his class from the University of Pennsylvania, married a great-granddaughter of Benjamin Franklin, had been a senator from Mississippi, and as secretary of the Treasury had put into place the free-trade Walker Tariff. Despite such previous distinctions, he would struggle with frontier legislation. He was only five-feet-two and weighed one hundred pounds, "a mere whiffet of a man," and was often in poor health.

In between the Geary and Walker administrations, one Leavenworth newspaper reported that Jim Lane was back at his law practice. This proslavery paper reported, "He says his voice is for peace and no longer war. We presume he sees no further chance to 'feather his nest' by gulling the northern people with the tales and rumors of wars." Of course it is just as likely Lane, and the rest of the Free State movement, was waiting for the new territorial governor to arrive and declare himself, and like everyone else he had to keep busy until then.

Walker arrived in Kansas on May 25. Two days later the new governor gave his inaugural address. Carefully vetted by the Buchanan administration, Walker's address gave support for the existing process of drafting a state constitution. However, it did call for all the legal voters in Kansas to be allowed to take part in the delegate election. Walker expressed hope that once the constitution was drafted it would be submitted to the people for a vote of approval before being allowed to become the law.

Walker's address presented a question to the Free State movement: was it now time to take part in the political process, or had the situation changed enough to warrant a new strategy? On the one hand, if they were beginning to outnumber the proslavery faction, that might overwhelm any efforts at ballot fraud by their opponents. On the other hand, the proslavery faction still controlled the territorial government. They had already "fixed" part of the process to draft a state constitution. Did they still have enough power to continue to rig things in their favor despite any possible numerical inferiority? The question of participation was one that the Free State movement would attempt to answer during the summer of 1857. Jim Lane would be at the center of that debate.

Lane returned to Kansas around April 1. He laid low for several weeks, keeping out of the public eye and meeting only with his friends. He resumed taking part in public meetings on June 9 when a mass convention gathered in Topeka to discuss the situation. As ever he was no shrinking violet. He was elected president of the convention and early on gave what William Cutler called "one of his characteristic speeches." Lane insisted on defiance of the territorial laws and the government established under them. With "great vehemence," at one point he said, "We will not obey the laws, we will not pay the taxes." He was not afraid of any new indictment lodged against him. "Governor Walker said, vote next week. What for? Have we not made our constitution? And do not the people of freedom like it? Is there any one of the Free-state party opposed to it? Can't we submit this to the people, and who wants another?"

Lane's view was not, in Cutler's words, "the unanimous reflex of the sentiments of the convention." However, he still had his admirers, "impressed by his rough eloquence and inspired by a heartfelt and all-absorbing hatred of slavery and all its minions." Among those admirers was the *Herald of Freedom,* which in its June 13 issue reported favorably on Lane's remarks and on a speech he gave in Lawrence a few days before.

Like previous conventions this one drafted a series of resolutions. But this convention also showed signs of division among the members of the Free State movement. The division was between those who thought resistance was the way to achieve the movement's goal and those who advocated participation and peaceful tactics. Lane by this time was leading the radicals, while the more moderate elements were under Charles Robinson. The divisions were smoothed over temporarily at Topeka on June 9, but they continued to present themselves as time went on.

On that same day, June 9, the Free State legislature met in Topeka. Unfortunately the members were never able to gather a quorum. Governor Walker was in Topeka at the time but decided against interfering with the session. Instead he gave a public address in which he repeated the policy he expressed at his inauguration. He did make one new point, that in October, "not under the act of the late Territorial Legislature, but under the laws of Congress, you, the whole people of Kansas, have the right to elect a delegate to Congress and to elect a Territorial Legislature." "This statement on due consideration had no small influence on the minds of many Free-state men in deciding them to participate in the election," wrote William Cutler.

Despite some interest in participating, the Free State faction chose not to take part in the election of delegates to the Lecompton constitutional convention. They might have been able to win, as there may have been only two thousand votes cast in that election. William Cutler speculated that this was less than a quarter of the residents of the territory according to the latest census. But had the Free Staters tried to take part, they might have faced another round of vote fraud, intimidation, and even violence.

There was another convention held in Topeka on July 15 and 16 on the election question and Lane was again chairman. This time Jim Lane was nominated to be the Free State delegate to Congress. Although he felt honored by the nomination, he refused to accept it. He said that he was not going "to leave Kansas [again] until her Missouri chains were broken and her people free under her own government." On the matter of the October territorial election, a recommendation was passed calling for a "mass convention at Grasshopper Falls, on the last Wednesday in August, to take such action as may be necessary in regard to that election."

During the convention Lane read a newspaper clipping that, according to the *Herald of Freedom,* had been put out "for his especial benefit." The reading was from the *Indiana Jeffersonian,* a "Democratic paper published in his old neighborhood." The *Jeffersonian* claimed that Lane, the "notorious freedom-shrieker," had recently "FRATERNIZED with 'bloody Atchison and with the monster Stringfellow'" and that he was "investing the proceeds of his freedom-shrieking speeches" in business ventures with the two men. The newspaper went on to claim that Lane was pocketing the money raised by his speeches to aid the Free State cause. To this charge, reported the *Herald,* "Gen. Lane replied that not one dollar of all the money that had come to Kansas had ever stuck to his hands." Two other men proclaimed the charges false and impugned the reliability of the Indiana editor.

The convention met at Grasshopper Falls on August 26. There had already been many local meetings held about the subject of the October election, so the hope for this meeting was that people's minds were now made up, and all the delegates had to do was ascertain the majority's sentiment and pass the relevant resolutions reflecting that view. Lane was at Grasshopper Falls, this time representing Doniphan County. He was placed on the Business Committee. As it happened, he and Charles Robinson were on the same side, arguing for participation in the October election. Opposing them and the idea of participation were men like James Redpath and Martin Conway.

Robinson alleged in his memoir that Lane favored participating in the election only because once at the convention he saw which way the majority was leaning. Yet in the *Herald of Freedom*'s report on the Topeka meeting in July, Lane had given the last speech, in which he said, "we must carry the October election." Later in his remarks Lane told the convention that the only use the Free Staters had for the territorial legislature was to "wrest it" from "the hands of our enemies." He also made clear that he still wanted the existing territorial government kept separate from the movement to admit Kansas under the Topeka constitution.

Lane and Robinson were not only allies, but theirs was the majority view. The resolutions adopted stated that since it was "of the most vital importance" that "the Territorial Government should be controlled by the bona-fide citizens," and since Governor Walker had pledged "a fair and full vote before impartial judges" at the October election, "we, the people of Kansas, in mass convention assembled, agree to participate in said election." They would rely on Walker's "faithful fulfillment" of his promise and ask him to review and correct "the wicked apportionment" that had been forced through by the proslavery legislature. The final resolution called for Lane to "be authorized and empowered" to offer Walker "the force organized by him" for "the protection of the ballot-box."

Governor Walker didn't quite take to that offer. On July 27 he wrote to Secretary of State Lewis Cass that Lane had been put in formal command of the Free State militia with the "professed object" of protecting the ballot box. However, Walker said, "no one of the constitutional party proposes to disturb" the election. He believed that the chance of another election-day invasion from Missouri was nonexistent, but he also requested that at least two thousand regular troops with artillery be stationed in the territory to preserve peace and enforce the law.

Enclosed with that letter were copies of two "General Orders" that Lane had issued. In the first order Lane called for towns and neighborhoods to raise companies to defend the polls. The second order contained Lane's outline for a militia force of four divisions, with two brigades to each division, each denoted by region. The superintendents of enrollments for each division and brigade were named as well. Walker was clearly alarmed by these detailed preparations and assumed the worst was going to occur once again in the fall.

By the end of 1857 a change had occurred within the Free State movement, as exemplified by the results of the Grasshopper Falls convention. The Topeka constitution was no longer seen as a valid method of rallying antislavery sentiment and resisting the proslavery authorities. The legislative election of October offered another chance for the Free State faction to take control of Kansas. But unlike previous elections, this time the antislavery advocates believed they had numbers on their side and a governor willing to enforce a free and fair balloting.

Still, though, Lane and the Free State militia went out to protect the polls from proslavery fraud. Kendall Bailes later wrote that Lane himself was at the village of Lanesfield (which was named for him) near present-day Edgerton in Johnson County. A detachment of regular soldiers was also sent to Lanesfield, leading to a tense meeting between Lane's men and the troopers. After the lieutenant in charge of the soldiers personally looked over Lane, amid laughs in the ranks of both groups, the soldiers left and Lane's men cast their ballots.

Election day was October 5, and historian Nicole Etcheson found that in most places the weather was "rainy and chilly." Army soldiers were posted at the polling places along with Free State men and calm largely prevailed. There was one obvious instance of fraud at Oxford in McGee County, where a village with six houses somehow polled over fifteen hundred voters, but Governor Walker refused to accept the bogus returns. Turnout was high, especially on the Free State side, and control of both houses of the territorial legislature went to the Free Staters.

Coming on the heels of the Free State victory were the results of the Lecompton convention. On September 7 a constitutional convention had been assembled at Lecompton to draft a proslavery state constitution. The convention met until September 11, when they adjourned to October 19. They met again from October 19 to November 3, when the delegates adjourned permanently. Not surprisingly, the constitution they drafted was ardently proslavery in character.

Article VII of the constitution said that "the right of property is before and higher than any constitutional sanction, and the right of the owner of a slave to such slave and its increase, is the same and as inviolable as the right of the owner of any property whatever." The state legislature would "have no power to pass laws for the emancipation of slaves without the consent of the owners," nor the "power to prevent immigrants to the State from bringing with them to the State such persons as are deemed slaves by the laws of any one of the United States or Territories," but they could "pass laws to permit the owners of slave to emancipate them." Anyone who harmed or killed a slave would "suffer such punishment as would be inflicted in case the like offense had been committed on a free white person," except "in case of insurrection of said slave." Furthermore, a section of the "Bill of Rights" read, "Free negroes shall not be permitted to live in the State under any circumstances."

The only concession the convention made to their opponents came in the process of approving the constitution before its submission to Congress. The document would be "submitted to all the white male, inhabitants of this Territory, for approval or disapproval." However, the vote would be either for the constitution with the slavery clause or without the slavery clause, not for or against the document itself. The delegates seemed to want to give the Free State faction a choice: vote for the constitution and hope that a future legislature might be able to erase the slavery clause later or vote against it, preserve what slavery existed, and prevent the state legislature from ever being able to remove slavery from Kansas.

The Free State faction was appalled at the document that had been drafted. "The people of Kansas scarcely needed exhortation to resist the Lecompton Constitution," wrote Leverett Spring. Lane threw his oratory behind the resistance to Lecompton. William Cutler, in his 1883 history of Kansas, wrote that on October 19, 1857, the Lecompton convention adjourned, and Lane and a crowd appeared in town. He "and his followers" were "exasperated at the [election] frauds in Johnson and McGee counties" and "openly threatened" to prevent the convention from meeting. Lane was the speaker and "as usual, aroused the crowd to the highest pitch of noisy enthusiasm." Resolutions were passed denouncing the frauds and calling for the convenient to adjourn, but there was no violence, and Walker, "true to his promises, [threw] out the fraudulent vote." The result of this noisy display, claimed T. Dwight Thacher, was that "for four days the members [of the convention] sneaked around Lecompton in the brush," afraid to assemble. Only when Governor Walker sent the army to Lecompton did the convention continue.

However, on November 14, 1857, Lane's continued anger over the proslavery constitution and the actions of the Lecompton convention, which had finally dispersed only two weeks earlier, erupted. While at Leavenworth, he said, "I am not going to advise war or bloodshed to-night, for perhaps there is no need of that. We have got the goats so separated from the sheep that we can easily kill them without committing crime. For I truly believe that should God show his special providence here to-night, we should see in these starry heavens his hand, commanding us to kill those damned villains."

Why should Jim Lane utter such a call? It appears quite intemperate for an aspiring senator to urge his supporters to set upon their opponents and kill them. One reason for such "red meat" rhetoric, one that some of his critics have leapt upon, was his association with a secret society known the "Danites." But here, as in many other aspects of Lane's life, there is a great deal of confusion. Much depends on partisan writings published long after these events were part of history.

Recently, author Todd Mildfelt wrote a biography of one of the more radical actors of the period. His book is also the first about the Kansas Danites. He found that the Danites were established late in 1855 in response to the secret groups Missourians created to push the cause for slavery in Kansas Territory. The term "Danite" springs from the Bible and means "the sons of Dan." Implied within the term is some ideal of a warrior for God. The Mormons picked up on that ideal in the late 1830s while living in Missouri. This group was often persecuted by their Protestant Missouri neighbors for their unconventional religious practices, so a radical band of Mormons established the Danites to fight back against persecution. The Mormon Danites failed in their efforts in

Missouri and disbanded, but the group was reformed in the 1850s when the Mormons came into conflict with the government in Washington. It was this second group of Mormon Danites that became the more well known of the two bands.

Early on in Kansas, Lane, Charles Robinson, and most of the Free State leadership joined the Danites. Robinson dropped out of the Danites when he became interested in nonviolent resistance, but Lane remained and at one point was their leader. According to James Legate, quoted in Richard Hinton's book about John Brown, Lane also "did in" the organization. He was "continuously calling meetings" in which some man would be singled out as a "pro-slavery hell-hound," a call would be issued for "his case to be investigated and adjudicated," and if found guilty there would be a decree issued for the man's execution. "Lane's 'Whereas' killed the society," Legate wrote, referring to the initial report on the "hell-hound" in question. The radical whom Todd Mildfelt wrote about, Charles Leonhardt, felt the same way.

In Alice Nichols' view the Danites were not so inactive. According to Nichols, Lane, along with his fellow Danites, planned to attack the Lecompton convention, a course of action discovered by Augustus Wattles, a partner in the *Herald of Freedom*. Wattles told the newspaper's editor, George W. Brown, who then assembled a meeting of Lawrence citizens. Lane was invited to the meeting, where Brown and the others confronted him about the plan. After some evasion Lane admitted that the rumor was true.

The meeting broke up, and another was set for that night, to be held outside. Speakers came to caution the crowd, but to no avail. Then an ally of Lane's, Joel Goodin, began to give an incendiary speech encouraging the shedding of blood. However, at the end of his speech, he said that no one "occasioned more strife" or had "been [a] more fruitful cause of our disturbances" than Lane. Goodin said that if Lane wanted blood, he ought to be "the first person to contribute." At that, Lane backed off his plan and agreed to join a "jubilation meeting" at Lecompton to celebrate Free State wins at the polls.

Nichols wrote that after this aborted effort the society was to go farther. Lane "and his Danites would wipe out all proslavery men still resident in the territory." She quotes on this subject James

Redpath, who attended a meeting and was to murder a proslavery newspaper editor. Redpath was "shocked" and denounced the scheme.

Nichols obtained her account of this story from a book on George Brown and from Charles Robinson's memoir, but she undermines her argument by relying on the explanations of two men who are at odds with one another and whose reliability she questions. Her own notes on the subject raise doubts about this incident. In one note she called George W. Brown "a famous liar," and in her text she wrote that Brown and Robinson often quarreled, even quoting Brown's comment that "circumstances will confine [Robinson] to oblivion." Furthermore, in the note on the incident itself, she does not quote the man she deemed "impartial," Leverett Spring. Spring himself gives no mention of Lane's plan in his book, *Prelude to the War for the Union,* nor in his article on Lane's career.

In his memoir, Robinson himself quoted Brown's article in its entirety, then printed two letters sent to Brown to back up the newspaperman's account, one from Goodin. John Speer, on the other hand, never mentioned any such meeting in his biography and even seemed dismissive of the notion that any secret societies of Free State men or abolitionists ever existed. So, did the secret assassination meeting in Lawrence really take place? The evidence is inconclusive but leans against it. In fact, a reading of the 1858 issues of the *Herald* suggests that G. W. Brown, early that year, had soured on Jim Lane as a leader of the movement against slavery in Kansas. It is entirely possible that Brown made the story up just to take one more shot at a man he had come to despise.

The supposed exposé of the Danites came in the short-lived *Crusader of Freedom,* published in Doniphan by James Redpath. It appeared in the February 3, 1858, issue, the same in which the first of a planned installment of an autobiography written by Jim Lane also appeared. The issue survives, and a reading of Redpath's piece hints at something other than what Lane's enemies have written.

The piece was framed as a letter written by Redpath to new territorial governor James Denver to back up Denver's claim of a secret Free State organization committing outrages. Redpath recounted that he was eating a "rather tough" chicken wing at a

James Denver took the office of governor of Kansas Territory as the conflict between the Free State and proslavery factions was winding down. He tried to blame Jim Lane for the spasm of violence that arose late in 1857. *Image courtesy the Kansas State Historical Society.*

Lawrence restaurant when he was approached by Jim Lane, "celebrated for his Adonis-like beauty of form and his zeal in the cause of Biblical Literature and of Foreign Missions." Lane asked if Redpath would join a "Secret Political Society for the establishment of the Topeka Constitution, the dissolution of this glorious Union, and the elevation of G. W. Brown" to "the Presidency of a Northern Republic."

"I feigned doubt," Redpath wrote. Lane then told him that his purpose was to become "President of the Religious Tract Society," a position Brown supposedly had promised to him. Lane, "if he succeeded in securing the vast powers now wielded by that body," would use his powers against the "pernicious and soul-destroying" habit of chewing and smoking tobacco. If Redpath went along, Lane would get him to the post of "Chaplain of the House of Representatives" or "even, perhaps, to the distinguished post of fifth assistant Postmaster" of a Kansas town. "Human nature is frail," Redpath admitted, and "against the seducing temptation thus skillfully presented," he joined. Lane told Redpath the time and place of the next meeting. Redpath went at the proper time to the "Church of the Holy Rifles." At the door he recognized Martin Conway.

> He was armed with a tomahawk, ten revolving pistols, a Sharpe's [*sic*] rifle, a United States sarbine [carbine], a musket with bayonet fixed, a breech-loading cannon, (a sixty pounder,) three dozen scalping knives, a gross of daggers and a hundred sword-canes—all of which were stuck in a leather belt, which also held his pantaloons up. In close proximity to where he stood, were several axes, broomsticks, rocks, bombshells, pen knives, scissors, clubs, cleavers, chairs, and other offensive munitions of domestic war. I noticed, too, that his finger nails were long and sharp.

Upon entering, Redpath was asked "the name of the most valiant of the sons of men" and the "worthy aspirant" of the "Presidency of our Free Northern Republic." He answered with G. W. Brown, was accepted, and told the secret password, "Kick me if you dare." A few sentences later Redpath wrote that he had "not the courage to proceed quite yet" with his account and would continue later. He closed the missive with, "Very falsely, &c., J. R."

Only the most biased reading of Redpath's "letter" would not observe that it was almost certainly a joke directed at Denver in response to his charges of Free State secret resistance. It might also be true that Redpath was directing a bit of ire at a fellow editor. As for Lane's involvement in the story, two things should be kept in mind. First, Denver had named Lane as the source of all the trouble in Kansas Territory. Second, Redpath and Lane had disagreed on whether the Free State residents should have voted in the election the previous October. Redpath could have been getting in a jab against a former opponent and his aspirations while simultaneously mocking Denver. It would seem that authors like Leverett Spring and Alice Nichols may have allowed themselves to be taken in by a journalistic prank.

A complicating factor in sorting out Redpath's comments is that he appears to have had a falling out with Lane later in 1858. By the end of May, Redpath was claiming that Lane had "organized a club of Danites in Doniphan County" and that he had privately told Redpath that if the territorial governor challenged him, Lane would send Danites after him. Naturally anti-Lane newspapers like the *Herald of Freedom* picked up on Redpath's change of tune. That change raises two questions: which of Redpath's stories about the Danites is true, the pro-Lane satire or the anti-Lane diatribe, and did Redpath's feelings cloud either or both accounts?

The Danite issue cropped up again around the end of 1857, when fighting broke out in southeastern Kansas between the proslavery and Free Sate factions. Back in 1856 many of the Free State residents of southeastern Kansas, including those in Bourbon County and around Fort Scott, were driven from the region by proslavery men. The following year many of those Free Staters returned to reclaim the lands they had been forced from, but the proslavery faction still controlled the county government. Free State citizens were frustrated in their efforts to obtain justice, and they formed a "squatter's court" in response. Naturally the proslavery county authorities refused to recognize the squatter's court and sent a posse to shut it down. A brief skirmish took place near the Free State stronghold of Fort Bain. That in turn caused the court's supporters to call for help from other Free State men in the territory.

The new Free State territorial legislature had appointed Lane major general of the militia on December 16. Lane assembled a force and marched on Bourbon County, arriving a few days after his appointment. It seems that Lane had been anticipating the contention and began the assembly recognizing what was coming.

Another Free State activist present in Bourbon County was Charles Leonhardt, the subject of Todd Mildfelt's book. Leonhardt was a German immigrant and a veteran of the Prussian army. He claimed to have served in the Hungarian revolt of 1848, but proof of such a claim is sketchy at best. He came to the United States in the 1850s and arrived in Kansas a dedicated abolitionist. At times he was active in the territory, but he also undertook speaking tours elsewhere.

Leonhardt met with Lane and his staff at a village in Franklin County called Ohio City around December 18. Lane's party was on their way to Fort Bain. Leonhardt, according to an unpublished autobiography, was inducted by Lane into the Order of the Danites. Supposedly, a few days later Lane inducted the whole assembly of Free State fighters at Sugar Mound in Linn County.

Militia member James Abbott, writing to his wife on December 22, made no mention of the Danites but did say that he and his fellow fighters had been "immediately mustered into the Service under the Law." He told her that he had hoped to return home "within a week at the most," but things were "most uncertain." Abbott was optimistic, though. "We have seen some hard times but never defeat. We have lost some by arrest but none in battle." He noted that "our little army" was up to 175 men and that the presence of Lane "had the effect to strengthen the hearts of my men and renew their hopes."

Another man, Joseph Trego, also wrote to his wife. In early January he said that in spite of war reports in the papers, the area was safe. There were far more Free State men present than ruffians. Most of his subsequent letters carried the same tone.

Within a month U.S. soldiers were dispatched to deal with the conflict. Lane was hesitant to attack them, so he made an overture, obtained assurances that the soldiers would not start conflict, then declared victory and sent his men home. At that point the governor stepped in to put an end to the trouble. He persuaded the proslavery county officials to resign and held new elections. A new slate of county leaders was elected, the governor confirmed them, and that ended the last official armed struggle between the proslavery and Free State forces in Kansas before the start of the Civil War.

But not everyone was happy about the onset of peace. Among those men were Charles Leonhardt and a friend of his, James Montgomery. Leonhardt and Montgomery had wanted Lane to pursue the proslavery forces. They did not care if such a battle might adversely affect Free State prospects or legitimize the Lecompton constitution. They wanted their enemies driven from the territory. By early 1858 they had soured on Lane and started to consider taking matters into their own hands.

Lloyd Lewis believed that more was made of the whole Danite controversy, or at least Lane's part in it, that there should have been. At one point in his 1939 address, Lewis told of how Lane, before his "election as senator by the revolutionary body of Free-State men here in Topeka," asked John Brown, Jr., for his support. When Brown hesitated, "Lane poured out compelling oratory" and "inducted young Brown then and there into a mysterious secret order" that "would fight the Missouri devils, fire with fire." Lane gave Brown a secret sign, told him an induction ritual, and even gave him a "signal of distress, 'Ho Kansas.'"

Brown voted for Lane, and the next day Lane gave him "the emblem of the order." "But that was all," said Lewis. "Brown said Lane never did anything more and the great secret order died from Jim's lack of attention." "Lane had used Brown, and Brown knew it, yet after a third of a century Brown would still say, 'But he had my heart and hand then; he has them still. I would not be divorced.'"

Questions about the Danite matter, radicalism, and Jim Lane's ties to both remain to this day. Was the fight in Bourbon County cooked up by Lane to cause trouble? The evidence suggests not. Was Lane at the head of a secret society pledged to eradicate slavery's supporters in the region? Probably not. If Lane had any connection to it, it was only to advance his political goals, and even then it seems that he dropped out or ignored it when the group proved untamable.

As much as his enemies wanted to portray Jim Lane as a radical, it should be remembered that he was always a politician first. As a politician, Lane used the threat of radicalism to obtain political compromises. When compromise was achieved, however, the radicals were left behind. By contrast, radicals eschew politics for direct action, using politics only when it suits their agenda and abandoning it as soon as they feel it is failing to accomplish their purposes.

The most that can be said about this in regard to Jim Lane is that there may have been a marriage of convenience between himself and radicals like John Brown. But because of their differing natures the alliance didn't last long. At any rate, the time for settling the Kansas question with bullets had been over for some time. Ballots would offer a final resolution to the matter.

At a mass meeting in Leavenworth on November 27, 1857, a resolution was passed repudiating the Lecompton constitution. Jim Lane spoke there and called for a special session of the new Free State legislature. On December 2 a Free State convention assembled in Lawrence. Robinson was the president of this gathering, and Lane was on a resolutions committee. This meeting called the Lecompton constitution "a fraud upon the people," an impending election on it set for December 21 a "swindle," and "the election of January 4, 1858, as a crime and a misdemeanor against the peace of this Territory, and the will of the majority." Only the legislature elected on October 5 was legitimate, and it could not be undermined without a fair and impartial vote.

On December 7 the Free State territorial legislature convened. There were cheers for Lane, Robinson, and "nearly every other person or thing that had the Free-State mark upon it," wrote William Cutler. A resolution was passed endorsing what was approved in Lawrence on December 2. However, the Topeka constitution was losing support. Lane in fact spoke out against further support of it, saying that submitting it again would be "a breach of faith with Secretary Stanton," to whom promises had been made that the session would stick to the Lecompton issue.

In mid-December word came that James W. Denver had been appointed the new territorial governor. Governor Walker was in

Washington at the time, trying to get instructions from the administration that would allow him to keep the promises he had made in Kansas. Unable to do so, Walker resigned on December 17. Denver took the oath of office in Lecompton on December 21, becoming the fifth man appointed governor since 1854. Born in Virginia in 1817, Denver had fought in the Mexican War, practiced law in Missouri, then moved to California, where he served in the state senate, as secretary of state, and as a congressman. In 1856 he was appointed commissioner of Indian Affairs and while in that post went to Kansas.

The day Denver took office was also the day previously set for the election on the Lecompton constitution. The Free State faction had already decided not to take part. When the votes were cast, the tally read: for the constitution with slavery, 6,143 votes, and for the constitution without slavery, 569 votes. There was again voter fraud; some 3,000 votes for admitting Kansas as a Slave State were found to be bogus.

After the election the Free State party began a debate over whether or not to assemble a ticket for state offices under Lecompton. To do so would be inconsistent with previous statements, would abandon the Topeka constitution, and would recognize Lecompton's. The supporters of participation argued that the success depended on keeping control of the government. In order to decide the will of the majority, another delegate convention was held in Lawrence on December 23. Over that day and the next the question of participation was debated.

Author Richard Cordley was present at that meeting, and he noted in 1882 that the Lecompton question was the sole topic of the gathering. Presiding over it was Charles Robinson, with most of the leading figures in the Free State movement there, including Jim Lane. Cordley noted that this time "opinions were more decided" and "feelings were more intense" than at Grasshopper Falls. The movement was split into two camps, the radicals and the conservatives.

The radical view was that "the whole Lecompton movement was a fraud." The conservative faction called for the movement to "come out of the clouds" and be realistic about the question. On the afternoon of December 24 a vote was taken: forty-five delegates were in favor of voting under Lecompton, and forty-five opposed.

To settle the deadlock, it was decided to count the vote by districts, with the delegates casting one vote for each district. That brought seventy-five no votes to sixty-four yes votes; the convention had decided against taking part in any Lecompton election. Those in favor of voting, including Charles Robinson, immediately called a mass meeting. The meeting resulted in a reversal of policy and the nomination of a Free State ticket.

This led to two elections set for January 4, 1858. One would elect state officials under the Lecompton constitution, while the other would be a referendum on the constitution. The former had been driven by the convention, while the latter by the Free State territorial legislature.

Governor Denver had trouble maintaining order. Free Staters stole a cannon from the Kickapoo Rangers and muskets from a proslavery doctor in Delaware City. James Montgomery led a Free State raid on the polls at Sugar Mound and destroyed the ballots. The proslavery faction resorted to their usual tactics of voter fraud by creating bogus returns.

The fraud was not enough to save the Lecompton constitution. More than ten thousand votes were cast against, while only two hundred votes were cast for it. The results were so one sided that Denver decided fraud in the other election would not give victory to the proslavery faction. Famously, one actual return was hidden in a candle box under a pile of wood and substituted for a bogus one. The box was found, the scheme exposed, and the proslavery party found themselves on the run.

However, the rejection of the Lecompton constitution in Kansas did not derail its progress. Instead, on February 2, 1858, President Buchanan sent the constitution to Congress with a recommendation that Kansas be admitted under it. The Senate voted in March in favor of Lecompton 33 to 25. The House was another matter; Buchanan needed 118 votes for it to pass there, but could count on only 100. He began an active campaign to garner the votes he needed, including offering federal patronage jobs to friends of representatives as well as cash for votes.

When House deliberations began on April 1, an amendment to the Senate bill was passed calling for a formal resubmission of Lecompton to the Kansas voters. The Senate refused to accept the bill with the amendment, and a conference committee was convened. At this point a compromise was offered by Rep. William English, a Democrat who opposed Lecompton. This compromise would give Kansas a land grant of 4 million acres if the voters approved the Lecompton constitution. Stephen Douglas, who had been opposed to Lecompton, decided to support the compromise. Anti-Lecompton Democrats were outraged, including many in his home state. Yet with Douglas on board and the backing of Buchanan, the bill was approved in the Senate 31 to 22 and in the House 112 to 103 on April 30.

Despite the constitution's acceptance in Washington, the vast majority of Kansans did not see the bill as a solution. The land-grant provision was an obvious bribe, and the Lecompton constitution remained wildly unpopular. When Kansans went to the polls on August 2, the balloting provided a resounding rejection that even Buchanan could not gloss over. The election was carried out with few problems and resulted in a defeat of the Lecompton document 11,300 to 1,788.

The defeat of the Lecompton document at the polls in 1858 signaled that the conflict over slavery in Kansas was coming to a close. It appeared that Kansas would be admitted to the union as a Free State; the only questions remaining were when and under what new constitution. Historians since then have debated who deserves the credit for the Free State victory. Inevitably the feud between Charles Robinson and Jim Lane surfaced in those debates.

One of Robinson's biographers, Don Wilson, claimed it was Robinson's "policy of peaceful resistance" that prevented "outright civil war in Kansas." This seems to fly in the face of the actual events of the summer and fall of 1856. It would seem that the lack of resistance encouraged the proslavery supporters to push as far as they had, and that the stiff resistance they met in the fall made them back down. Furthermore, it can be argued that it was Robinson's policy that brought on the sack of Lawrence, which provoked John Brown to commit murder on Pottawatomie Creek, leading to the fighting in August and September. Robinson's strategy failed in Kansas for the reason it went awry in California: a ruthless opponent. The proslavery movement used its power to try to stifle any dissent, to arrest any opponent on any pretext, and to employ any method of fraud to remain in power. How long, one wonders, was Robinson willing to submit to this treatment in hopes of it succeeding?

And then there is the letter Robinson wrote to Eli Thayer in April 1855. Toward the close of his letter he said to Thayer, "If they give us occasion to settle the question of slavery in this country with the bayonet let us improve it." Two sentences later he asked Thayer, "Wouldn't it be rich to march an army through the slave holding states & roll up a black cloud that should spread dismay & terror to the ranks of the oppressors?" It does seem remarkable that the man who would so criticize Lane and John Brown for their willingness to resort to force would essentially call for precisely that sort of campaign against slavery in 1855.

In Robinson's own 1892 memoir he tried to split hairs while at the same time glossing over any mention of the "Fabian policy." He claimed it had been the strategy of the Free State movement "to act strictly on the defensive as to Federal authority, but to thwart and baffle the usurpation [of that authority by the proslavery side] till the Federal authority itself should be compelled by the popular outcry" to uphold the will of the Free State majority. He accused Lane and John Brown of being opposed to that policy by waging war against federal authorities.

But this begs the question, Did Robinson think Lane was fighting federal authorities at Fort Saunders or Hickory Point? If so, Robinson's actual strategy was not what he claimed. If not, then Robinson appears to have wanted to have his cake and eat it too. Either way it would seem that, at least toward the end of his life, Charles Robinson did believe that the Free State movement should not have allowed their opponents to gain the initiative in the territorial conflict.

One of Robinson's supporters, Leverett Spring, perhaps inadvertently gave Jim Lane credit when he quoted a speech Lane gave on February 15, 1858. Lane's speech contained a review of the tactics of the Free State movement. "At the great delegate convention held at Big Springs in September, 1855," Lane said, it had been unanimously decided "not to organize in resistance" to the proslavery territorial government. "We adopted the let alone policy, neither resorting to nor resisting it. This plan was embraced as the peacefully legal one in preference to organized resistance to the territorial laws, to save the effusion of blood and to avoid those laws instead of coming in conflict with them." The "patriotic, patient and peace-loving" Free State citizens of Kansas had been victims of the kinds of fraud that would have driven others "into bloodshed and civil war." But the movement had not armed themselves "except to resist invasion from other states" and after appeals for protection from federal troops had been refused.

Spring, quoting this speech after telling of Lane's Danite scheme in his piece on Lane's life, admitted that "his statement [was] true in regard to the tactics which the antislavery party adopted and on the whole successfully carried out." Up to that point the Free State movement had acted on the defensive. It therefore follows that when Lawrence was sacked by the proslavery forces, the Free State movement felt it had no choice but to take up arms and fight their enemy in the field.

Lloyd Lewis put his own spin on this question when he spoke about Lane in the late 1930s. He did classify Lane as a radical along with "Old John Brown of Osawatomie." But, said Lewis, Brown "scorned politicians" and "dreamed of blood and war." "It was really Lane who did more than any other one soul to make Kansas free. He knew the tricks with which to overcome Sen. Davy Atchison from Missouri; he knew the ruses with which to outlast, outmaneuver the whole administration machine from Washington."

> For when everything has been said and done, it was Jim Lane, more than any other man, who made Kansas free soil. He was the organizer of victory; he was the shrewd, scheming politician who knew what weakling to buy and what strong man to inspire. He was the man who called the neighborhood meetings by the side of the road, the mass meetings in churches, the delegate conventions in big halls. When civil war came to Kansas in 1856 and the name "Bleeding Kansas" was on the front page of every newspaper and was the great theme for debates in the United States senate, it was Jim Lane who led the fighting men, riding the night, directing the raids, the burnings, the stratagems—wily as an Indian, dramatic as General Sheridan in the timeliness of his arrivals on the field.
>
> Kansas laughed about him then, we laugh at him now, but just

the same it was Lane who was the head of the executive committees, it was Lane who was chairman in the meeting of that Free-
State experiment in revolution, it was Lane who was general of
the fighting forces, Lane who wrote the resolutions, Lane who
drafted the memorials and appeals for statehood, and when the
Free-Soil men of Kansas territory had something formal to present
to congress, it was Lane who was sent to do it. . . .

The amazing propaganda that he spread did cow the Pro-slave
bands, and it did inspire the Free Staters to a superb burst of
activity, with men marching through the night to bombard
enemy blockhouses, burn and shoot. And it was a matter for
cheering when through the darkness the marching men heard,
"Here comes Captain Cook," and turned to see it was Old Jim,
his eyes a-fire.

This was the campaign which swept the border, and settled the
fate of Kansas so far as armed force was concerned, and it is
known elsewhere than in your state.

What such claims fail to consider is the possibility that credit for
the defeat of slavery in Kansas may not go to any one man, but to
a population. After all, what ousted the proslavery politicians from
the territorial legislature was the large numbers of Free State voters. Their numbers were large enough to overcome any fraud by
their opponents and large enough to make accepting fraud politically unsafe for the latter territorial governors. That more than
anything swung the balance of power in Kansas.

Credit should also be given to John Geary and James Denver. Geary
was the first territorial governor to stand up to the proslavery side and
win the confidence of the Free Staters while in office. By asserting
himself and trying to deal fairly with both sides, he was able to bring
a measure of calm to Kansas in the fall and winter of 1856. Denver
seems to have followed Geary's example and that brought about the
elections of 1857 that were freer and fairer than previous polls. It is
unlikely that the end of the conflict would have been as quiet as it was
had not both men tried to be "honest brokers" to both sides.

With the proslavery movement in retreat, many believed that
peace would finally come to Kansas. But there would be no peace
for Jim Lane. There would be more work for the cause and a personal crisis that would threaten to end his career permanently.

VIII.

During the Calm

While Jim Lane was hard at work trying to make Kansas a Free State, his personal life had taken a turn. His wife, Mary, had returned to Indiana, perhaps in 1856, and filed for divorce. She had waited some nine months for him to contact her, but he had been too busy with his cause to bother. Her divorce was granted on grounds of abandonment, and she moved in with relatives of hers.

Then in 1857, Jim Lane returned to Indiana to try to reconcile with his wife. Whatever he said or did worked, for not only did they reconcile but they also remarried. However, she seems to have told him that she was tired of dealing with the illnesses that scourged the frontier in those days and tired of the danger of being Mrs. Jim Lane in Kansas Territory. She told her husband that she would stay in Indiana until the situation in Kansas improved to her satisfaction. He agreed, and she remained outside of Kansas until 1858.

The Free State movement had gotten into the habit of holding meetings on a regular basis to express views, hash out grievances, and draft all manner of documents on their cause. Although in early 1858 the Lecompton constitution was still alive nationally, in Kansas Territory it was dead. That meant another assembly would have to gather, this time to draft a new Free State constitution. The old Topeka document seemed to be outdated and to encapsulate too many contentious issues to be revived.

To these ends on February 10, 1858, the territorial legislature passed a bill calling for a new constitutional convention. Gov. James

Denver withheld signing the bill, but the legislature passed it again on February 13 then adjourned their session. The maneuver, although making the bill effective, would eventually cast doubt on the convention's proceedings. The delegate election occurred on March 9, with some nine thousand largely legal votes cast. The delegates met in the village of Minneola in north-central Franklin County.

The first settlement in that area came in 1854 with the creation of two towns, Minneola and Centropolis. The former was Free State and the latter proslavery. Centropolis thrived for a time but withered when one of its prominent men, a store owner, moved his business to Minneola. Soon there were several important Free State leader attached to the town company. Jim Lane even gave the newspaper, the *Statesman,* its new name.

Denver admitted some twenty years later, in speaking about this convention, that although Lecompton was "a poor place to live," Minneola was worse. The site was "out on the prairie, with not a shade tree anywhere near it." About the only factor Minneola had in its favor was that several of the members of the territorial legislature "were interested in lots in the proposed new capital." The legislators probably hoped to profit from the sale of town lots if the seat of government was moved.

The convention began on March 23, with Lane elected president, and the first issue it took on was the question of the capital of Kansas. Opponents of Minneola alleged that the effort to make that town the capital was pursued only to make its investors rich. Supporters replied that once the capital moved from Lecompton some town would profit. Minneola was also in the center of the territory and thus a good location for the territorial government. As the public was against Minneola, a motion was made to adjourn the convention elsewhere.

A later pioneer of the area, quoted in an Ottawa newspaper over fifty years later, claimed this first motion was to adjourn to Lawrence. It was, he said, a "sham fight" to uncover delegate sentiment on a state capital. The debate carried on until lunch. After a break a new motion was set forward for the delegates to adjourn to Leavenworth.

It was at this point that Lane rose to speak. None of the newspapers of the time carried Lane's speech or quoted from it. The only record of his remarks are found in a speech T. Dwight Thacher gave in 1883 to the Kansas State Historical Society. Thacher said that Lane stood up in the "dimly-lighted room," with the darkness of night outside, and spoke to such a "pitch of excitement" that Thacher had never seen before.

Lane began by speaking about the Free State party. He said that a "crisis" was facing the party and reminded the delegates of their responsibilities in dealing with the crisis. "He then alluded to the threats" of Minneola's backers, warning that if they failed to get their way they might break up the party. Lane "then said that if in the momentous and supreme hour of the party's struggle they were bound to leave it on account of a few paltry shares in Minneola, then let them go—and go to hell!"

Joel Goodin tried to defend Minneola's bid for the capital, but the damage was done. Still, the debate over the question went on through the night and into the next morning. Finally a delegate from Minneola changed his vote and the convention adjourned to Leavenworth. Although technically Minneola remained the capital, the territorial legislature refused to meet there and eventually Topeka would become the government center. Once Minneola lost its bid, its prominence and its population drastically declined.

On March 25 the convention reassembled at Melodeon Hall in Leavenworth. Lane resigned as president, stating that he "did not wish to hinder a vote in Congress by his acting as President of the Convention." Dwight Thacher wrote many years later that this resignation was also at the behest of Martin Conway, who had chided Lane at Minneola for "wanting to accumulate honors upon himself unduly." Thus chagrined, Lane stepped aside in favor of Conway, who became president of the convention.

The convention resumed working until April 3. There were two factions among the seventy-two delegates who met at Minneola, according to William Cutler. A radical faction favored a constitution formulated on the basis of the Topeka constitution, while a more conservative element preferred "framing the Constitution, and organizing a State government only in strict conformity with the prescribed forms of law."

With such dissension, compromises were forced. The matter of black law was altered drastically; the Leavenworth constitution granted the right to vote to "every male citizen." However, provision was also given for the matter to be submitted for a final decision by a vote of the people. Other than this, the Leavenworth constitution was largely a copy of the Topeka constitution. The vote for its adoption was set for May 18, 1858, the same day as an election for state officers. On April 28 and 29 a convention was held in Topeka to select a ticket under the Leavenworth constitution, in which Henry J. Adams of Leavenworth was nominated for governor. Nowhere among the other candidates were Jim Lane or Charles Robinson.

Dwight Thacher was one of the delegates to that convention, and he noted that Lane took little part in the deliberations. He supported the radicals but "rendered them little assistance on the floor." This can also be seen in the official journal of the convention kept by Samuel Tappan. Lane made one motion on the Topeka document before resigning on March 26. He led one committee, on phraseology, that reported on April 1. Lane was present but seemed hardly active. However, Issac Goodnow of Manhattan, who was also present, wrote to a "friend Sherman" in early April that Lane was "the *ruling spirit* which directed and inspired" the delegates.

At the May 18 election the problems of the Leavenworth constitution, mainly over black suffrage, caught up with it. Although the balloting was three to one in favor, only about four thousand votes were cast. It was presented to Congress, but even the most ardent Republicans admitted that it had little support. For the rest of 1858 no further attempts were made to draft a constitution for Kansas.

Lane's time in Kansas from 1858 to 1860, and indeed to a lesser extent the rest of his life, would be dominated by one incident: his fatal shooting of Gaius Jenkins in June 1858. Lane's enemies then and later would use this killing as the cornerstone of their impeachment of his character. They would describe it as the murder of a man over something as trivial as a water well. But the facts of the case, and the land dispute that led up to it, are far more complicated than that.

Land was at the heart of the trouble between Gaius Jenkins and Jim Lane. Specifically, it was a piece of land immediately west of the original townsite of Lawrence. Both men had claims to the land that were tied together in a messy dispute over ownership and preemption law. While Lane's enemies would claim that he was willing to do anything to get the land, the facts suggest otherwise.

One of the more insightful views about land disputes on the antebellum frontier comes from Englishman Thomas Gladstone. He was in Kansas reporting on the situation in 1856 and had a chance to see firsthand how squatting for land worked. He wrote that the process began with someone finding a piece of land that appeared unclaimed by another. That squatter would post notice of his claim on the land and with a government authority. A few years later, when an official survey was conducted and a land office opened, the squatter would offer "the upset price of $1¼ per acre, over which no one bids against him," and he would obtain legal title to the land.

Gladstone noted that although this "rough method" often worked, there could be abuses of this system. The most common, and the most relevant to the Lane-Jenkins feud, was the practice known as jumping a claim. This was the act of claiming land on which someone else already had made a preemptive claim. "The temptation to jump lies in the advantage of entering into another man's labours," he wrote, "and becoming the happy possessor of improvements without the necessity of toiling for them." This almost always led to a fight, and often the weaker party would go "to the wall."

In the case of Lane and Jenkins, Jenkins always insisted he had established his claim first. A "musty old paper of the times" that John Speer owned, in reality a list of the early settlers around Lawrence and their claims, had printed next to Jenkins' name the date April 30, 1854, supposedly the date of his preemption claim. But as Speer pointed out in his Lane biography, that would mean Jenkins was claiming land before the Kansas-Nebraska Act had become law. As such, Jenkins would have had no legal basis to claim the property in question.

In determining the validity of Jenkins' claim, Lane's enemies often relied on two statements made by another of Lane's opponents, James Blood, that supposedly had some bearing on when Jenkins made his claim. Chronologically first was a notarized statement dated October 12, 1857. In it Blood said he and Jenkins came to the site in September 1854. They camped on a hill south of Lawrence, and Jenkins told Blood he planned to preempt a claim nearby. However, according to Blood it was a year later, in September or October 1855, that he witnessed Jenkins improving his claim.

The second statement appeared in 1884. In that Blood largely followed the timeline of the 1857 document. The only addition was a sentence asserting that Lane had sold a "double-log house" to Jenkins in December 1855. John Speer observed that neither statement actually helped Jenkins' side of the claim dispute. He noted that Blood could have "named a single day he saw Jenkins residing on the place" and Blood "would gladly have stated it," for under laws of the time, any claimant who was absent from his claim for more than thirty days would forfeit his right to it.

The next problem with Jenkins' claim, as Speer and others have written, was the manner in which Jenkins made it. When Speer arrived in Kansas City in late September 1855, he met Gaius Jenkins, who was the proprietor of a hotel in Kansas City. Jenkins told Speer as they traveled from Kansas City to the Lawrence area that one of his employees, Edward Chapman, was residing on the land he had claimed in order to secure the title to it. Speer replied that he had heard that Chapman already had sold part of this land to the town company forming Lawrence. Speer wrote that Jenkins then "spoke very bitterly of Chapman's treachery."

Speer ended up on a committee to settle the dispute. Although Speer said that the "links of friendship and neighborly kindness" had been forged between himself and Jenkins and were never broken, he agreed with the committee decision in Chapman's favor. This in turn caused Jenkins to place a notice in the *Kansas Tribune* of September 15, 1855. Jenkins asserted the right to his claim, and people were warned "not to purchase lots or city interests" on the land Chapman had sold. The notice concluded with Jenkins saying that he was "in favor of the movement now being made by the Outsiders [proslavery men trying to fight the establishment of Lawrence] to break up the settlement of March last." That notice also appeared in the *Herald of Freedom* as late as November 24, 1855. "This advertisement is clearly in evidence against Mr. Jenkins," Speer wrote.

Speer discovered another obstacle to the claim in the words of John Shimmons. Shimmons was a friend of Lane's and knew his case against Jenkins intimately. According to him, Jenkins and Chapman had entered into an agreement over the claim. Chapman had taken an interest in land claimed by a Dr. Lykins of Kansas City over the summer of 1854. Chapman did not have the money to make improvements such as building a house, but Jenkins did. Jenkins agreed to provide the money if Chapman would give him half the land.

In March 1855, Chapman sold his half of the land to the Lawrence town company. He also paid Jenkins for his part of the land with a personal note, and Jenkins accepted the note. Chapman then took a claim south of what he had sold and in April sold that property to Jim Lane for six hundred dollars. A few months later Jenkins began feuding with Chapman over the note and placed his advertisement.

Around this time Jenkins bought half of Lane's claim for eight hundred dollars, "payable in cash and notes." They agreed to share in the preemption payment and pledged their families to support each other's claim if one of them died. But when the section lines were finally drawn on the land, Lane's and Jenkins' residences ended up in the same quarter-section. Lane offered to divide the quarter-section with Jenkins, but Jenkins refused the deal. At this point, said Shimmons, Lane's legal team brought up Chapman's personal note, which suggested that Jenkins had recognized Chapman's sale and therefore had no valid claim to the land. It was at that point that the two men engaged in a legal case to settle the ownership question.

Kendall Bailes in his biography of Lane found evidence that Jenkins was so intent on claiming the land he engaged in some rather extralegal activties. In 1856, when Lane was forced to exit the territory to promote the Free State cause, Jenkins pried open the lock on Lane's house and took his furniture to Lawrence. When Lane finally returned home on May 28, 1857, he was compelled to stay awake all night with a pistol in his hand, for Jenkins had appropriated the house for his farm hands and throughout the night came in and out "swearing and threatening" Lane. In addition to these problems, Bailes believed that although Lane's legal case was strong, the men in the land office who would decide the matter were proslavery partisans in Lecompton.

There appear to have been other factors contributing to the dispute between Lane and Jenkins aside from the land claim. William Connelley, who published a detailed account of the feud in one of the Kansas State Historical Society's *Collections,* found letters from James Christian, who knew both men. At least one of those letters was published in the *Arkansas City Traveler* in 1878. In it, Christian stated that there were already tensions among the two groups of Free State partisans in Lawrence, those from New England and those from the Western states. Jenkins' friends were mostly New Englanders, while Lane's supporters were the Westerners.

Christian wrote that Jenkins could be "a generous, whole-souled, warm friend" when sober, but had "an impulsive, violent temper" when drunk, which he said was frequent. Lane, on the other hand, was "cool and deliberate." John Speer gave a similar description of Jenkins. He wrote that Jenkins could be "good-hearted, generous and hospitable" but had an "irascible temper" and was "given to indulgence in strong drink," which made Jenkins "quite passionate."

Christian claimed that the conflicting temperaments between Jenkins and Lane were illustrated when the two men were in Lecompton one day. Someone joked to them that "the best way" to "settle the difficulty" between them was to go outside and fight. Jenkins leapt up, taking the remark seriously, and loudly pro-claimed his willingness to do so. Lane, invoking an incident where a slave had been ordered to arrest Jenkins, "sneered" to Jenkins that he had no business talking to him about a fight. At that point the register of the land office appeared and demanded silence and deliberation in the claim dispute.

The *Traveler* story on the feud suggested yet another reason for the heated passions of Lane and Jenkins. During his time in Kansas one of Lane's daughters died, and she was buried on the disputed land. Lane and his family left the area during the 1856 troubles, and when they returned, "all traces of the grave were gone." Lane believed that Jenkins had torn up the grave and became enraged. He called Jenkins a "ghoul" and vowed that if he found proof of Jenkins' guilt, he would kill him "at first sight." According to the story, Lane believed "until the day of his death" that Jenkins had defiled his daughter's grave.

(When Speer made note of Christian's letters, he expressed skepticism that Jenkins had been so vindictive as to dig up a child's grave. Speer wondered if it wasn't a grave robber or a "careless" farm hand who had desecrated the grave, and then wrote, "Let us hope for some other cause than brutal malignity toward the living and the dead.")

An additional view of the men's mindsets comes from the pen of Edward Fitch, a resident of the Lawrence area. He wrote to his parents on June 5 about Lane's murder of Jenkins. He told them that Jenkins "had been drinking freely" on the day the murder happened and implied, as James Christian said later, that Jenkins drank liquor often. By contrast, Fitch wrote that Lane was and had been "for some time a member of the Temperance Society of Good Templars," a fraternal organization devoted to the prohibition of alcohol.

Before the disagreement turned violent, however, the case between Gaius Jenkins and Jim Lane went to the land office in Lecompton. Twice, in 1884 and again in 1894, John Speer wrote to commissioners in the General Land Office to find out how the case had been resolved. The latter response revealed that the register and the receiver at the land office in Lecompton issued a report on October 19, 1857, in which they stated that they had been unable to render a decision in the case. On December 16 the two officers were instructed to obtain more testimony and make a decision. That was how the matter stood on the fateful day of June 3, 1858.

According to a contemporary account discovered by William Connelley, the day before the shooting Jenkins went to the gated water well near Lane's house. Lane confronted him and Jenkins left. The next day, June 3, Jenkins sent one of his hired men to the well for water. Lane ordered the man away. Jenkins sent word to Lane that he intended to get water from the well, and Lane sent word back that he would shoot him if he tried. That afternoon Jenkins came to the Lane home with as many as four friends. Jenkins was armed, at least one of his friends had a pistol, and another carried an ax with which to demolish the lock on the gate of the well. Lane warned them to leave. When they moved on the well, Lane went into his house to get his shotgun.

When Lane came out of his house, according to some eyewitnesses, one of Jenkins' friends fired or tried to fire at Lane. Lane responded by shooting Jenkins, and one of the four shot Lane in the leg with his pistol. The men carried Jenkins away, and he died that same day. Lane was later arrested and charged with murder.

Albert Richardson was at the office of the *Herald of Freedom* the day of the shooting. He heard about the murder when a voice from the street called out, "Jim Lane has killed Gaius Jenkins, and a mob has gathered around his house to hang him." Richardson dashed to the Lane home and discovered that out of the two or three hundred people around, only "a few" were calling for Lane's lynching.

Richardson was able to enter the homes of both men. Lane was lying in bed, "a pistol [wound] in the knee," with his wife and children around him in tears. The same scene was played out in the Jenkins household, with his widow and children shrieking over "the bloody corpse of the husband and father." Richardson thought Lane had fired first but conceded that whether he had or had not, he "did exactly what two out of three frontier settlers would have done under the circumstances."

Newspapers of the time were becoming divided over Jim Lane's political career, and as such were also divided in their reporting of the shooting. The first news of the shooting appeared in the *Herald of Freedom* on June 5. In that account the "bloody tragedy" occurred due to "a contested land claim." There was only a slight bias toward Jenkins, namely because of the claim that Jenkins had felt obliged to bring friends with him because of "threats made by Lane." Editor George W. Brown's tone changed a week later. Then, he wrote that Jenkins was "beloved by all peoples," he accused Lane of being a "trespasser" on the disputed claim, and he ignored Jenkins' aid to the proslavery faction in the Lawrence land dispute just three years earlier.

The *Republican* in Lawrence took a balanced approach in its account of June 10. "It is unpleasant to say anything that may seem to reflect in the least unfavorably upon the actions of the dead," it commented at one point, "as it is also to impune [*sic*] criminality to the actions of the living; and in touching on this, we are treading upon rather dangerous ground, and will leave it with the proper tribunal to decide" who was in the right.

Editor John Martin of the *Freedom's Champion* in Atchison, in the report of June 12, was rather confused in his sympathies. At first his account sided with the Jenkins view. Then he reprinted a story from a proslavery paper in Leavenworth that called Lane's actions self-defense. That was followed by a letter from a "reliable gentleman" in Lawrence who said Lane's shooting was a deliberate murder, even going so far as to claim Lane had said he "had made arrangements to kill a man at one o'clock."

The tone of the "reliable gentleman" sounded quite a bit like that of George W. Brown in his account in the *Herald*. Brown had already come to dislike Jim Lane. That can be seen in a mock editorial of May 29, in which he endorsed Lane as the Republican candidate for president in the 1860 election. The other contenders, wrote Brown, were not as "progressive" as Lane was, since just a few years ago Lane had tried to "buy a female slave in Lawrence" and had been "making conservative speeches, tickling the ears of pro-slavery men, inducing them to vote for him."

The politics and personal biases of the newspaper editors determined the slant other papers took on the shooting. Sol Miller of the *White Cloud Chief* wrote that though there were "thrilling accounts" of Lane's battles with Border Ruffians, now when "we hear of him killing a man, it is a Free State man." Added J. E. Jones at the *Fort Scott Democrat,* "We always thought that Jim would reach the gallows or the penitentiary, before he did the U. S. Senate." On the other hand, when anti-Lane coverage appeared in the *Freemen's Champion* of Prairie City on June 10, it was with this comment: "We copy them for the purpose of showing our readers how unfair an unscrupulous enemy can be at the misfortune of the object of its venom."

Unlike the majority of its counterparts, the *Leavenworth Times* followed the *Republican* in taking a responsible position on the matter. It noted in its story on June 12 that accounts of what happened were biased either in favor of Lane or of Jenkins. "In this state of affairs," the newspaper stated, "it is evident, that we cannot get at the exact truth, until the witnesses on the stand shall swear to what they know."

Lane's trial began on June 15 and lasted just over two weeks. Among the prosecuting attorneys were George Collamore, future mayor of Lawrence; Samuel Wood, future editor of the Emporia newspaper; and former territorial secretary and acting governor Frederick Stanton. Lane's defense attorneys included James Christian and Thomas Ewing, Jr., son of a prominent Ohio senator and a future general. William Connelley found a detailed news account of Lane's trial published in the *Missouri Democrat* of St. Louis. He had the stories printed in full in volume 16 of the *Kansas Historical Collections.*

Testimony began with the doctor who had examined Jenkins' corpse to determine the cause of his death. The second day and part of the third were taken up with the questioning of Ray Green, one of Jenkins' friends who was present at the time of the shooting. Jenkins' nephew Henry, also present, testified on the third day as well. Four witnesses were questioned the next day, including Jenkins' widow. Around the end of that day or the beginning of the fifth the prosecution rested its case.

Lane, still recovering from his own wound when the trial started, was seen to be regaining his strength by the time the defense began its case on the fifth day. The witnesses for the defense tried to contradict the state's witnesses, a process that continued through the sixth day, with an interesting comment from Douglas County sheriff Samuel Walker. Immediately after the shooting he had arrested Lane and asked him who shot him. Lane told Walker that the men responsible for shooting him had returned to the Jenkins home. At the stable outside that home Walker found three men. He asked if they had been with Jenkins during the shooting. One man said he was and told Walker that "if his pistol had not gone off Lane would not have killed Jenkins." Walker testified that his response to this was, "That puts another face on the whole affair."

The reason for Walker's comment was simple. It clearly would have been murder had Lane shot Jenkins without provocation. Trespassing would not have been justification enough for Lane to respond with violence. But if one of Jenkins' friends had fired first, then Lane would have been justified in returning shots.

The reporter for the *Democrat* stated that the testimony on the seventh day aided Lane's defense. The prosecution put on rebuttal witnesses on the eighth, ninth, tenth, and part of the eleventh days. On the rest of the eleventh day, the defense responded with rebuttal witnesses of their own. The prosecution made its closing argument on the twelfth day, while the defense took two days to present its closing.

The trial had been held before three judges. They rendered their verdict on June 30, finding that the prosecution had not proven Lane had committed willful murder. Lane was discharged, and that ended the trial.

Regarding the claim dispute, on September 12 the receiver decided in favor of Jenkins. The register refused to agree with the decision, but on October 6 he changed his mind. Lane appealed the decision, and on July 20, 1861, the decision was overturned. Jenkins' heirs then appealed, but the secretary of the interior upheld the finding for Lane on December 31, 1861, on December 27, 1862, and again on February 21, 1863.

Leverett Spring wrote that in the wake of the killing of Jenkins, Lane's moods varied wildly. He said that someone "who met him on the streets of Lawrence in these dark days described him as 'care-worn, haggard, reduced almost to a skeleton, the picture of despair.'" Yet on another occasion Spring noted that when someone said to Lane that the killing might hinder his ambitions, Lane replied, "Oh that won't make any difference. General Jackson was a duelist and I don't believe that the killing of a man in self-defense will hurt me."

Just as Lane may have been conflicted about the killing of Jenkins, history too has had trouble dealing with this incident. Those who resented Lane often portrayed the killing as cold-blooded murder while avoiding the messy facts. However, Lane's defenders have had to struggle with the reality that a man—a Free State activist—died at his hands.

Still, the defenders seem to have a better case than Lane's critics. Lane was exonerated of murder in a territorial court not likely to be friendly to him. He was outnumbered on the fatal day and was not armed when the confrontation began. He probably did harbor genuine regret for his actions, despite the evidence that he had justification for the shooting.

For Lane's enemies during his life and afterward, facts such as these were often unfortunate inconveniences to be ignored or dismissed. The killing of Jenkins was more "proof" of Lane's bloodthirsty fanaticism and immoral conduct. Lane's enemies could be vitriolic in their hatred of him and the truth was rarely an obstacle to their animus. It is possible that the death of Gaius Jenkins haunted Jim Lane for the rest of his life. But the misstatements about that death haunt his critics far more, undermining any points they have and demonstrating the depths that resentment of a man can take his rivals. If this incident says anything at all, it is that Jim Lane's life is a tangled thicket to be unraveled rather than simplified with severe pruning.

According to Leverett Spring, in August 1859, Lane sought religion in an attempt to cure his remorseful spirit. Spring quoted a reverend who said he baptized Lane "during a camp-meeting near Baldwin City" on August 29. Lane, said the minister, "manifested much feeling and answered all the questions readily." Most viewed Lane's faith as John J. Ingalls did, who once wrote that Lane "partook of the sacrament as a political device."

Yet Lane might have been sincere. At another revival meeting in Lawrence, Lane said,

> Sixteen years ago an aged, pious and widowed mother lay dying. She called her eldest son to her bedside and said, "Henry, it is my desire that you should have religion, and that, if consistent with your feelings, you should find it within the Methodist church." What could that son do but make the pledge? To-night he appears before you to redeem it. Wicked as he may have been, he desires to be received on probation into the church of which she was a life-long and consistent member.

Leverett Spring wrote that one of the ministers present then said, "My dear brother Lane, we rejoice to hear your decision, but you will have a very narrow way to walk in. It will go out, 'Lane has joined the church.' Let men and devils know that you are earnest and honest."

Spring, ever the Lane critic, would have none of it. "As these periods of piety were fragmentary and often coincided with periods when 'endorsements' and fresh certificates of good character would be useful," he wrote, skeptics like him "regarded Lane's connection with the church as a move in the game of politics and nothing more."

Lane seemingly was good-humored about this skepticism. While giving a speech in Leavenworth that Spring said "fairly smoked with profanity," Lane was admonished by some members of the audience, who complained about this violation of God's law. Lane shot back, "Why, I am a pious man. Just now, to be sure, I may not be quite up to the devotional point!"

Whether or not Lane turned to religion to reverse his fortunes, he did use his rhetorical gifts to such effect. On March 17, 1859, he released a letter through the *Lawrence Republican* rebutting comparisons between himself and a notorious proslavery leader accused of murder. He began by referring to the Jenkins shooting, saying, "It is true that Mr. Jenkins fell by my hand, and no one has more deeply felt or more grievously mourned that misfortune, than myself." However, he was facing "four armed men" who had fired at him first. "During the whole attack, I desisted from firing upon my assailants until the last possible moment." Lane asked the newspaper's readers, "Although I have never asked any one to endorse my conduct in this affair, I am compelled to inquire whether there is any one who candidly believes that, surrounded by the same circumstances, he would not have acted in the same manner?"

While Jim Lane fought to restore his name, there was another change in the office of territorial governor. James Denver resigned the post, telling President Buchanan that Kansas had been pacified. His replacement was Samuel Medary, a politician from Ohio who was an ally of Sen. Stephen Douglas. The parade of governors in and out of the territory had been so fast since 1856 that Medary's barber, perhaps jokingly, told him to pay by the shave rather than monthly.

By early 1859 plans were under way to form a Republican Party organization in the territory. Raymond Gaeddert, writing about the early years of Kansas as a state, believed Lane was a strong influence behind the effort. So did *Herald of Freedom* editor G. W. Brown, who made a sour note in his January 29 issue of an early meeting Lane led.

Favoring the movement was the *Lawrence Republican,* now edited by Dwight Thacher and his brother Solon. Their first editorial on the idea, appearing January 20, stated that it was not leaders who would make a Republican Party but "the ideas which inform the party and constitute its basis." On February 17 the newspaper published a call for an organizing convention in Osawatomie for May 18. In endorsing the call, the *Republican* argued that the time was right and that the Democrats who controlled the government of the territory were already organized and therefore had to be countered.

G. W. Brown at the *Herald* was the main Free State opponent of the effort. On January 29 he stated that he would "sustain the Big Springs Platform until Kansas is a State in the Union." On March 5 he again expressed opposition, but this time because Jim Lane seemed to be behind the convention. By this time Brown was also becoming a critic of Charles Robinson, Lane's chief political rival. Back on January 15 he had reprinted a *New York Herald* piece calling Robinson a "schemer." Brown not only heartily endorsed the insult and warned "the people of Lawrence" to oppose everything Robinson supported, but even went so far as to accuse Robinson of plotting to become president so as to "turn the Republic into a *Monarchy*." Brown's stance was supported by the Democrats in Kansas. One of their organs, the *Wyandotte Weekly Western Argus,* claimed that the territorial legislature "had passed an act opening the jails of the Territory" so as to assist in the formation of the Republican Party.

The convention was held on May 18 and 19 in Osawatomie. It began at eleven in the morning with Henry Fox of Shawnee County being appointed temporary chairman and Dwight Thacher as secretary pro tem. A credentials committee was put in place, the convention adjourned for lunch, and afterward the committee reported the names of the delegates and the counties they represented. Neither Jim Lane nor Charles Robinson were reported as being present at the convention. Although Lane does not appear to have been present in Osawatomie, he was believed to have had some influence not only on its call but on the proceedings themselves.

The other bit of afternoon business was the creation of a committee on permanent organization. Nominations were accepted, a platform committee was created, and the convention adjourned for the day. The next day the platform was read out and approved. It called on the convention set to meet in Wyandotte to draft a new state constitution to completely prohibit slavery in Kansas. Although it did not make an open call for a convention to draft candidates to run for state offices, such a convention was held in October.

Lane may have also had a hand in another convention in 1860. This one met in Topeka on October 17 to draft an overall plan for the construction of a Kansas railroad. Raymond Gaeddert believed that Lane, while not present, acted through William Weer and convention president W. Y. Roberts. One of the railroad projects under discussion was the Leavenworth, Pawnee & Western, which was to connect Leavenworth to Lawrence and Topeka and then travel westward to the Rockies and perhaps the Pacific Ocean. Both Lane and Charles Robinson had interests in the LP&W project, but even here they were divided. Robinson favored the railroad entering Lawrence north of the Kansas River, while Lane preferred an entry south of the river.

When Robinson and his allies failed to get their way on a question of representation, the Robinson faction bolted from the convention. The question was between company interests and population, and the majority decided on the former. Robinson's action had little impact, and the convention drafted a plan that, with just one exception, was actually realized during the 1860s.

John Brown had, since the time he had first come to Kansas, believed that only the shedding of blood could put an end to slavery. He joined with James Montgomery on a few of his raids in 1858, and late that year he liberated several slaves himself from Missouri, but events in the territory to some degree passed him by. By the end of the year, Brown had decided that Kansas was not where he should be in his struggle against slavery. He wanted to go into the South itself and wage his war there.

To that end Brown assembled some of his sons as well as men both white and black who were as determined as he. These he shaped into the core of a force that would initiate a slave uprising. He took his band to the area around Harpers Ferry, Virginia, home to a military arsenal. Under the disguise of a farmer, Brown trained his force of between twenty and thirty men through the summer and into the fall of 1859.

On the night of October 16, Brown began his attack. His men

were able to take control of the arsenal, seize hostages, and cut the telegraph lines. It was well into the following day before the residents of Harpers Ferry were aware that Brown's men had control of the federal armory. But once they became aware they moved, surrounding Brown's men and exchanging fire with them. A contingent of marines under Col. Robert E. Lee was sent to capture Brown's men. Brown himself was identified by another army officer under Lee, Lt. J. E. B. "Jeb" Stuart, who had served in Kansas and knew Brown. Stuart was sent to ask Brown to surrender, Brown refused, and Lee sent in the marines. Brown was wounded but taken alive, along with the surviving members of his band.

Brown was charged with treason against the state of Virginia, convicted, and hanged before the year was over. His raid, trial, and execution electrified and polarized the nation. Southerners feared Brown would be the first of a horde of abolitionists who would come to kill them. Northerners might decry Brown's tactics, but many agreed with his goals. With a looming presidential election that was sure to further exacerbate the nation's differences, the United States seemed to be careening toward a civil war over the issue of slavery.

Democrats tried to pin Brown to the Republican Party as the election campaign of 1860 began. However, the Republican Party had by then spread throughout the Northern states and was that year largely unified. The Democratic Party by contrast fractured along sectional lines with a Northern wing nominating Stephen Douglas and a Southern wing nominating Vice President John Breckinridge. The Republicans met in Chicago to decide their candidate for president. The main contestants for the nomination were Sen. William Seward, Sen. Salmon Chase, Simon Cameron from Pennsylvania, Missourian Edward Bates, and Abraham Lincoln.

Abraham Lincoln was a lawyer from Illinois. He had served one term in Congress, where he had opposed the Mexican War and had risen to national prominence in 1858 when running for Stephen Douglas's Senate seat. He had engaged Douglas in a series of debates that were dominated by slavery issues, including the question of the Lecompton constitution. Lincoln had articulated the Republican opposition to the extension of slavery in such a manner as to enhance his standing nationally. Although a dark-horse prospect, Lincoln had hopes that he might be able to obtain the party's nomination for president in the 1860 election.

Lincoln came to Kansas in December 1859 at the behest of a friend, Mark W. Delahay, and spoke in the towns of Elwood, Troy, Doniphan, Atchison, and finally Leavenworth. It was in Leavenworth that Jim Lane met Abraham Lincoln for the first time. Wendell Stephenson noted that it may have been at that personal meeting that Lincoln's view of Lane changed. In October he had written to Delahay his concern in allying himself with Lane, but the following March, Lincoln asked Delahay to tell Lane that if his "friendship for you could be of any advantage" to let Lane know that he had it and that "I shall be pleased to hear from him at any time."

Senator Seward was the leading contender as the Republicans met in Chicago. However, Seward was too radical for moderates in the party, and he was tied to corruption in New York state politics through a campaign manager. Chase too was thought overly radical to obtain mainstream support, while Bates was too conservative. Cameron had flirted with too many political parties in the past to seem viable. That left Lincoln as a compromise candidate.

Lincoln had strengths of his own that lifted him above simple acceptability. From the crucial state of Illinois, he was moderate enough to have broad voter appeal, but radical enough to satisfy the party faithful. His personal rags-to-riches story could strike a chord with many Americans. It also symbolized the values not related to slavery that Republicans prized. Finally, and perhaps most important, there arose a perception in the party that Lincoln had a far better chance of winning Western states than did Seward.

Lincoln won the nomination on the third ballot. It energized the hometown crowd at the convention, and that in turn energized Republicans throughout the Northern states. The Democrats were divided into two sectional parties, and a third party, the Constitutional Unionists, emerged from the remains of the Southern Whig Party to nominate Tennessean John Bell.

The presidential election split into two contests, Douglas against Lincoln in the North, and Breckinridge against Bell in the South. Douglas was the only candidate to offer himself as a national one, but Southerners would not forgive him for turning from the Lecompton constitution. Southerners also despised Lincoln and claimed that a Lincoln victory would force them to attempt to leave the union. Northerners, who had heard similar talk in the 1856 election, ignored the warnings. Breckinridge and Bell made no campaign efforts outside the South.

Jim Lane stumped for Abraham Lincoln in the 1860 election in Kansas and Indiana. His appearance in his old congressional district in September caused a Democratic newspaper there, the *Register,* to dig up all manner of slanders against him. It threw at him the Jenkins shooting, his dispute with General Lane in Mexico, a few other personal feuds, and called him an abolitionist to boot.

In the election Bell took three Southern states, Breckinridge the rest, and Douglas only New Jersey and Missouri. Lincoln won majorities or pluralities in the rest of the states and earned 180 electoral votes; he only needed 152 to win. Though Lincoln only took 40 percent of the popular vote, he won a majority of the votes cast in the North. Abraham Lincoln thus became the sixteenth president.

But Southerners had been quite serious about secession if a Republican were elected. Within weeks of the election the South was swept up in a mass movement toward secession from the union. South Carolina was first on December 20 and was followed by Mississippi, Florida, Alabama, Georgia, Louisiana, and Texas by February 1, 1861. Virginia seceded two months later, and after it so did Arkansas, North Carolina, and Tennessee. Kentucky and Maryland wavered, and many of its sons would fight for the new Confederate States of America, but both states' governments remained loyal. That left Missouri as the last Slave State to decide upon its allegiance. That decision would naturally be important to Kansas, and Kansans kept a close eye on their neighbor in the first months of 1861.

Kansans also had to look to their own interests. Kansas was admitted to the union on January 29, and that meant it had to finally form a state government and send representatives to Washington. For Jim Lane, this would be his chance to realize his ambitions, or have the last several years amount to nothing.

IX.

Statehood and Secret Deals

In the summer of 1859, one last constitutional convention was held, this one in Wyandotte. It drafted a constitution that barred slavery from Kansas. This constitution would be approved by Congress early in 1861, allowing Kansas at last to enter the Union a Free State. With the passage of the Wyandotte constitution in October 1859, politicians in Kansas Territory moved to elect state officers in the expectation that as soon as the constitution was submitted to the federal government, Kansas would be admitted as a state. The Republican Party met first, on October 12 in Topeka. There were two candidates for the party's nominee for governor, Charles Robinson and H. P. Johnston. Robinson won the nomination forty-three to thirty-four. Running with him for lieutenant governor would be J. P. Root. Among the other Republican candidates were Martin Conway for congressman and Robinson ally Thomas Ewing, Jr., for chief justice of the state supreme court. The Democrats met in Lawrence on October 25 and nominated Samuel Medary for governor.

Between the two nominating conventions John Brown's raid on Harpers Ferry took place, so the Democrats tried to use Brown's association with the antislavery party to beat the Republicans. The tactic failed, and may have even backfired, for when the election was held on December 1, the whole Republican slate was chosen to lead Kansas. The election also put in place a state legislature overwhelmingly controlled by Republicans. Of the seventy-five members of the state House of Representatives, sixty-four were

Republicans; of the twenty-five state senators, only three were Democrats. Clearly party divisions were to play no role in legislature. What division there would be came from the split in the Republican Party between the allies of Jim Lane and Charles Robinson.

Governor Robinson sent his first message to the legislature on March 30, 1861, over two months after the state had been admitted to the union and those elected in 1859 had taken their seats. Robinson's message outlined what he thought ought to be accomplished during the first year of state government. Laws had to be passed to organize state offices and set out the duties of state officials. An effort was needed to get the federal government to take over the territorial financial debt, and the new state must find sources of revenue. Electoral districts had to be set out, consistency with the territorial code had to be provided for, and locations for state institutions such as a university and a prison had to be located.

The first order of business for the new state legislature was the election of two U.S. senators. The matter of who would be chosen senator was not only of interest to the candidates, as a letter from John J. Ingalls indicates. Writing to his father on March 21, Ingalls said that President Lincoln had made it clear no federal appointments would be made in or for Kansas until the state had two senators.

At the time most federal positions had no qualification requirements, so it was perfectly acceptable for senators and congressmen to reward their supporters with government posts. Presidents went along with this patronage to win and maintain allies in Congress and in state party organizations. President Lincoln therefore was unwilling to award any patronage jobs until he knew who would be representing Kansas.

In his letter, Ingalls voiced his opinions of the four main contenders for senator, Marcus Parrott, Samuel Pomeroy, Frederick Stanton, and Jim Lane. Of them Ingalls seemed to think that Stanton had the smallest chance, as he was "an eleventh-hour Republican." Ingalls was uncertain about Pomeroy; the man had guts, "but if brains enter the contest somewhat, his chances are small." Parrott had been the territorial delegate and therefore would "probably succeed."

And then there was Lane. Ingalls called him "one of the most remarkable men I ever knew." Lane was "a perfect demagogue, charlatan," and "knave," "everything that is infamous and detestable in private life." Yet he said Lane also had "a certain indefatigable energy, magnetism and nerve, which conquers adversity and achieves success." As to his becoming senator, Ingalls wrote, "The chances are immensely in his favor."

Raymond Gaeddert, writing about the "birth" of the state, said that Stanton might have been the darkest horse in the race. He had been a Democrat while in the post of secretary of the territory and had only joined the Republicans late in 1859. Nevertheless, he did live south of the Kansas River, and sentiment in the state at the time was for one senator from north of the river and one from the south. In that way Stanton was a direct competitor to Lane.

Marcus Parrott was from Leavenworth, and therefore one of the northside candidates. Although not totally popular in his hometown, he did have the support of many in northern Kansas. They viewed him as a friend of their railroad ambitions. In mid-February, Parrott and Lane decided to form an alliance to strengthen their chances at winning the election.

Parrott's chief rival was Samuel Pomeroy. Pomeroy had been an agent of the New England Emigrant Aid Company and through that was well known in Kansas. He became even more acclaimed (and perhaps connected) by taking the lead in efforts to relieve Kansans suffering during the drought of 1859-60. His support was very mixed; some northerners were behind his candidacy, others opposed, in part due to Pomeroy's uncertain alliances with a variety of railroad companies. Although willing to win at any cost, Pomeroy seemed to be caught by the Lane-Parrott combination.

Lane of course had been working Kansas for months to secure his election. As early as October 1859, Lane had joined forces with Martin Conway, who aspired to be a congressman from Kansas. Lane also tried to forge an alliance with the supporters of Marcus Parrott. One such supporter was P. P. Elder, who noted in 1893 that he was one of the few Parrott backers who also backed Lane's candidacy. Elder wrote that initially many of the Parrott men were willing to "vote for Lane to save Parrott," but their mood changed as the start of the session approached.

In fact, as John Speer wrote in 1896, Lane's initial plan was to first secure election to senator through the territorial legislature. There was concern in Kansas that the state would not be admitted before Congress went into its new session and perhaps not until the spring. He would get the territorial legislature to elect him, add that to the standing vote under the Topeka constitution, and head to Washington to "control more effectually" federal patronage and to "prevent any appointment" made while the Lincoln administration waited for Kansas to formally send two senators.

Another example of how Lane laid the groundwork for his candidacy is found in a letter he wrote to Mark Delahay dated December 18, 1860. He began the letter by reporting that he had arranged for John Speer, now one of Lane's "most faithful friends," to gain control of the *Lawrence Republican* newspaper, provided he could raise five hundred dollars for his campaign. Lane boasted that with control of the *Republican* and their influence over two other newspapers in Kansas, "we can accomplish almost anything." Lane vowed to Delahay that his opponents "shall not beat [me] over by corruption"; "the people are for me, the [members of the state legislature] are for me," and "by [G]od they shall not defraud me out of my election."

Some of the newspapers in Kansas had already expressed their views on Lane's candidacy. When William Phillips gave a speech in late October 1859 supporting Lane's bid, the *Republican* printed the speech and the *Herald of Freedom* denounced it. That appeared to be the end of the election "war" until it came time for the state legislature to cast votes for senators.

By that time, the newspaper opposing Lane's bid was the *Topeka Tribune*. In its issue of February 16, 1861, it printed two pieces expressing its views. One was a letter from an Indiana Republican that said Lane "was not the most suitable man" to be a senator. The other was a letter from Lawrence that confidently predicted Lane would not be elected because he had lost support in the legislature. This was followed by a piece on March 2 that claimed Lane had not done more for the Free State movement than anyone else and therefore was not entitled to be a senator. Finally, on March 29 the newspaper derided sentiments that Lane was an honest enough man to make a good senator.

Not that Lane's foes were above reproach either. The *Kansas State Record* of Topeka reprinted a piece from a Mound City newspaper on March 23 that stated Lane's enemies there were using means "both foul and fair" to defeat him. The *Emporia News* noted in its February 13 issue that all manner of "below par" candidates were jockeying for Senate seats, making odd alliances and extravagant promises.

John Speer was just as unrestrained in his praises of Lane's candidacy. His "Senatorial" commentary in the March 21 issue of the *Republican* did what the *Tribune* had warned against: giving Lane sole credit for the antislavery triumph in Kansas. Surprisingly, another newspaper backing Lane's chances was the *Fort Scott Democrat,* which on March 16 called him "the smartest hound in the pack." As for the two Republican newspapers in Leavenworth, the *Daily Times* and the *Daily Conservative,* both supported Lane's election because, as the latter put it, Lane had "always been true to [Leavenworth's] interests."

Lane's chief rival in state politics was still Gov. Charles Robinson. In a letter to his wife, Sara, written on January 11, the governor was confident that Lane's efforts would be in vain. "Lane has undertaken a personal fight on me for the purpose of destroying my influence at [Washington]," he told her. But he said that "by paying a little attention to the matter [he could] make him smell worse than ever. He & his friends are already beginning to falter in their course for fear that I will turn the tables on them which I can do with ease."

Robinson was counting on an appointment to the post of commissioner of Indian Affairs. His plan was to use that position to get control of federal patronage in Kansas and secure the election of Lane's rivals to the Senate. To that end he visited the nation's capital in late December 1860 and remained through January. Robinson also delayed the start of the session of the state legislature to put off a vote on the senatorial election until he could consolidate his power. As the *Missouri Republican* of St. Louis noted, "If the state legislature is called at an early day, Lane will certainly be elected Senator, so the Governor announces his intention of not convening it before spring, no doubt devoutly hoping some combination may be formed before that time to defeat his enemy."

Aiding Robinson was one of the dark-horse candidates for senator, Thomas Ewing, Jr. On January 17 he told his brother Hugh that he was going to Washington to help Robinson achieve his appointment as commissioner. With Robinson appointed, he said, "I will go to the Senate, *sure.*" A few days later he told a friend, Caleb Smith, that he was at work and on January 22 told another, Thomas Corwin, that Robinson "will be recommended to the new administration" for the post. That same day he wrote to J. J. Coombs that he would "succeed" as a Senate candidate because he had Robinson's backing, and only a combination between Lane and either Parrott or Pomeroy could defeat him.

However, Robinson's delaying tactic failed to win him allies. Sen. Lymon Trumbull wrote to Mark Delahay about this on February 16, 1861. He said that Robinson's delay in convening the state legislature was "utterly inexcusable" because the "bill to admit Kansas was hurried through for the very purpose of getting the Kansas Senators [to Washington] before the 4th of March." The governor had to have known that, added Trumbull, and that the nation's fate "may depend on two votes." For his part Senator Trumbull was willing to have any Kansas appointments to federal offices put on hold until the new senators arrived. This may also have been the view of the president, for in a letter from Washington written by Alfred Gray to Marcus Parrott, Gray noted that "Robinson is not in favor with the new administration," in part because of his delaying scheme. That assessment is also backed by John Speer, who wrote in 1896 that Martin Conway had already gotten Lincoln to sign off on withholding federal appointments until senators were elected.

The governor's other hope to best Lane early in 1861 also came to naught. President Lincoln appointed an Indiana man to the post of Indian commissioner. That man had been very helpful in getting Lincoln both the Republican nomination and the presidency. It also seems to have hurt that Robinson stalled in assembling the state legislature. Robinson's plans to stop Lane failed entirely as the month of March ended and the state legislature finally convened.

Lane's enemies had only a short time to figure out a new scheme, but on the night of March 31 they concocted another plan to thwart his ambition. Backers of Stanton, Parrott, and Pomeroy joined with the Democrats to call for a vote in the state Senate the next day to elect a senator from south of the Kansas River. It seemed that the disdain many of the Parrott men had for Lane overcame their will to support the Lane-Parrott alliance. They were aided in their scheme by Thomas Ewing, Jr., the son of an Ohio senator, an ally of Governor Robinson, and the man chosen to be chief justice of the state supreme court. Friends of Ewing and Robinson came to the April 1 session expecting to pull one up on Lane.

That morning one of Parrott's backers presented the motion. It caught the Lane faction completely by surprise, but it also led to confusion in the Senate as a whole. A parliamentary battle ensued that lasted all morning and resulted in the nomination for senator of Lane, Parrott, Stanton, and a man named A. J. Isacks. The nomination split the Lane-Parrott combination and led to Stanton getting the most votes.

Lane's enemies thought that had gotten the better of him. There was only one thing wrong with their scheme. Senators were usually elected during joint sessions of state houses and senates. If Lane's allies could get the vote of April 1 overturned with a call for a joint session, they could recapture their momentum. With the alliance between Lane and Parrott broken, Lane's friends went in search of a new combination.

Isaac Goodnow, one of the founders of Manhattan and of Kansas State University, was an ally of Samuel Pomeroy in 1861. Writing more than thirty years later, Goodnow recalled that he advised Pomeroy to align himself with Lane if he wished to be elected senator. Pomeroy chose instead to take his chances on his own but found himself coming up short against Parrott. He then decided on an alliance with Lane and sent Goodnow to meet him and lobby on his behalf.

When Goodnow arrived at Lane's headquarters, he wrote that Lane was "terribly disheartened and sick." But when Goodnow told him that Pomeroy wanted to join forces with him, "his face shone with some new lustre." "I have been ready all the time to act with General Pomeroy," Lane said to Goodnow, "but for some reason he has stood aloof. I am ready now to consult with him."

The new alliance kicked in the next day, April 2, when the House voted to go into joint session on April 4 to elect the senators. Stanton's supporters tried to fight the motion in the state Senate, but lost on a close vote. It didn't help Stanton's chances that Parrott's men were split on the motion. So on the afternoon of April 4 the state legislature assembled to elect two U.S. senators.

The members were supposed to stand and announce the two candidates they were voting for, state senators first, then members of the state House. For the next two hours confusion reigned as members switched votes, and support for the various candidates rose and fell. In the end Lane captured approximately fifty-five votes, Pomeroy fifty-two, Parrott forty-nine, Stanton twenty-one, and Isacks eleven. The final seven votes were split amount four others. Jim Lane and Samuel Pomeroy were now senators representing Kansas in Washington.

Even though many writers since that election have admitted there was a certain inevitability in Lane's ascension, many have in the same breath suggested that Lane bought his way into the U.S. Senate. Sidney Clarke, in writing about Lane in 1879, said, "there were men in Kansas who honestly believed that Lane bought votes for his first election to the senate." Indeed, Clarke added, there were probably as many "yet living who are so perfectly certain that [everybody] but themselves is corrupt in politics." But this was not how Lane obtained his support, Clarke insisted. He had traveled with Lane from Lawrence to Topeka in early 1861 to be present at the session of the new state legislature. On the way the pair stopped in the village of Big Springs for dinner. Paying for their meal "exhausted our finances to such an extent" that when they made an "honest count" of their funds after dinner the two men had all of $2.50. This small sum would have been unsuccessful in buying a senatorial position.

Even ardent Lane critic Leverett Spring admitted that at this time Lane was broke. "The wolf was often at his door," he wrote in 1898. "When the senatorial contest opened, Lane succeeded in borrowing twenty dollars, proceeded to the capital and opened headquarters in one of the hotels. Efforts were made to induce his landlord to turn him out of doors on the ground that he could never pay his bills, but the plot failed. If it should succeed he swore that he 'would move into a dry-goods box and get ahead of the hounds.'"

Lane was never a rich man, no matter how much power he had. Sidney Clarke recalled that Lane usually had to borrow money from his friends to pay his bills, friends who were often "nearly as poor as himself." Yet Lane was no big spender, and even when he had money his habits "were temperate and frugal."

Verres Smith, although no Lane man, wrote in *Lippincott's* that Lane had ways other than bribery to get votes for his Senate bid. Well after the votes were cast, Smith claimed that Lane had stated that of the fifty-six or so men who had voted him into the Senate, forty-five "now wear shoulder-straps," alluding to the fact that once in the Senate, Lane had some power to obtain or recommend commissions in the army.

Newspaper reaction to Lane's victory was mixed. The *Emporia News* of April 13 expressed some disappointment that Pomeroy had bested Parrott, but also noted that with Lane as senator and Robinson as governor "it almost seems as if old Topeka days were revived." The *State Record* went further, stating on April 20 that Lane's election was "an ample vindication" of the work of the Free State movement. John Speer noted with some glee in the April 25 issue of the *Republican* that Missouri newspapers were "terribly troubled" by Lane's election.

Another newspaper that had opposed Lane's candidacy was the *Kansas State Journal* of Lawrence. But on April 11, after Lane's election, it expressed the view that it would back Lane as long as he put Kansas ahead of his friends. Sol Miller in White Cloud would have none of it. "Ask us to eat an onion," he wrote on April 11, "to have all our teeth extracted, or to consent to being circumcised, and we might submit, under certain circumstances; but do not ask us to cheerfully acquiesce in the election of Lane and Pomeroy to the United States Senate!"

One week later Miller, in reporting on a speech Lane gave in Atchison, observed that at this "big hurrah" Lane made many promises. There would be "tremendous crops" harvested that year; the Pacific Railroad would build along the Kansas River; and the state would prosper generally. "As Jim promises to deal in the miraculous," Miller concluded, "perhaps he can tell us whether he intends to bring poor Jenkins to life again!" A week after that, when news came that Lane was promising Marcus Parrott a chance at Martin Conway's seat in Congress, Miller wrote that "Lane has no more right to bargain off that nomination than his distinguished ancestor had to promise the whole world to Christ."

Before Lane could assume his seat, he had to briefly put aside the controversies swirling around his election to the Senate in order to carry out his duties as a father. Namely he had to give away his daughter Ella at her wedding to Charles Adams. "It was a very humble wedding in a very humble pioneer cabin," wrote John Speer. There were only a few close friends in attendance, but as all had been helpful in Lane's recent campaign, Speer asked one of them "when the caucus would begin." Lane said a few words to them before he left. One of the things he said, as Speer and many others have written since, was this: "Now we shall see what a live man can do."

The Washington that Lane arrived in on April 13 was a city under siege. Lincoln had issued his call for seventy-five thousand volunteers after the attack on Fort Sumter, and two days later Virginia chose to join the Confederacy. Maryland was hovering on the brink of secession; no one was certain if Union soldiers coming through the state to Washington would make it unscathed.

That first night Lane and Samuel Pomeroy took to the street in front of their hotel to make speeches. As soon as Lane stepped up, Confederate sympathizers shouted, "Mob him!" Lane, as ever in his element, met the calls with a threat of his own. His voice rising, he yelled, "Mob and be damned!" He warned his opponents that he had "a hundred men from Kansas in the crowd, all armed, all fighting men, just from the *victorious* fields of Kansas! They will shoot every damned man of you who again cries 'Mob,' 'Mob.'" Lane's supporters cheered loudly as the hammers on their pistols were cocked.

The Kansans were in the city not just to support the government cause. Since the days of Andrew Jackson, new congressmen and senators were followed by men from their home state looking for federal jobs. The ability of these legislators to reward men with patronage often determined if they would remain in office.

The next day, Maj. David Hunter came to Lane's hotel room. Hunter was a member of Gen. Winfield Scott's staff, and he asked for Lane's help. There were few Union soldiers in Washington, and word had it that Confederates or their allies might try to capture President Lincoln. Hunter asked Lane to organize the Kansans in the capital into a company to guard the White House.

The list of the men Lane assembled for this "Frontier Guard" now reads like a who's who of early Kansas. There were no prominent men among the officers, but the list of privates included Daniel Anthony, future mayor of Leavenworth and brother to suffragette Susan B. Anthony; Sidney Clarke, future congressman; Thomas Ewing, Jr., relative of William T. Sherman, head of the LP&W railroad, and a future general; Marcus J. Parrott, who had just lost the contest for senator; and the other senator from Kansas, Samuel Pomeroy.

In spite of its pedigree, the Frontier Guard seems to have been limited to one duty, albeit a prestigious one. According to the *New York Tribune*, Lane's men camped in the East Room of the White House to protect the president. They remained on guard for at least a week. On April 25 a correspondent for the *Tribune* remarked on the odd sight of these rough Kansas "guests" posted in the "gorgeous apartment," but added that in case of an attack the "guests would show they were meant rather for use than ornament."

Lane's Frontier Guard even managed to be the first to capture a rebel flag, according to former member and consul general to China, D. H. Bailey, who spoke about his experiences to an Emporia newspaper in 1882. The story of the capture began in April when a rumor surfaced that Confederate sympathizers were planning to take a bridge over the Potomac River. Lane's men were ordered to the scene, along with another volunteer company composed of Kentuckians. No enemy soldiers were found, but on the other side of the river there was a house flying a rebel flag. The owner of the house was badgered into lowering the flag, which Lane proudly displayed near his room at the Willard Hotel.

As Union regiments finally arrived in Washington toward the end of April, the need for irregular units such as the Frontier Guard ended. In early May, Lane assembled the guard and marched them to the White House. They were met by President

Lincoln, who thanked them for services rendered. After that, according to the *Republican* of May 9, the guard returned to the Willard Hotel, "exchanged compliments with each other, and adjourned till the next meeting."

Naturally enough, Lane's allies would call the guard's service vital to the nation's security, while his enemies would dismiss it as useless political theater. Author Edgar Langsdorf researched and wrote a brief history of the guard that was published in 1940. "It must be remembered that Washington in 1861 was in a condition of hysteria," he wrote, "and the Guard was a psychological factor of real importance in helping to calm the city's nerves, no matter what its military value may have been."

Most authors writing about Jim Lane have agreed that it was around this time that he went from being an ally of President Lincoln to being something close to a friend. From that point on, Lane visited Lincoln every day he was in Washington. Views of this relationship largely depend on whether the author liked or disliked Lane. Leverett Spring, decades later, neatly summarized how Robinson and his allies saw the matter.

> Lane's singular influence over Mr. Lincoln and the secretary of war, Mr. Stanton, is one of the most inexplicable and disastrous facts that concern Kansas. It was the source of the heaviest calamities that visited the commonwealth during this period, because it put him in a position to gratify mischievous ambitions, to pursue personal feuds, to assume duties and offices that belonged to others, to popularize the corruptest political methods, and to organize semi-predatory military expeditions. His conduct not only embarrassed the state executive and threw state affairs into confusion, but provoked sanguinary reprisals from Missouri.

In 2001, Craig Miner devoted a whole article in *Kansas History* to the relationship between Lane and Lincoln. He found that the senator and the president had much more in common than did the governor and the president. Lane and Lincoln were Westerners who spent some part of their lives in Indiana. They were born five years apart, Lincoln in 1809 and Lane in 1814. They were both strong public speakers. They both liked a good laugh and a good story. Perhaps more deeply, both men had melancholy streaks to their natures, dark moods that could drive them to despair. Recognizing such traits in each other might have led Lane and Lincoln to something more than just a political alliance, perhaps even to an actual friendship.

Too, though they were opposed to slavery, neither was an abolitionist as Robinson was. Miner likened Lane's eventual radicalism over slavery to the zeal of a religious convert or to the former alcoholic who becomes a temperance activist. Lincoln intensely disliked slavery, but he refused for almost a year and a half to make it an open aim of the war. He feared that doing so too soon would drive away the Border States and make recruiting in much of the country too difficult. Indeed, it may have been that Lincoln allowed Lane to make his radical statements on slavery in 1861 and 1862 as part of an overall strategy to prepare the public to take such a step. By contrast, the abolitionist in Robinson probably would not have allowed himself to be used in that way, and the independent politician in him would have caused him to speak out against Lincoln for not carrying through on the "proper" policy.

And Robinson had faults of his own that made it hard for him to get as close to Lincoln as Lane did. William Cutler noted that he was not a "party politician," meaning that Robinson would not follow Lincoln out of party loyalty, but only out of duty or personal loyalty. Robinson also failed to spend time in Washington presenting his side in any dispute with Lane that involved the president.

There may have been something else that prevented Robinson from getting very far with Lincoln. The president would have needed men of action and decisiveness to carry out his policies and prosecute the war. Not even Jim Lane's enemies would have doubted that he was a man of action. Yet Charles Robinson appears to have been if anything a man of inaction. Although personally brave, Robinson seemed to shrink from outright confrontation. Lane, on the other hand, was more than willing to do just about anything to ensure that his side would come out on top. With the nation in the grip of civil war, such willingness was not just favorable, but could also be vital. Lane's tactics might not always be ethical, but as long as there was a means to rein him in, Lincoln would have thought Lane useful.

On July 18, 1861, according to Sidney Clarke, Lane delivered his first speech in the Senate on what the nation's policy should be now that war had begun.

> I represent a constituency whose rights have been trampled under foot by the slave oligarchy of this country. Fraud, cruelty, barbarism were inflicted on them by that power. The attempt is now being made by that power to overthrow the government— to destroy the Union. They have brought upon this conflict. If, in that conflict, the institution of slavery perish[es], we will thank God that He has brought upon us this war. I do believe, Mr. President, that the institution of slavery will not survive, in any State of this Union, the march of Union armies, and I thank God that is so.

Lane's political enemies were not willing to grant him an inch, on this speech or on any other. Leverett Spring alleged that once Lane had gained the Senate, his "eloquence did practically cease." "On one or two occasions he broke through the restraints of the place and spoke in his natural vein. 'Old Jim thinks he's at Baldwin City,' was the comment of a Kansan in the gallery."

Lane's supporters, however, did not think he ought to restrict himself to making speeches to aid the war effort. Early in 1861 an editorial in the *Leavenworth Conservative* said, "Put Jim Lane at the head of our armies, and instead of months of idleness we shall have victories every day and a restored union in six months." Lane himself seemed to agree, and that would lead to yet another controversial episode in an already contentious life.

X.

The Lane Brigade

In 1860, Missouri elected the pro-Southern Democrat Claiborne Jackson as governor. Early the next year Jackson tried to organize a pro-secession convention but was foiled by pro-Union politicians. When President Lincoln demanded volunteers after the firing at Fort Sumter, Jackson called up a Missouri militia to resist Federal authority. This official action, sanctioned by the Missouri constitution, was thwarted when a pro-Confederate mob failed in their attempt to seize arms at the Federal arsenal in St. Louis. Capt. Nathaniel Lyon had seized the arms at the arsenal and moved the supplies out of state. Lyon furthered the Union cause in Missouri in May when men under his command captured a camp where militia under Jackson were being trained. At that point Lyon took over most Union forces in the state.

Meanwhile Jackson had appointed Sterling Price commander of the state's militia units. However, Price and Jackson, along with the body of the state militia, were forced to retreat from Jefferson City by Lyon's aggressive march on the capital. Price ultimately had to flee to southwestern Missouri, but there he was able to drill his men in peace. When he felt his army was ready, Price sent it on the offensive and in early July defeated a Union force at Carthage. Price was then joined by Benjamin McCulloch, commanding regiments from Arkansas and Louisiana, and by the end of July, Price had pushed Lyon back to Springfield.

Although outnumbered, Lyon (now a general) knew his men were better trained and supplied than the Confederates. Early on

August 10, 1861, General Lyon launched a two-pronged attack on the Confederate camp along Wilson's Creek. The Union assault succeeded early in holding off rebels on the north side of the field, and the flanking column under Col. Franz Sigel was able to push forward. Then a Louisiana regiment, supposedly wearing uniforms similar to those worn by an Iowa regiment, marched on Sigel. The colonel held his fire long enough to let the Louisiana troops attack, and they drove his column back. The rest of the rebels concentrated their forces on Lyon's main body; at around 10:30 A.M. Lyon was killed, and soon after, the main body pulled back to Springfield.

Lyon's actions had been against the advice of his superior, John C. Frémont. The man famous across America as the "Pathfinder" and the first Republican Party candidate for president had been put in charge of the Western Department by Lincoln in July. Lincoln hoped that Frémont could beat the Confederate forces in Missouri while keeping slave-owning Unionists in the state loyal to Washington. Complicating Frémont's mission were Senator Lane's next moves.

As early as April 27, 1861, there was speculation about Sen. Jim Lane taking a military post. On that day the *Press* in Council Grove reported that he had "been placed at the head of 1,000 troops" and would therefore resign his seat. A week later the *Times* of Leavenworth stated that Lane was being given the power to recruit three cavalry companies and an artillery battalion, while on May 11 the *Conservative* claimed that Lane would be assigned the task of recapturing Fort Smith, Arkansas, from the rebels.

Not everyone thought Lane ought to have a hand in military affairs. On May 11 the *Topeka Tribune* expressed dismay that on returning to Kansas both Lane and Senator Pomeroy were making promises that they had the power to recruit soldiers for the new Union army. Only Governor Robinson had that power, and he had already offered a thousand men for Federal service. Additionally, and perhaps in spite of reality, the *Tribune* noted that every day the mails "bring us tidings of peace from the State of Missouri."

A week later the *State Record* reported that Lane only wanted to "assist" in forming the two regiments the president had said he was willing to accept. On May 30, John Speer wrote in the *Republican* that there was no reason why Lane ought not use his "talismanic name" to aid in recruitment, but the *Tribune* of May 25 claimed that Lane was not just using his name to bring in men; he was angling to be appointed a brigadier general. In an issue the following week, the newspaper went so far as to accuse Lane of interfering with Governor Robinson's power to raise troops for the national army.

This of course brought Lane back into conflict with Robinson. Pro-Robinson papers such as the *State Journal* wondered about Lane's "talismanic name" and asked, "Where is the regiment that prefers him for a leader?" But to papers trying to strike some sort of balance, as was the *Conservative,* the feud was an annoyance. "On all public questions there is a Robinson version and a Lane version," wrote editor D. W. Wilder, "and neither is the truth." Still, there was a war on, and Lane seemed interested in doing more than making pro-Union speeches in the Senate.

On June 20, President Lincoln informed Secretary of War Simon Cameron that he had been considering what to do with Lane. "I have been reflecting upon the subject, and have concluded that we need the services of such a man out there at once," the president said. They had "better appoint him a brigadier-general of volunteers to-day, and send him off with such authority to raise a force . . . as you think will get him into actual work quickest." Cameron endorsed the comment with, "General Lane has been authorized to raise two additional regiments of volunteers."

The *White Cloud Chief,* among other newspapers, printed in early July an announcement from Lane dated June 25. The announcement stated that the Department of War would accept two regiments into service in addition to the three Governor Robinson was already raising. (After Lincoln issued the initial order for regiments, he authorized Robinson's ally Frederick Stanton to raise a third regiment.) Senator Lane would have the power to raise these two new regiments, and William Weer and James Montgomery would take command of each regiment. Lane would continue to serve as senator, even though he was planning to take command of a Kansas Brigade around July 20.

To Robinson this authority meant that Lane was no longer a senator, despite his intentions, and he promptly dispatched Frederick Stanton to take Lane's seat. When Sol Miller in White Cloud made note of this on July 18, he asked when the state would "be purged of the curse of the Robinson and Lane wrangle?" John Speer, of course, wrote in the *Republican* on that same day that Kansas was "disgraced" by Robinson's action. Lane himself was quoted in the *Conservative* as saying he thought this was "an attempt to bury a man before he was dead." However, events would move fast and prevent Stanton and Robinson from succeeding in their takeover of the Senate seat.

Lane's regiments shortly were mustered at Fort Scott. In fact three regiments, not two, would compose what would become known as the "Lane Brigade." According to William Cutler, military records did not call these regiments the Third, Fourth, and Fifth Kansas. The first of these was the Fifth Regiment Kansas Volunteer Cavalry, commanded by Hampton Johnson. The second was the Sixth Volunteer Cavalry under William Judson. The last was the Seventh, with Charles Jennison in command. Lane made his headquarters at Fort Scott, where he housed his brigade before moving them into action.

Two weeks after Wilson's Creek, Lane was informed by Col. James Montgomery "from sources hitherto reliable" that 1,000 rebels were heading to Fort Scott. The informant also claimed that McCulloch was "sending 4,000 picked men from Springfield, and armed with Colt's, Sharp's, Maynard, and minié rifles." However, two days later Brig. Gen. Ulysses Grant, in command at Jefferson City, reported that McCulloch was moving on him.

That same day, August 25, Lane sent a dispatch to the commander of Fort Leavenworth that shows just how muddled the situation on the border was. He wrote that one Confederate force had been within thirty miles of Fort Scott, reported that he had information that "500 rebels" "were threatening Paola and Osawatomie," and hinted that Fort Leavenworth might be in danger, but he still wanted the artillery from there because "a large force is marching upon us."

Two days after that, a letter was sent to Secretary of War Simon Cameron that told of "rebel camps forming undisturbed" through Missouri and relayed that "their early concentration into another formidable army may reasonably be looked for." "It is the opinion of some of our best-informed citizens," the author continued, "obtained from their Southern correspondence, that the possession of Missouri is regarded of the utmost importance to the Southern cause." He added that "[t]he possession of the lead mine of that State by the rebels will also be a most unfortunate thing for the country." That lead mine, which was shipping lead out through the town of Osceola, would be a key to future actions by Lane and his men.

Meanwhile on September 1, Governor Robinson had sent his own opinion of the situation to Frémont. "I desire to say that we are in no danger of invasion," he wrote, "provided the Government stores at Fort Scott are sent back to Leavenworth and the Lane brigade is removed from the border." He emphasized, "But what we have to fear, and do fear, is that Lane's brigade will get up a war by going over the line, committing depredations, and then returning into our State."

While Lane organized his men and planned his campaign, he created the town of Fort Lincoln along the Little Osage River in northern Bourbon County, about four miles west of the present-day village of Fulton, as a pro-Union base for his forces. He felt his headquarters of Fort Scott were still rife with Southern sympathizers and briefly had even considered burning it. Fort Lincoln would not last long, but it seems to have been active enough while Lane and his men were nearby.

Not all the men under Lane at this time appreciated his attempt to create a new community. Charles Cory served in the Sixth Kansas Cavalry, which was formed out of units of the Fort Scott home guards and other companies. In speaking to the Kansas State Historical Society in 1908, Cory alleged that Lane did give orders for the burning of Fort Scott. However, the men of the Sixth and their commander, Lt. Col. Lewis Jewell, refused to carry out the order. Instead Jewell fortified the town and armed the citizens to defend against a Confederate attack.

Whatever the facts regarding this matter, Lane continued to carry on his campaign. Writing an official report of the action on September 3, Lane claimed that his men "drove back the advanced guard of the enemy," engaging "the whole force of the enemy yesterday for two hours 12 miles east of Fort Scott." Lane's command fell back to Fort Lincoln, but he allowed his cavalry forces to remain behind "to amuse the enemy until we could establish ourselves here and remove our good stores from Fort Scott." He reported his losses as five killed and six wounded, adding that "the enemy has suffered considerably." He also called for reinforcements, stating that he was "surrounded by a superior force." "I am compelled to make a stand here," he said defiantly, "or give up Kansas to disgrace and destruction."

In Lane's next message to his superiors, dated September 4, he stated that he had 800 men at Fort Scott and 250 men in Barnesville, a dozen miles northeast of Fort Scott. Overall, he claimed to have "a regular force of about 1,200 men" and "an irregular force" of between 400 and 600 against a Confederate army "in the neighborhood of 6,000" in fortified positions on Dry Wood Creek. Along with those numbers, he had "seven pieces of artillery, either one or two 12-pounder howitzers," a "6-pounder," and "1,000 mounted men." Again he asked for more men and artillery.

On September 10, Lane reported to the commander of Fort Leavenworth that he was moving east. He planned, he said, "to march east as far as Papinsville, if possible, clearing out the valley of the Osage." From there he would turn north, "clearing out the valley of the Marais-des-Cygnes, Butler, Harrisonville, Osceola, and Clinton." He related that "if attacked by on overwhelming superior force, I will, of cause, fall back on Kansas." Lane had under his command twelve hundred infantry, eight hundred cavalry, and two pieces of artillery. He left two hundred men at Fort Scott, three hundred at Fort Lincoln, and two hundred at Barnesville.

Two days before, on September 8, Confederate raiders attacked the town of Humboldt in Allen County. The raiders stole property belonging to the residents, but no buildings were destroyed and no one was killed. As a result of that raid, on September 12, Lane sent about eight hundred men back to Fort Scott, some of whom were ordered "to follow the marauders who attacked Humboldt" and either pursue them "to the Arkansas line or take them." That pursuit force was led by Lt. Col. James G. Blunt. They caught up with Capt. John Matthews' band and in a sharp fight killed the guerilla leader. Unfortunately for Humboldt, that fight brought rebels back to the town on October 14 and they burned most of the buildings in the village.

On September 16, Lane sent some six hundred men and two howitzers against a rebel camp at Morristown, Missouri, in Cass County. "They succeeded in routing the enemy," he wrote, "killing

7, capturing their entire camp equipage, tents, wagons, &c., some 100 horses and horse equipments." Union losses were two killed and six wounded, with four of them having "mere flesh wounds." However, one of the dead was an officer in his brigade, Col. H. P. Johnson.

Following this successful attack was one of the most controversial military actions Lane and his men undertook. On September 22, 1861, Lane's brigade moved on Osceola, Missouri, burning and looting the town and leaving some men dead. Reports vary as to what actually took place. Lane's first report of the action, dated September 24, stated that Confederates had "ambushed the approaches to the town" and "after being driven from them by the advance under Colonels Montgomery and Weer, they took refuge in the buildings . . . to annoy us. We were compelled to shell them out, and in doing so the place was burned to ashes" and "15 or 20 of them killed and wounded."

Although having strong Union sympathies, Leverett Spring wrote what became an accepted account of events when he said that Lane "sacked and burned" the town and "a score of inhabitants" were killed. Spring even charged Lane's chaplain of stealing "Confederate altars in the interest of his unfinished church at home."

John Speer went to Osceola around the turn of the century to discover what people there said had happened. One man told Speer that Lane boxed up the records in the county courthouse before setting the town on fire. Another speculated that because the town had a large quantity of supplies on hand, Lane fired it to prevent them from falling into the hands of Price's army. Everyone whom Speer talked to agreed on several facts. The first was that whoever was killed died in the skirmish before Lane's men entered town. The town was prosperous due to the steamboat trade and could have been used as a base of supply for Confederate forces, thus providing some justification for Lane's raid. There was a great quantity of whiskey in town, but Lane had it burned rather than given to his men. Lane's men did not commit any "outrages" against the women of Osceola, and they did not plunder the town, rob the bank, or perform atrocities against the citizens.

Whatever the truth was of Lane's attack on Osceola, there was plenty of criticism of it and of his men. In the summer of 1861 the pro-Confederate *Argus* wrote of fifty-two "ragamuffins and cut-throats" on their way to join Lane. The newspaper also claimed that Lane's men could not "fight honest Americans in daylight." At least one Kansan wrote to his half-brother denouncing stories of Lane's pillaging, saying that the cause of the elimination of slavery is too important "to allow a base desire for plunder." Later, Maj. Gen. Henry Halleck would say that all Jayhawkers, including Lane's men, had "turned against us many thousands who were formerly Union men."

The attitude of the men following Lane was radically different from Halleck's observation. A soldier of Company K, Seventh Kansas, wrote three letters to the *Enterprise* of Mishawaka, Indiana. In the first, dated November 15, he said, "We think this is the proper way and the only way to crush this rebellion. Take every thing that can be of value to the traitors and they will be [unable] to continue this rebellion." On January 1, 1862, he reported, "The [First] Kansas Cavalry have liberated more slaves than there are men in the regiment. . . . Had the Government adopted this plan in the beginning, the cause of this war would be well nigh wiped out by spring."

Even young Samuel Reader, who had denounced plunder in October, expressed pleasure in January of the prospect of Lane taking command of all Kansas units. Reader wrote that Lane "knows how to carry on the war amongst our [Border Ruffian] neighbors."

More than that, Lloyd Lewis said in 1938, was that "the Missouri army had been kept out of Kansas." The point may not be an entirely accurate one. Lane's raid into Missouri seemed to figure very little into the campaign plans of Sterling Price, but it does raise a valid question: had Lane's men not been in western Missouri, would Price have marched his army north from Wilson's Creek looking for supplies, or would he instead have gone west toward Fort Scott or northwest toward Fort Leavenworth?

On September 18, 1861, General Frémont ordered Lane "to march with your forces on the State Line road to Kansas City," make contact with Brig. Gen. Samuel Sturgis at Lexington, and "co-operate with him to defeat the enemy." Lane did not reply until September 24, when he wrote to Frémont, "Although

Lexington has fallen since your order of September 18, I propose to move on Kansas City, there to form a junction with General Sturgis." Lane added that "rumors are rife" that rebels were moving toward the southern parts of Kansas. "If such is the case," he said, "God only knows what is to become of Kansas when we move on Kansas City."

Within a week Lane had arrived at Kansas City. On October 3 he reported to Frémont that between two thousand and three thousand rebels were moving south. He gave orders to Lieutenant Colonel Blunt at Fort Scott to move north to intercept them, while he would move south along with General Sturgis's command to defeat them.

The next day Sturgis sent Lane a letter he had received from Frémont and asked for "any opinion you may have formed after reading" it. The letter, dated September 29, ordered Sturgis "to fall immediately back upon Fort Leavenworth," join "any regular troops at Leavenworth," and "proceed by railroad to Chillicothe." Lane immediately replied, "Are you not satisfied it [Frémont's order] was predicated upon the fact that the enemy crossed a force on the north side of the river that we know had recrossed?"

To this question Sturgis told Lane, "I am so confident that [Frémont's order] is founded in misconception of the enemy's movements, and intentions, that I do again earnestly solicit a conference with you before a single step is taken in the premises. To obey the order is to give up the contest in the West, to stampede the people of Kansas, and to devastate it. Not until a battle is fought and a defeat suffered should Kansas City be given up to the enemy."

Much of this confusion stemmed from Frémont's increasing inability to deal with his command. When he had arrived in St. Louis at the end of July his vision was of a two-objective strategy. The first was to put down the rebellion in Missouri, while the second was a move down the Mississippi River to take Memphis, Tennessee. Progress on the second objective seemed to go smoothly, but the first gave Frémont problems. Part of his trouble with subduing Missouri did lie with the independent actions of Lane and Nathaniel Lyon. However, a significant part came from his declaration of martial law in the state on August 30.

Frémont's declaration went far beyond his mandate in two crucial aspects. First, it called for the execution of Confederate "guerillas" captured behind Union lines. Not only did this order invite retaliation, but Frémont's front lines were not well defined. Second, Frémont ordered his men to seize the property of Southern sympathizers, which included freeing their slaves. This order cheered abolitionists, but it gave Lincoln problems with slave-owning Unionists in the Border States.

On September 2, Lincoln sent a private letter to Frémont. He ordered Frémont not to carry out any executions without presidential approval and asked him to modify his orders about freeing slaves. Hoping that the general would not misinterpret his tone, Lincoln told him that the message was "written in a spirit of caution, and not of censure." However, Frémont chose not to take Lincoln's letter as a gently worded order, but as unsolicited advice. He told the president that he would not change anything in his declaration without a formal order to do so.

By then events were getting well away from Frémont. In addition to Lane's raid into western Missouri, Gen. Sterling Price had moved north from the Springfield area and attacked Lexington, an important town between Jefferson City and Kansas City. Price's men conducted a three-day siege of the Union garrison at Lexington and captured it on September 20. Frémont was roundly criticized for doing nothing to prevent the fall of Lexington, though in some fairness to him he seemed to have had few resources at hand with which to have intervened.

Aware that his reputation was now at stake, Frémont decided to assemble what forces he had and pursue Price's army. He seems to have had some notion that once Price was dealt with he would march toward New Orleans. But he hesitated when his army assembled at Springfield at the beginning of November. Before Frémont could make up his mind about his course of action, orders reached him that Lincoln had removed him from command. He remained until about November 3, when his replacement, Gen. David Hunter, arrived to take command.

This final movement marked the formal end of what was known as the Lane Brigade. The regiments Lane had formed were incorporated into the overall Union army in the region and given their own assignments. Hunter himself came under the command of

Henry Halleck, who was put in charge of the Department of the Missouri.

Lane's first effort to take total control of the military situation west of the Mississippi came as early as October 9, 1861. On that day he wrote to President Lincoln from Leavenworth. He began by justifying what he had done, saying that he had "labored earnestly and incessantly, as commander of the Kansas Brigade, to put down the great insurrection in Missouri." Because state officials "had failed to collect a force worthy of the name," he raised a "gallant and effective" brigade whose "operations are a part of the history of the country."

Despite that "to a man" his army was "exceedingly desirous of continuing in the service under my command," Lane said he felt "compelled to abandon the field." Part of this was because Governor Robinson was trying to disband the brigade. "There being no hope of improvement in this condition of things so long as I am in my present position," Lane wrote, but hoping "that I may with my brigade remain in the field," that "the Government be sustained in this region," and to protect Kansas "from invasion from Missouri," Lane requested that a new military department be established. He wanted the department "composed of Kansas, the Indian country, and so much of Arkansas and the Territories as may be thought advisable to include therein." Lane believed that the commander of the department should be able to assemble a force of "at least 10,000 troops."

"If this can be done, and I can have the command of the department," he promised, "I will cheerfully accept it, resign my seat in the Senate, and devote all my thoughts and energies to the prosecution of the war."

On November 16 the *Republican* in Lawrence reported on the creation of a Department of Kansas with Gen. David Hunter in charge. The newspaper gave no notice of an expedition south, the area of Lane's interest. That had to wait until January 9, 1862, when it reprinted a story from the east that Lane "will have such an army and such a command as he desires to have." That story speculated that Confederates in Indian Territory would be the objective of Lane's army. Later in the month the *Emporia News* reported that Lane had met with the new Union commander, Gen. George McClellan, who had given Lane the "authority to conduct the campaign on his own principles."

What those principles were has been a subject of debate ever since the news of the planned expedition first became public. A thirst for glory was what John J. Ingalls thought Lane's motivation was in establishing the expedition. In writing to his father in late February, he said that Lane had told him it would give the farmers of Kansas "a market for all their forage" and make the state rich. This would naturally build up his reputation and power in the state.

But that was not how Lloyd Lewis viewed Lane's motivation. Lewis said in 1938 that Lane was opposed to "the milk-and-water policy of the West Pointers" like Gen. George McClellan. Lane wanted to "break secession" by carrying the war to the South, in this case Texas, Arkansas, and Louisiana. Lane critic Verres Smith claimed that when Lane actually met with General McClellan, who asked him what he would do if he found "no Union sentiment" on his way south, Lane responded, "I will leave no rebel sentiment behind me," will make the land "a howling wilderness," and will give the lands of "white rebels" to "loyal blacks."

Lane expressed his views on the matter in speeches he gave around the country toward the end of 1861. The first was held in Springfield, Missouri, on November 8 when he was serenaded by men of the Twenty-fourth Indiana. After reclaiming his Indiana heritage he told the Hoosier soldiers that "the point of difference" between himself and his "compeers in command" was slavery, "the Pandora's box from which has issued all our national troubles." He declared, "My creed is, *let slavery take care of itself*." But to him this did not mean returning escaped slaves to rebel masters; indeed just the opposite. "Abduct from [a rebel family] a slave, and kill in arms a son, and the loss of the slave will be regarded as the greater misfortune," he said to the soldiers. "This war is for slavery," and the Union ought to "make it the mighty engine for slavery's destruction."

Lane returned to that theme when he spoke in Boston on November 31. To his audience at Tremont Temple, he called slavery "the disease" that was sustaining the rebellion. "Ask the soldiers of General Price what they are fighting for," he said. "They will answer 'slavery.' . . . 'Slavery' is written on their banners, and what is ours,—is it not substantially the same, when we war for the old Union?" Toward the end of his remarks he said this: "You cannot with the same army crush out treason and preserve slavery."

Finally there was his speech at a party in his honor in Washington on December 2. Here he told the gathering that slavery was the "weak spot" of the rebellion, and the Union owed it "to the commerce of the country and the world, to the orphans that are being made, to the widows and the wounded that are multiplying, to the loyal brave who are laying down their lives, to the humanity around us, and to the God above us" to strike at that weak spot.

Maj. Gen. David Hunter may or may not have agreed with Lane's ideals about striking at slavery to end the rebellion. All that mattered to him was that Lane was misrepresenting his views on the expedition to Washington. On January 24, 1862, Hunter got word from his superiors that if Lane's expedition took to the field, Lane would not have an independent command, but was "to operate to all proper extent under your supervision and control, and if you deem proper you may yourself command the expedition which may be undertaken."

Neither Lincoln nor his generals were going to let Lane command the expedition. In fact, on January 31, Lincoln told Cameron, "General Lane has been told by me many times that he is under the command of General Hunter, and assented to it as often as told. It was the distinct agreement between him and me when I appointed him that he was to be under Hunter." John Hay, Lincoln's secretary, noted in his biography of Lincoln that although the president recognized "Lane's great energy and influence in Kansas," he had no intention of giving the senator "the superior direction or management" of military operations in the state.

Despite Lincoln's assurances to the contrary, Lane continued to insist on running the show, and with apparent frustration Hunter wrote to Maj. Gen. Henry Halleck on February 8. "It seems," Hunter said, "from all the evidence before me, that Senator J. H. Lane has been trading at Washington on a capital partly made up of his own Senatorial position and partly of such scraps of influence as I may have possessed in the confidence or esteem of the President, said scraps having been 'jayhawked' by the Kansas Senator without due consent of the proper owner." Lane's "great Southern expedition" had been sanctioned by Lincoln "under misrepresentations" that it was "the joint design and wish of Senator Lane and myself." That was not true, said Hunter. "Never to this hour has Senator Lane consulted me on the subject directly or indirectly."

Hunter was not the only one angry over Lane's drive to be a field commander. Kansan Abelard Guthrie was in Washington in early 1862 apparently on his own business. In January he looked for an attorney to represent him in some federal matter. On January 17 he went to Lane for help, but Lane referred him to another attorney. "This would not have been necessary had he attended to his business as Senator or redeemed his promises as friend," he wrote in his diary. Lane was being constantly "beset by an army of sycophants who pander to his vanity as he turns a cold shoulder to his old and real friends."

By the end of the month Guthrie noted that there was a move afoot to have Lane ousted from his committee assignments in the Senate, including the Committee on Military Affairs. Guthrie spoke to Rep. Martin Conway to express his preference that Pomeroy take over Lane's assignments. Conway objected by saying he was "uncertain about Lane's going into the army" and reminded Guthrie that Lane "would be displeased with this premature removal." For his part, Guthrie thought Pomeroy "industrious and faithful" and "more reliable and attentive to business," but conceded that Lane had "more influence."

Concerning Lane's interest in the expedition, Guthrie thought Lane was "acting very strangely if not insanely." On February 4, Guthrie wrote in his diary that he had sent a letter urging Lane to remain in the Senate, but the message was useless, as Lane had "a thirst for military fame." Even as late as February 27, Lane was still angling for command, much to Guthrie's frustration. He wrote in an oft-quoted statement, "There seems to me a species of insanity in some of this man's eccentricities."

Finally, on February 10, Lincoln wrote to both Lane and Hunter.

He repeated his previous statement that Hunter would be in command of the expedition. Lane either would have to "report to General Hunter for duty" or else "decline the service." With that, wrote Lincoln biographers Nicolay and Hay, "Lane lost his interest in the expedition." Halleck's continued opposition ensured that there would be no expedition, and on March 11, Hunter's command was subsumed into Halleck's.

Lane was said by one person with him at the time to be very angry at failing to get command of the expedition. While on a train trip from Washington back to Kansas, Lane supposedly called Lincoln a "d——d liar, a demagogue, and a scoundrel." This left the senator looking like "a braggart, a fool, and a humbug."

Those quotations appeared in the *White Cloud Chief,* already an anti-Lane paper, a few months after the expedition had come to naught. In a statement to the state legislature published in the *Conservative* on February 28, Lane was more subdued. He expressed his "conviction" that "a satisfactory arrangement would be made with Major General Hunter" about his leadership of a southward military movement. He said he had intended to resign from the Senate and accept a commission as a brigadier general. He made "every effort which self-respect would permit" to arrange matters with Hunter; "I failed." He thought he would be unable to serve under Hunter "without degradation," but as he was "thwarted in this," he had decided to return to the Senate.

Of course, his return to the Senate did not mean Lane would not have a hand in military matters in Kansas. He simply would not have direct control. Although the expedition plan had failed, Lane gained an opportunity to have influence without surrendering the Senate seat he had so long struggled to obtain. He could act through a friendly commissioned officer, and Lane may already have had someone in mind.

The following month one of the officers who had served in the Lane Brigade, James G. Blunt, was promoted from colonel to brigadier general. The public reaction to the promotion was largely unfavorable. The *Emporia News* called Blunt's advancement over another Kansas colonel, George Dietzler, a "gross injustice." Charles Jennison resigned in part due to Blunt's promotion, and

James Blunt was elevated to the rank of general by Jim Lane. Many Lane critics accused Blunt of being Lane's henchman in military affairs in Kansas. However, by the summer of 1864, Blunt's faults appear to have become too much for even Lane to tolerate. *Photograph courtesy the Baxter Springs Heritage Center.*

his friends at the *Conservative* expressed their dissatisfaction as well. Virtually the only newspaper to support Blunt's promotion was the *Lawrence Republican,* edited by Lane's friend John Speer.

Prior to Blunt's promotion David Hunter had been in charge of the Department of Kansas, comprising Kansas, Nebraska, Colorado, and the Indian Territory. He was replaced by Samuel Sturgis, who in May was replaced by Blunt. In Sturgis's time as head of the department he had quickly become unpopular. Indeed Sturgis was so unpopular that when Blunt replaced him newspaper sentiment changed drastically. Sol Miller of the *Chief* wrote of the change under the headline "THANK THE LORD!" The *Conservative* wrote, "The Department of Kansas is restored and a man is placed in command who knows his rights and knowing dare maintain."

For his part, Blunt admitted after the war that he was "inexperienced in the routine of military affairs" but had decided to accept the post. Blunt wrote that among the challenges facing him as commander of the Department of Kansas were protecting wagon trains along the Santa Fe Trail, defending Kansas from rebel incursions, and dealing with reports of rebel armies assembling in Arkansas and Indian Territory. To cope with the last problem Blunt asked for reinforcements from the secretary of war. None were to be had, but "authority would be given to raise new regiments within the department." To that end Lane was appointed commissioner of recruiting.

While those units were being raised, Blunt decided to deal with the rebels directly south of Kansas. In June 1862 he organized a force consisting of about six thousand men under Col. William Weer. Weer's men captured the capital of the Cherokee Nation, Tahlequah, and one of the principal chiefs, John Ross, surrendered and joined the Union army with enough men to form the Third Indian Regiment.

Shortly after these triumphs the expedition was plunged into turmoil. The men were short on clean drinking water and Weer got into a dispute with another colonel about returning to headquarters in the face of their lack of supplies. That colonel had Weer arrested and brought the troops back to Kansas. Blunt had intended to sort out the matter, but by the time he met the force personally in mid-August, the Confederates were on the move in Missouri.

Back in May, Maj. Gen. Thomas C. Hindman had taken over Confederate forces in Missouri, Arkansas, and northern Louisiana. He spent the summer assembling a new army to retake Missouri. That army got moving in September and defeated a Union force at Newtonia, Missouri, on September 30. Blunt moved his division to counter the movement, and Hindman pulled his men back into Arkansas.

Blunt's division then attacked a rebel force under Col. Douglas Cooper at Old Fort Wayne on the Arkansas-Indian Territory border on October 22. Cooper's forces were routed in half an hour. Union general John Schofield's forces took Fayetteville, Arkansas, late in October and, deciding his objectives were achieved and with an illness coming on, he returned to St. Louis on November 20. He moved part of the Army of the Frontier under Gen. Francis Herron back to Springfield and left Blunt with the rest in northern Arkansas.

Responding to moves by part of Hindman's force under General Marmaduke, Blunt attacked the rebels at Cane Hill on November 27. Despite orders to pull back to Little Rock, Hindman decided to counter Blunt. The Union general discovered Hindman on the move around December 3 and called for Herron to march to his aid. Herron marched his men at a forced pace and were within twelve miles of Blunt's position on December 6.

Hindman decided he would defeat Herron first then attack Blunt's rear. On December 7, 1862, Hindman's cavalry under Marmaduke flanked Blunt and attacked Herron near Prairie Grove Church, north of Cane Hill. Herron strengthened his line and drove Marmaduke back. Hindman then brought up his main body but hesitated to attack. Blunt was able to get his division moving and by early afternoon his units were pitching into the Confederates. The battle at Prairie Grove was a draw, but it turned into a Union victory when Hindman withdrew his army to the Fort Smith area.

About three weeks later Blunt raided Van Buren, a town across the Arkansas River from Fort Smith. The Union forces won a surprise victory, driving the Confederates further from the area.

Blunt's men also captured four steamboats loaded with supplies for the rebel troops. Except for Fort Smith itself, the Union army had taken over most of northwestern Arkansas and eastern Indian Territory.

Blunt's string of successes were hailed in Kansas and throughout the nation. The *St. Louis Democrat* praised him as being "clear-headed" in victory while having been in "the very thickest of the fight." The *New York Times* said that although Blunt was a "civilian General," he was a "magnificent commander" who should be allowed to march on Texas. The *Leavenworth Conservative* called for Blunt to be promoted to major general.

Blunt's standing couldn't have been higher in Kansas as 1863 began. He had won victories at a time when overall Union prospects seemed low, and his achievements seemed to have proven Senator Lane right in advancing Blunt in rank. Lane's own standing would be just as high. He had managed, in about a year, to gain complete control of Kansas politics. He had done so largely through a scandal that permanently tarnished his chief rival, Charles Robinson.

XI.

The Scandal

Through the end of 1861 and the first few months of 1862, Robinson's rivalry with Lane had few successes. Robinson tried to remove Lane from the Senate under the reasoning that he thought Lane was also to serve as a brigadier general in the Union army, and according to the Constitution, no one could serve in two positions in the federal government. Lane, on the Senate floor and in a letter to the state legislature, said that although he had been commissioned, he had never formally accepted the rank.

In mid-October 1861, the Republican State Central Committee gathered because two statewide offices, those of attorney general and state treasurer, had become vacant. An election was planned for November to fill those vacancies, and the party assembled to nominate their candidates. At the same time the *Leavenworth Conservative* called for an entire ticket of candidates for state offices to be nominated.

Ostensibly this call was made because of a reading of the state constitution that suggested that the current state officeholders had been elected in 1859 and thus had fulfilled their two-year terms. Members of the central committee tied to Lane decided that this interpretation would give them the chance to oust Lane's rival. A full slate of candidates was approved, including George A. Crawford for governor, and they began a short run for office. Crawford managed to win the election, but the state board of election canvassers, of which Robinson was a member, refused to certify the results. Crawford sued but lost the case before the Supreme Court of the State of Kansas.

By the time the legislature came back into session in early 1862, Robinson's influence as governor had waned. He and his career would be ruined by the bond scandal that dwarfed almost everything else that year in Kansas. The controversy was the culmination of the feud between Charles Robinson and Jim Lane, and it left the reputation of the former in tatters and made the latter the undisputed master of Kansas politics.

The scandal began with the 1861 legislative session, when lawmakers approved two bond issues so the state could pay for its needs and its participation in the war effort. The first issue was for $150,000 in 7 percent bonds, the second for $20,000 in 10 percent bonds. Two Leavenworth men were given the negotiating power in order to sell the bonds; however, after seventy days the bonds remained unsold.

Governor Robinson contacted a New York banking firm for help, but the firm's representatives told him prospects were poor for the sale of the bonds. The legislature gave Robinson, the secretary of state, and the state auditor the power to sell $100,000 of state bonds for a price of at least 70 cents on the dollar. But they had no luck in selling the bonds either. The state's financial picture looked quite bleak.

Then, as the state's treasurer, H. R. Dutton, was returning from New York he ran into Robert S. Stevens. Stevens was a friend of Governor Robinson, a fellow director in a Lawrence bank, and impressively connected in Washington. Stevens asked Dutton for $31,000 of the state's 10 percent bonds for a price of 40 cents on the dollar. Dutton agreed to Stevens' terms and gave him $29,000 worth of the 7 percent bonds. Stevens went on to Washington, met with Secretary of the Interior Caleb Smith, and sold him $26,000 of the 10 percent bonds at 95 cents on the dollar. Stevens netted almost $15,000 from the sale.

After his profitable transaction, Stevens headed back to Kansas by way of Dayton, Ohio. There he met with Thomas Corwin, a brother-in-law of Secretary Smith and a claims agent in Washington. It appears that here Stevens and Corwin joined forces to get their hands on more Kansas bonds. Stevens returned to Kansas, obtained another $29,000 worth of bonds, and sent them to Corwin by the end of October.

Around this time Sen. Samuel Pomeroy became involved in the

bond sales. He sent word to Kansas's Secretary of State J. W. Robinson that the secretary of the interior might be willing to buy more bonds. Robinson and the state auditor, George Hillyer, assembled what bonds they could and arrived in Washington at the end of October. But then Pomeroy told Hillyer that interest had waned at the Interior Department and advised Hillyer to allow Stevens to act as an agent for the Kansas bonds. By the end of November they had granted that power to Stevens.

This led to a fateful meeting at the Pomeroy house in Washington on December 1 between Secretary Robinson, Hillyer, Stevens, Corwin, and Pomeroy. While Pomeroy's wife entertained the two state officials, Pomeroy, Stevens, and Corwin met. It was later alleged that it was at this time that the three men plotted to defraud the state, with the two officials as their unknowing dupes. The trio came out of their private conversation with a contract to grant Stevens full power to sell all the outstanding state bonds.

It was as a result of these events that Governor Robinson's reputation first ran aground. The agreement to sell the bonds was backdated to October 25 in part because Secretary Robinson not only signed his name to it but Governor Robinson's as well. The two state officials later claimed that the governor had consented to "any arrangement" to sell the bonds. The governor, for his part, would say that he had supported any legal arrangement to dispose of the bonds. This contradiction is significant. If the state officers were telling the truth, Governor Robinson was part of the scheme; if he was being truthful, he was no party to it.

Once Stevens obtained the authority to sell the state bonds, he returned to the secretary of the interior. He offered to sell the bonds, about $150,000 worth, at 85 cents on the dollar. The secretary agreed and obtained President Lincoln's approval of the purchase. Corwin then wrote a letter that the members of the Kansas delegation, Senators Lane and Pomeroy and Congressman Martin Conway, would sign to give final approval of the bond sales. Of course Pomeroy went along, and so did Conway.

Lane held out, according to Raymond Gaeddert, largely because of fears among his advisors that Stevens was angling to become senator. But Lane did sign the letter, either because Stevens paid the senator's private secretary one thousand dollars or because Lane was induced to sign it without reading it. Either way his signature was on it and the sale went through by the end of December. Not more than a month later, questions were being asked about the sale of the bonds, and an investigation in the state legislature followed quickly thereafter.

Around the time that news of the bond sales broke in Kansas, John J. Ingalls wrote a letter to his father that hints at the reaction in the state to that news. On February 23, Ingalls reported that just as Kansas was emerging from "famine and starvation" came word that the state had "in a single transaction been swindled by our state officers out of One Hundred and Fifty Eight Thousand Dollars." Ingalls was no admirer of Jim Lane, yet tellingly he wrote, "The probability is that this last swindle could have remained concealed had it not been for the rage and disappointment of that crazy humbug and charlatan, the 'Grim Chieftain' Jim Lane." Ingalls was certain that Lane knew of the "fraud" and had "participated in the profits," but "his audacity is sublime." "The people detest Governor Robinson," and Lane was therefore exploiting the story to "divert attention" from the failure of his Texas expedition and to enhance his reputation "as the friend of the masses."

The Kansas House of Representatives formed a committee to investigate the matter and report if any officials needed to face impeachment trials. The committee reported on February 14, calling for the impeachment of Gov. Charles Robinson, Secretary of State John W. Robinson, and State Auditor George S. Hillyer for high misdemeanors in office. Among the signers of the report were two Lane allies, Sidney Clarke and Thomas Carney. The House voted sixty-five to zero for a resolution of impeachment, and the Senate assembled as a Court of Impeachment on June 2.

During the investigation of the matter in the state House, Robert Stevens was called to testify. When asked to name his negotiating partners and those who shared in his profits, Stevens declined to answer. He did say that those persons were "not residents of the State." He was also asked if state officials were involved; he responded by saying that if they were, they could speak for themselves. Raymond Gaeddert concluded that this statement to some degree absolved the governor, the secretary of state, and the auditor from having shared in Stevens' profits.

The first tried by the impeachment court was John Robinson. He was found guilty on the first article of impeachment and was acquitted on the second through the eighth articles. On a vote of eighteen to three, Secretary Robinson was removed from office. The trial of George Hillyer followed; he too was convicted on the first article and acquitted on the others, and he was removed from office by a vote of eighteen to two.

The trial of Governor Robinson came last and took all of one day. He faced only five articles of impeachment. He was acquitted on every article by a vote so nearly unanimous, wrote author William Culter about twenty years later, "as to render the trial a complete vindication of his honesty." Robinson's role in the bond sales seemed so minor as to appear nonexistent, so on the surface his acquittal appears to have been perfectly logical.

But there may have been other reasons for Robinson's acquittal. Author Raymond Gaeddert pointed out that Lane had packed the state Senate against Robinson. Leverett Spring in his book went farther, saying that "the whole movement" toward impeachment had originated with Lane and "was aimed at Robinson." If such claims are true, why wasn't Robinson convicted and impeached?

Gaeddert believed that a deal had been arranged between the two factions by Thomas Ewing, Jr. Ewing had been a Robinson man, but by the spring of 1862 the chief justice of the state supreme court was an ally of Lane's. Ewing was eager for the U.S. Senate to pass the Pottawatomie Treaty to benefit his LP&W railroad project, but he needed Senator Pomeroy's support, and according to Gaeddert, Pomeroy was allied with Governor Robinson through Robert Stevens. Convicting Robinson would have angered Pomeroy and turned the senator against the treaty. Therefore, Ewing mediated a deal that turned over the state auditor and treasurer as scapegoats, allowing the factions to avoid further danger to their plans and reputations and getting the treaty passed in the Senate. Gaeddert admitted that the evidence for this arrangement was "missing" at the time he put forward his hypothesis in 1940, but he believed the facts supported the case for an arrangement.

However, little new information has come to light since then to suggest that the two factions made any such deals. One compelling argument against such a deal was that a few months after the impeachment, Thomas Ewing left the railroad company and joined the Union army. If he was so passionate about the railroad that he would broker a deal between Robinson and Lane, why would he then abandon it for military service? Most authors who have written about Ewing have agreed that he tended to look out for his own interests. His entry into the army, although into a regiment Lane had helped recruit, was to advance his own political ambitions. He seemed to care about the railroad so long as he made money and it kept him connected to men in power.

Another issue raised when considering the possibility of a deal is Pomeroy's position in the affair. The evidence is very strong that Pomeroy was at the heart of the scandal. From Lane's point of view, he was a challenger to his control of federal patronage. Therefore, Lane ought to have wanted the investigation to turn next to his rival senator, thus removing any political opposition to his power over Kansas, rather than wanting to make any deals with him. As for Robinson, exposing Pomeroy's role in the swindle might have restored some of the governor's reputation. It would seem then that if any arrangement were to be made between Robinson and Lane, it would have been advantageous for both factions to turn on Pomeroy instead of simply scapegoating the two state officials.

These ambiguous motivations lead to the question that historians and partisans of the two politicians have grappled with since news of the scandal emerged: did Gov. Charles Robinson in fact do anything wrong?

Raymond Gaeddert believed that Robinson was innocent and pointed the finger at Stevens, Pomeroy, and Thomas Corwin as the men who had "plotted the scheme to defraud the State." Other Robinson supporters such as biographer Don Wilson and historians Leverett Spring and Albert Castel insisted that the governor was merely the victim of Lane's wrath.

Kenneth Davis was not so certain. In his bicentennial history of Kansas, he pointed out that Stevens was one of Robinson's "close associates." Although there was no proof that Robinson profited from the bond transactions, Davis believed that Robinson had to have made something from the deal. Indeed, it would seem remarkable that Robinson's friend and business partner had profited and Robinson had not.

Robinson's 1892 book says little about the scandal. He claimed it was Lane, Pomeroy, and Martin Conway who pointed Hillyer and John Robinson toward the secretary of the interior and that Stevens was "employed" by the two state officials to undertake negotiations. Interestingly, Robinson wrote that Stevens "received no more than the usual rate for his services." Not only are these assertions strange considering the facts, but even stranger is that Robinson did not bother to note that Stevens was a friend of his. Perhaps this spin was in part due to Robinson's hatred of Lane, and in part due to a guilty conscience.

The impeachment trial was not the end of the effort to correct the state's financial condition. The remainder of the 1861 bonds were sold into 1863, when the state legislature issued more bonds. Robinson's successor took a hand in the sales of those bonds and perhaps took profits as well. Since that new governor was a Lane man, at least in the beginning, no investigation of him was ever conducted.

Author and historian William Connelley wrote of the impact of the scandal, stating in his history of Kansas that the state was referred to in newspapers as "the rotten Commonwealth." Though that reputation did not harm the state's finances—for "at the close of the Civil War," he noted, "Kansas made ample provision for the payment of all her obligations"—there was one longterm effect: "This bond transaction destroyed Governor Robinson politically."

Although Charles Robinson could and did blame Lane for his downfall, his own actions and faults were just as responsible. His close ties to Robert Stevens certainly played a role in his diminished reputation, and his stubbornness prevented him from trying to personally lobby Abraham Lincoln to counter Lane's influence. In fact, Robinson so came to dislike Lincoln during the war that in a letter to Amos Lawrence, sent days before Gettysburg, Robinson wrote, "if Genl. Lee would take the President & Secretary [of War] prisoners . . . we [the Union] would be the gainers even though Washington was lost at the same time."

Indeed, one of Robinson's longtime supporters, Sol Miller at the *Kansas Chief,* wrote some twenty-five years later that "it has often occurred to [me] that Gov. Robinson never considered how much he himself was responsible" for his ruin. The occasion for Miller's comments was a speech Robinson gave in January 1889 to a group called the Loyal Legion. The former governor touched on his feud with Lane in his talk. That gave Miller the chance to voice his own opinion on how Robinson became marginalized after the bond scandal.

Miller believed that had the former governor been patient and maintained his Republican alliances, eventually Lane would have "play[ed] himself out" during the war, leaving Robinson still standing. "Robinson had only to wait," he wrote, "making his fight within the Republican party," and when Lane "went under, Robinson would have become the great leader of the Republican party of Kansas—the party would have instinctively turned to and rallied around their first Governor."

Instead, Miller observed, Robinson "became soured on the whole party" and turned "revengeful." "He hit the Republican party a lick whenever he could do so," which hurt friends and foes alike. He appointed Democrats to the state offices left vacant by the impeachment trial. He also appointed a Democrat to the state supreme court when Ewing left to join the army. Not only was this "absolutely paralyzing" to his friends within the party, it "made it impossible for them" to show they were loyal Republicans.

Charles Robinson would blame Jim Lane for his political disgrace, but it would seem that Lane did nothing more than exploit Robinson's questionable alliances and stubborn nature. Robinson had made his own bed, and his reluctance to lie in it is more telling about his character than Lane's.

The bond scandal was not quite the end of the feud between the senator and the governor. Jim Lane had been advocating the enlistment of freed slaves and black freedmen into the Union army for months. He called for such enlistments in a June speech in New York and at a war meeting in Leavenworth in August. It would be in the summer of 1862 that Lane would try to put this policy into action, and it would be over that that Lane and Robinson tangled one last time in their official capacities.

President Lincoln and his administration were reluctant to take so-called colored regiments into the army as the war began. There was considerable racism in the North among Midwesterners, unions, and even foreign-born citizens. Too, Lincoln worried that recruiting blacks would antagonize loyal slaveholders in the Border States that had not yet seceded. There was even a view in government and among the public that raising such regiments would be an open admission of an inability of white soldiers to suppress the rebellion.

In Kansas, however, sentiment was leaning in favor of the enlistment of blacks. In 1861, Senator Pomeroy introduced a bill outlawing slavery in the Confederate states. When word of the bill came to Kansas, one young settler near Topeka wrote that he felt "proud that a senator of Kansas first presented" such a bill. A few sentences later he added, "All I want is the entire destruction of human slavery."

In his speeches in late 1861 in Boston and Washington, Lane expressed his view that the war was being fought to overthrow slavery. Samuel Reader wrote in mid-January 1862 to his half-brother that he agreed with Lane. "Jim Lane knew what course to pursue in [Missouri] in respect to slaves," he wrote. Later that summer Reader expressed his support for the enlistment of blacks, saying that he would prefer them armed for the duration of the conflict rather than wait until the nation had no choice but to enlist them. He also expressed the sentiment that whites should not be drafted when slaves and former slaves were willing to fight. In Topeka in 1862, Samuel Reader wrote that Lane had said, "We have a great many men who sympathize so strongly with the negroes that they wish to keep them in a Band box away from the war while white men are to be killed by the thousands."

When he returned to Kansas in the summer of 1862, Lane brought with him the power to raise more regiments. He began this crusade in earnest at the beginning of August when he opened a recruiting office in Leavenworth. The office would accept whites and blacks, the latter only as laborers. Lincoln had already told the press that this was as far as he was willing to go. Lane was willing to go farther, and he dispatched two officers to recruit black men in the state's interior.

Opposition to these recruitments came from all quarters. Missouri slaveholders howled about their "property" running off to join the army. Local authorities tried to charge recruiters with theft. And some blacks were concerned, either because they feared retaliation against their families still in bondage or because they were worried about poor treatment from white soldiers and officers. In July a Fort Scott newspaper warned that the black recruits should be kept away from white soldiers, as they would have "as much to fear [from their white counterparts] as from the rebels."

On July 22, 1862, Secretary of War Edwin Stanton appointed Lane a "commissioner for recruiting in the Department of Kansas." Lane was allowed to raise "one or more brigades of volunteer infantry" to serve for three years. The senator decided to creatively interpret his orders, for on August 5 he reported, "Recruiting opens up beautifully. Good for four regiments of whites and two of blacks." Perhaps having a modest attack of conscience about exceeding his authority, the next day he communicated to Stanton, "I am receiving negroes under the late act of Congress. Is there any objection? Answer by telegraph."

Lane believed his authority came from a law of 1795 that had been amended on July 17, 1862, and called for the "militia to execute the laws of the Union" to "suppress and repel invasions." The amendment allowed the president "to receive into the service of the United States" "persons of African descent" to perform labor. Lane also viewed another section of the law, which freed slaves who owed "labor to any person" who had "borne arms against the United States," as favorable to his position.

One objection came from Maj. T. J. Weed, the assistant adjutant general in Kansas. The same day Lane sent his telegram to Stanton, August 6, Weed wrote the secretary of war about Lane's action. Weed received a reply from Stanton and from Major General Halleck that said, "The law of July 17, 1862, authorizes the President only to receive into the military service of the United States persons of African descent. As the President has not authorized recruiting officers to receive into the service of the United States such persons for general military purposes, the inclosed order of General Lane is without the authority of law."

Weed sent word of Halleck's rejection to Lane, but that failed to stop him from raising his two regiments, for on August 20, Governor Robinson wrote to Stanton. "General Lane is recruiting a regiment of colored men in Kansas," he said. "Shall I commission the officers? Has a draft been made on this State?" The next day

Stanton told Robinson, "If General Lane has applied to you to commission any officers for a regiment of colored men, please give the name of the person and rank of the officers for whom application has been made and instruction will be given you on the subject."

Two days later Stanton finally communicated to Lane directly. Regarding the two regiments of black soldiers, he replied, "you are informed that regiments of persons of African descent can only be raised upon express and special authority of the President. He has not given authority to raise such troops in Kansas, and it is not comprehended in the authority issued to you." Stanton forwarded this message to Robinson on August 28 but admitted to the governor, "The extent of that authority and how far the action of General Lane comports with it you can judge of as well as any one else."

Orders from Washington did not stop Lane from allowing blacks to be accepted into the regiments. Nor, it seems, did it stop more direct methods of "recruiting," according to one Edward M. Samuel of Liberty, Missouri. Samuel wrote a statement on September 8 that claimed that "some 15 persons" from Kansas entered Clay County, Missouri, to, as they said, "recruit negroes for General Lane's negro brigade." Samuel said these men "took forcible possession of some 25 negro men and about 40 horses from persons indiscriminately."

Lane would later say on the Senate floor, "I had the honor of organizing the first regiment of colored soldiers in this war." Leverett Spring said he also admitted to the irregular method of its organization when he added that he had raised the regiment "by one swoop—just by sending out patrols the men were brought right in."

This was quite a change for a man whom his opponents claimed in 1855 thought Kansas ought to become a Slave State if the climate was right for hemp. Spring himself noted that change but seemed to miss its implications. "Lane was a pro-slavery Democrat when he came to Kansas in 1855," Spring wrote in 1898. "Two years in the territory effected a great change in his sentiments."

Critics of Lane were always willing to accuse him of following popular sentiment, but if that was true and Lane was radical enough not just to support the raising of black troops but to call for equal treatment of black and white soldiers, it stands to reason that his constituents had become just as radical. Lane's progressive stance would have put him ahead of President Lincoln, who until early 1863 was unwilling to have black soldiers accepted into the Union army. This change in Lane, and the fact that events were radicalizing the nation, were notions that authors like Spring had trouble accepting.

In Spring's case, he revealed his hesitancy to welcome this Lane by starting his next paragraph with, "Yet Lane advocated colonization." He wrote that in the summer of 1861, Lane gave a speech in which he said, "South America ought to be given up to the negro." Lane returned to that idea in 1864, but with certain modifications. This time Lane wanted "to set aside" the state of South Carolina or the "territory of the Rio Grande" "as the future home of the colored man." For Spring, this implied that Lane was a hypocrite on the issue of race. What Spring seems to have forgotten was that Lincoln entertained the idea of colonization until September 1862, when he finally decided to issue his Emancipation Proclamation.

In contrast, John Speer in his biography related a story that showed how far Lane was going in terms of race relations. While in Washington on his Senate duties in 1862, Lane saw a black maid being forced to ride on the steps of a streetcar while the child she was escorting was allowed to ride inside. Lane promptly tried to help the black woman into the car "over the protests and threats of the conductor." In the Senate, Lane proposed a bill to revoke the streetcar company's charter unless it did away with segregated cars. The company backed down, and the man who had once advocated black law won a victory against racial segregation.

Lane's efforts at assembling a regiment of black soldiers did pay off and by the end of September, a First Regiment of Kansas Colored Volunteers was being drilled in a camp near Wyandotte. Late the following month they marched into Missouri and fought with a guerilla band near Butler. It was the first time that black soldiers had entered battle for the Federal army during the Civil War. The men were rewarded on January 13, 1863, when six companies were enrolled into the Union army. They were designated the First Regiment, Kansas Colored Volunteers, and as the Seventy-ninth U.S. Colored Infantry. Even though the regiment was the fourth such unit to formally enter the army, it did have the distinction of having the first black veterans from any Northern state.

Administration policy toward the enlistment of black soldiers had changed during the fall of 1862, for President Lincoln decided that the Civil War had to be about more than just restoring the union. It had to be about putting an end to slavery. To that end he wrote the Emancipation Proclamation, which he planned to issue after a Union victory. Although the battle of Antietam was not much of a victory, it did force the Confederates to retreat from Maryland and provided Lincoln the platform for his announcement. Lincoln publicly announced his new policy, and it took effect on January 1, 1863.

The proclamation abolished slavery only in those states in rebellion; in those still loyal, slavery remained legal. Although it freed slaves only in those areas outside the control of Union authorities, the proclamation was in effect a seizure of enemy property in order to reduce that enemy's ability to fight. Many Northerners who still abhorred abolitionism supported emancipation for that reason. Though some abolitionist leaders thought the proclamation too weak, others saw it as transforming the war into a moral crusade against slavery, and they rallied behind Lincoln. Finally, the proclamation made it all but impossible for Britain and France, who had long since outlawed slavery, to recognize the Confederacy.

As the fall of 1862 approached, election season heated up once again, although this time everyone recognized that the elections in Kansas would be legal. With Charles Robinson's reputation in tatters and Jim Lane in the ascendancy, it was clear that the Republicans would nominate a new candidate for governor, along with all the other offices up for contention.

Two letters to the *Conservative* in Leavenworth that were published on September 3 lobbied for two separate Republican nominees. Party members in southern Kansas still favored George Crawford's bid. Leavenworth interests, however, promoted the candidacy of local businessman Thomas Carney. When the Republicans gathered for their state convention, Carney became their favorite and was chosen as the party's nominee for governor.

A. C. Wilder, another Leavenworth man closely associated with the *Conservative*, was nominated for congressman. Crawford did not leave empty-handed, however; he was nominated for John Robinson's old post, secretary of state.

There were still many Republicans who disliked Lane and refused to support the ticket. Those anti-Lane Republicans decided to ally themselves with Kansas Democrats to nominate a "Union" or "Union Republican" ticket. They put forward W. R. Wagstaff for governor, John Ingalls for lieutenant governor, and Marcus Parrott for congressmen. The Democrats did put up one nominee of their own, one William G. Mathias for congressman.

Anti-Lane newspapers praised the combination ticket and denounced the Republicans. The *Topeka Tribune* wrote that the Union nominations comprised "undoubtedly honest, capable, and otherwise worthy" men, while the *State Journal* called the Republican slate "the property for all political intents and purposes of Lane & Co." The *Times* of Leavenworth believed the alliance was the only hope for broadly loyal Republicans and Democrats, and that in the heat of war, party politics should not matter.

Of course, the *Times*, like other anti-Lane organs, was not so objective that its editors could keep their own vitriol in check. Repeatedly, the *Times* claimed that Lane was threatening to arrest anyone who voted against the Republican ticket. On November 4, on the eve of the election, it warned that fraudulent ballots were being printed up to fool Leavenworth voters, though on that same day it printed a letter backing Carney's bid for governor.

Although there was very vocal dissent for the Lane-backed Republicans, Parrott's split with the senator was possibly problematic for the anti-Lane ticket. Back in August, Parrott and Lane had spoken at a meeting in Leavenworth. After Lane spoke, Parrott, according to the *Kansas Chief*, "ridiculed him" and mocked Lane's statements that "Kansas was in danger" from Confederate guerillas. Although Sol Miller wrote that Lane dealt "largely in humbug," Parrott's attacks were "ill-chosen" and there was "no sort of doubt" in Miller's mind that the threat from "rebel raids" was real.

Naturally enough the pro-Lane press leaped on the opposition slate with a vengeance. The October 4 issue of the *Emporia News* called the gathering that had put forward the slate a "Union Ass

Thomas Carney was elected the second governor of Kansas. He began his political career as a Lane ally, but by 1864 he had turned on Lane in an attempt to make himself the state's most powerful politician. By the end of Lane's life Carney was again a friend. *Photograph courtesy the Kansas State Historical Society.*

Convention" filled with "sore-headed Republicans," "pro-slavery Democrats," "Robinson men," and "political fossils." A correspondent for the *Conservative* on September 30 wrote that the abilities of the men at the convention "will be below mediocrity" and that no one "of any special prominence" would be attending. He then compared their effort to the futile crusades of Don Quixote. On October 2 the *Conservative* claimed that the convention had "dared not utter" anything about President Lincoln's Emancipation Proclamation so as "not [to] offend the sensibilities of the ex-border-ruffians whom they were wooing for their support." By October 10 it was calling the slate the "Mongrel ticket" and linking it with the unpopular Governor Robinson.

In the end the Republican ticket was just too popular for the anti-Lane alliance to handle. Thomas Carney was elected governor, A. C. Wilder was elected congressman, and Jim Lane had once and for all triumphed over his longtime rival Charles Robinson.

Kansas politics appeared to quiet down during the first half of 1863. Lane and Carney tried to work together. There was some clashing over the organization of new regiments, but the rancor of 1862 subsided. Attention in Kansas was directed toward military operations to the south. In that, Lane's favored general, James Blunt, was given more chances to win accolades for himself and further prove Lane correct in his advancement. Despite such a fortuitous start to the year, more trouble for Lane was on the horizon.

XII.

Lane, Quantrill, and Lawrence

The chief architect of the coming events was an Ohio settler who had come to Kansas opposed to slavery. William Clarke Quantrill moved to the territory in 1857. He was a young man who had hoped to establish a farm and make enough money to send back to his mother and siblings. He became a schoolteacher, but when his farm failed he took a series of rough jobs on the Plains.

During that time something seems to have happened to him, although authors such as Thomas Goodrich have never been able to explain what. What is known is that in 1859 he was expressing contempt for John Brown's raid on Harpers Ferry, and in 1860 he was indicted in Lawrence for returning slaves to bondage, though that year he had participated in some Free State raids on Missouri. Quantrill managed to avoid arrest, but then he joined in a raid on a Missouri plantation.

It is at this point that his life took a fateful turn. Accounts vary as to what occurred during the raid. Nicole Etcheson wrote that he warned the plantation's owners in advance; others have said the raid went awry and Quantrill was captured. Whatever happened during the attack, afterward Quantrill claimed that his brother had been killed by Jayhawkers under James Montgomery and that he had lured the raiders to the Missouri plantation to exact revenge. In fact his brother was alive in Ohio, but that didn't matter to the Southern sympathizers of Missouri. They took him in as one of their own.

In 1861 he joined the Confederate-leaning Missouri state militia

William Quantrill was a young man from Ohio who became a leader of Missouri's Confederate guerillas. In 1863 he led the attack on Lawrence that killed over 150 men. *Image courtesy the Kansas State Historical Society.*

under Claiborne Jackson and Sterling Price. Frustrated and angry with Price's retreat after the battle at Lexington, Quantrill decided to become a guerilla. His goal was not only to fight the Union occupation of Missouri, but also to launch retaliatory strikes against Kansas. To that end he drew some of the most ruthless partisan riders of the Civil War to his side.

There was "Bloody" Bill Anderson, part of a family of pro-Confederate Missourians who had settled around Council Grove. In 1862 his father had been accused of horse theft. When the older man tried to face down his accuser, he was killed. Anderson fled, only to later return, kill the local judge who had made the accusation, and burn down his store. George Todd, Dick Yager, and Coleman Younger were the sons of prominent and prosperous families with Confederate sympathies who had been attacked by Jayhawkers. Frank James, like Quantrill, had served in the militia, and his Unionist neighbors retaliated against his family. These men and others, many of them teenagers, became part of Quantrill's force of rebel raiders.

Their first strike came in March 1862, when they attacked the town of Aubrey, Kansas, about thirty miles south of Leavenworth. A week later they captured the Union garrison at Liberty, Missouri. After a bloody battle in August his men captured Independence, Missouri. In September they attacked Olathe, killing three men and robbing several homes and stores. The next month Quantrill led an attack on Shawnee, Kansas; two men were murdered and several houses burned. They returned to the region in 1863. In May there was a raid on Plattsburg, Missouri, while that same month Yager led an attack on Diamond Springs, west of Council Grove.

Union authorities began to crack down on captured guerillas to discourage them. General Blunt approved of the executions of them as spies. His replacement as the military defender of the Kansas border, Thomas Ewing, Jr., decided to take steps to defend that part of his Department of Kansas. He established a series of posts from Leavenworth to Fort Scott, stationed troops at each post, and gave them orders to report any suspicious activity not only to him but to neighboring posts as well. Ewing even went so far as to consider the arrest and detention of the families of the most notorious of the partisans.

Ewing's men very quickly filled the jails in and around Kansas City with suspected rebels and their families. For more detention space a brick building was taken over. The three-story structure was poorly constructed and appeared unstable, but several women, a few children, and one man were placed inside as prisoners. After complaints an initial inspection on August 13 found the building unsafe, but a second inspection later that morning cleared it. Unfortunately, just after lunch the building collapsed. One of Bill Anderson's sisters was killed and another injured, while a cousin of Coleman Younger also died. Five women in all lost their lives in the collapse and two were seriously wounded.

The guerillas related to the victims were eager for revenge. Both Thomas Goodrich and Nicole Etcheson believed that Quantrill had already been considering a bold stroke before the building collapse, but the deaths fueled his anger. His attention had fallen on Lawrence. It seemed to symbolize all the things his men hated about their Yankee foes: "liberated" and runaway slaves had gravitated there; stolen property from pro-Confederate families was rumored to be sold in the stores and displayed in the homes of Lawrence citizens; most of all, it was the hometown of men they hated, men like Jim Lane.

The people of Lawrence, although seemingly confident in their security because of their distance from the state border, were not completely oblivious to their town's danger of attack. Rumors of a raid struck Lawrence in the summer of 1861 and in November 1862. The most serious of these rumors came on July 31, 1863, when it seemed Quantrill might attack the city during a full moon. But when nothing happened the people laughed off their fears and went back to their lives.

In spite of the warnings and the close call, the people of Lawrence assumed they were safe. However, in August, Quantrill decided to attack Lawrence. His men would get their revenge for Kansas City, Osceola, and every other outrage real or imagined. They would strike a blow for the cause, which was suffering in the wake of Union victories at Gettysburg and Vicksburg. Quantrill gathered between three hundred and four hundred guerillas in Missouri, and on Thursday, August 20, they set out for Kansas.

Capt. J. A. Pike at Aubrey was aware of the movement of

Quantrill's force at around 5:30 on the evening of August 20. Captain Pike immediately sent word up and down the line of posts guarding the border as well as to district headquarters at Fort Leavenworth. An hour and a half later he discovered that Quantrill's men had crossed into Kansas. Instead of setting out after the Confederates, Pike simply reported the information to Fort Leavenworth and to Capt. C. F. Coleman at Little Santa Fe.

Coleman gathered some two hundred men and set out to find Quantrill. Unfortunately for him, Quantrill's men were moving over open country and did not leave an obvious trail. Coleman's efforts were further hampered when Quantrill split his force to throw off any pursuit. By the time Coleman's men reached Gardner in southwestern Johnson County, the raiders had a six-hour lead on him.

After the second message from Pike arrived at Fort Leavenworth, Maj. Preston Plumb, Ewing's chief of staff, assembled fifty men and headed south. By dawn he had reached Olathe. A few miles farther, Major Plumb overtook Captain Coleman and together they continued the pursuit. They made it to within six miles of Lawrence by 10:30 the morning of August 21. But by then it was too late.

Much has been written about the August 21 attack on Lawrence by Quantrill's men. Several survivors wrote down their experiences, and author Thomas Goodrich devoted a whole book, *Bloody Dawn,* just to the "Lawrence massacre." For the purposes of this work, only a few of the most notable accounts will be retold.

About two miles east of Lawrence, Quantrill and his men reached the farm of Rev. S. S. Snyder of the United Brethren church. According to author Richard Cordley, Snyder was a lieutenant of in one of the regiments of black troops raised in Kansas "and this was doubtless the reason they singled him out." While in his barnyard at dawn, perhaps going to milk some cows, he was shot and killed. Snyder was the first man killed during the Lawrence raid. From his farmstead the guerillas surged into town, shooting, killing, and burning.

Charles Robinson had left his home on the north side of Lawrence for the stone barn he owned on the south part of Mount

Oread early that morning. He was preparing for his usual morning carriage ride when Quantrill's men rode into town. He remained at the barn during the assault, apparently able to see guerillas going house to house setting fires and shooting men. It was still a close escape for him, as some of the raiders were sent up to Mount Oread to keep watch for any approaching Union troops.

John Speer was also able to avoid becoming a victim, but two of his three sons were not so lucky. One was shot in the street, fleeing the invasion. He was shot twice; after the first bullet he played dead, but then a second guerilla shot him in the head. Another son was burned to death in one of the business buildings set on fire. A third son hid under a sidewalk, but nearby fires forced him into the street. Wrote Richard Cordley, "He went boldly up to some of them and offered his services in holding their horses. They asked him his name, and thinking the name of John Speer might be too familiar, he answered 'John Smith.' Under that name he remained among them till they left and was not harmed."

Speer's friend Jim Lane would be spared any such grief, but his escape was, according to at least two sources, by a very slim margin. Reverend Cordley wrote that "Lane was naturally in demand among" Quantrill's men. "They seemed to know he was in town, and were determined to get him." Naturally they headed for the Lane mansion.

According to an issue of the *New York Times* published in early September 1863, Lane at first thought the sounds coming from Lawrence were firecrackers. He was convinced of the danger when a black person ran by his house saying that "the rebels were in town." He dressed and asked his wife, Mary, to retrieve the two guns he kept in their house. When they couldn't be found, he grabbed the sword he had from his Mexican War days, still intent on fighting back. His wife and children begged him not to fight, but to flee. He finally did so, heading out the back door of his house just as guerillas were riding up to the front gate.

Richard Cordley wrote that it was Mrs. Lane who met the raiders. They told her that they "'wanted to see the general.' She told them 'he was not in.' They broke up his furniture, smashed the piano, and then set the house on fire." Cordley thought Quantrill himself was at the head of this party, for he wrote that upon leaving, "Quantrill tipped his hat to Mrs. Lane, and 'wished her to give his compliments to General Lane and tell him he would have been very glad to meet him.' Mrs. Lane assured him that 'Mr. Lane would be no less glad to meet him under different circumstances, but it was not convenient that morning.'"

In notes in Wendell Stephenson's biography of Lane, William Connelley wrote that among the items stolen from the Lane home were the sword he had been given by the men of the Fifth Indiana back in 1849 and the flag presented to him by the people of Mexico City. In the case of the latter, the guerillas assumed this was a mythical black flag the ladies of Leavenworth gave Lane to carry into Missouri in 1861. The raiders tore it in two and carried it out of Lawrence under their clothes. However, the flag addition to the story seems odd, considering that the flag supposedly had the arms of Mexico on it and inscriptions either in English or in Spanish. Certainly, though, these items did disappear from the Lane home; only the sword's sheath was ever recovered.

For his part Jim Lane fled his house through a ravine and a cornfield until he reached the edge of town. According to the *Times,* at that point Lane tried to find a horse and ride out, but he ended up hiding until the raid was over. Other accounts state that Lane did get a horse and ride over the Kansas River and find safety some distance away. What is true is that Jim Lane escaped Lawrence with his life and not much else.

Others also had fortunate escapes, but many did not. Almost all the businesses downtown were looted and burned. Two of the three banks in town were robbed of everything. Many houses were destroyed by fire, and many more were robbed and everything of value stolen. A church serving blacks in town was burned, but other churches in town were spared. The loss of life was high; between 150 and 200 men and boys were killed that August morning. Only one of Quantrill's men was killed, and that man died after the raid when he became separated from the main body and was ambushed by a scouting party.

Almost as soon as the raiders had left and news of the Lawrence massacre spread, people tried to find someone to blame for what had happened. Inevitably, the effort to fix blame went back to Lane and his 1861 expedition into Missouri.

Leverett Spring was among those who accepted the notion that the Lawrence raid was retaliation for depredations committed by Lane and his Kansas Jayhawkers. He attributed his view to a quote from one of Quantrill's men: "Jennison has laid waste our homes. . . . Houses have been plundered and burned, defenseless men shot down, and women outraged. We are here for revenge—and we have got it!"

John Speer was unwilling to accept such a rationalization. Writing at the turn of the century, he pointed out that eyewitnesses to the Osceola raid told him that Lane executed no one, stole nothing, and only burned the town to prevent its loaded stores from falling into the hands of Price's army. By contrast, Speer claimed, there was no strategic value to the burning of Lawrence. Whereas Lane's men had committed no atrocities on the civilians themselves, Quantrill's men dragged several women from their houses and killed their husbands in front of them. They compelled one woman to help them search for her husband. Several boys were believed to have burned to death in various fires, as had one of Speer's own sons. Some men staying at the Eldrige Hotel surrendered only to be executed by the raiders. "The statements about Quantrill having 'a grievance' are all false," Speer concluded flatly.

Lloyd Lewis, in his 1938 speech, made little mention of Lane and the Lawrence massacre. Yet about the Lane expedition of 1861, he said, "What Lane had proposed doing in the winter of 1861-1862 was substantially what William Tecumseh Sherman did in the winter of 1864-1865." He added, "'Jayhawking' became a great feat when the regulars performed it."

If this rationale is accepted, then any blame held against Lane was not for the actions he performed, but in the claim that his actions did not go far enough toward subduing rebel forces. Sherman's march through Georgia and Sheridan's march through the Shenandoah not only destroyed those areas' ability to support the Confederate armies, but smashed all Confederate military forces. Lane's brigade destroyed supplies but did not destroy the rebel bands.

This is all speculation, of course, yet it points to the fact that trying to place responsibility on any one person for what happened in Lawrence on August 21, 1863, is a futile exercise. Albert Castel, no supporter of Lane, found several causes for the success of Quantrill at Lawrence. Gen. John Schofield had shifted troops from Kansas to the east, leaving border protection to a smaller force. Captain Pike failed to send word to his superiors of what was happening, and so did the people along Quantrill's route. Also to blame was the "carelessness of the people of Lawrence" in not keeping the roads leading into town constantly patrolled.

Regarding Lane, Castel could only say that perhaps his disagreements with Governor Carney might have contributed. This blame only went so far as Lane's effort to keep Carney from raising a regiment to guard the border. Castel conceded that there was little proof that if such a regiment were in the field, it could have stopped Quantrill, but he felt that its existence might have saved the town.

Castel gave credit for Lawrence to Quantrill himself for his talent and audacity. "His ability should not be overlooked because of his cruelty," Castel wrote. Quantrill's raid succeeded due to "a nearly perfect combination of timing and execution," and he did much to keep from having to rely on luck. Military and civil authorities never expected Quantrill to strike so far into Kansas, and thus they were unprepared for him when he did.

Even those who blamed Lane for Quantrill's attack on Lawrence had to admit that in the hours afterward, Lane put his life on the line to strike a blow against the guerilla leader and his band. As with much of Lane's life this was a controversial action and many would question his motives.

When Jim Lane returned to Lawrence, he was horrified at the destruction. Rather than take part in any recovery efforts, Lane wanted to go after the raiders. While this seems bizarre, even selfish, sources including the *Conservative* and the *New York Times* reported that around fifty men from Lawrence agreed to join Lane in his pursuit of Quantrill. The trail wasn't hard to follow, as the *Times* noted, for "everything on the road from Lawrence to Prairie City was in flames."

Meanwhile, Maj. Preston Plumb's command, in pursuit of the raiders, was within six miles of Lawrence at eleven on the morning of August 21. According to his report, Plumb's men did make it to

Lawrence, but only after Quantrill's men had departed. Plumb decided to continue following the guerillas. His men found a trail leading south and intercepted Quantrill's band at Palmyra. Quantrill ordered about one hundred of his men to form a line of battle behind his main force to delay their enemy. By the time the Union men formed their own line, the raiders had fired one volley, remounted, and retreated. Despite his weary men and horses, Plumb kept his troops in the chase until they reached Paola. Three miles north of town a sharp fight broke out. Shortly thereafter, the raiders broke off and split up. When Plumb's men tried to find their trail, they could not, so the major took his men into Paola to rest and to feed his hungry soldiers.

Sometime before the skirmish broke out, Lane and his citizen-soldiers met Plumb's troops. William Connelley wrote in his history of Kansas that when Lane met Plumb, he demanded the major turn over command to him. A witness, wrote Connelley, heard "some high words" pass between the men when Plumb refused. Lane appears to have backed down, and as long as he was in the field pursuing the guerillas, he followed orders. Indeed, a story in the August 26 issue of the *Leavenworth Times* reported that ever since the pursuit ended, Lane had been praising Plumb and his actions to anyone who would listen.

Having gotten word from Captain Pike of Quantrill's movements, while Plumb and Lane pursued the raiders, Lt. Col. C. S. Clark at Coldwater Grove assembled the soldiers posted south of him. He took his men north and struck Gardner late in the morning. From there he was updated on the situation and took his small command toward Paola, arriving there around five in the evening. He tried to stop the guerillas along a creek three miles south of town, but after engaging Plumb, Quantrill's men managed to avoid Clark.

Lieutenant Colonel Clark was now the senior officer at Paola, but instead of ordering an immediate pursuit, he held off sending anyone after Quantrill until daybreak. By then the trail had grown cold. Quantrill was able to avoid other Union forces converging on the Paola area, a squad of the Linn County militia, and elements of the Fourth Missouri Militia near the border. Quantrill's men scattered for good when they reached the middle fork of the Grand River in Missouri.

General Ewing missed the active pursuit entirely. He wrote in his official report that he finally read Pike's messages at quarter to eleven in the morning. He returned to Fort 'Leavenworth only to find that no cavalry was stationed at the fort. There were five companies of the Eleventh Ohio preparing to leave for Fort Laramie, but they had no weapons. It was not until one in the afternoon that Ewing was able to march from Fort Leavenworth with about three hundred soldiers.

Ewing then received information that Quantrill's men were planning to attack Topeka after having finished with Lawrence. Ewing took his men south to De Soto, wasted five hours crossing the Kansas River, then took his force to Lanesfield. There he was informed of events around Paola, and at that point he turned east toward the Grand River. About the only interaction Ewing could claim with the raiders was that one unit from Missouri was able to get close enough to Quantrill's tail to compel them to abandon the plunder they had stolen from Lawrence.

Governor Carney wrote to General Schofield about the attack on August 24. "Disaster has again fallen on our State," he said tersely. "Lawrence is in ashes," and "nearly 200 lives of our best citizens have been sacrificed. . . . I must hold Missouri responsible for his fearful, fiendish raid." He believed that a force as large as Quantrill's "could [not] have been gathered together without the people residing in Western Missouri knowing everything about it. . . . Such people cannot be considered loyal." There would be "no peace in Missouri," and there would be "utter desolation in Kansas" unless the region was "made to feel promptly the rigor of military law." Feelings were "intense all over the State," and at the very least "a court of inquiry" had to be convened to investigate how the tragedy had occurred.

Schofield replied to Carney on August 29, telling him that he had asked for that court of inquiry. He called on the governor to keep the people from trying to resort to a revenge attack on Missouri, for that would lead to more retaliation and eventually "utter desolation on both sides of the border." Schofield promised Carney firearms for the state militia and other unspecified measures to deal with Quantrill and his men.

Three days after Carney sent his report to Schofield, Jim Lane spoke in Leavenworth about what had happened in Lawrence and what he thought should be done in response to the massacre. According to the *Leavenworth Times,* Lane began by offering a resolution that called for as "many of the loyal men of the border as can be spared from home protection" to assemble at Paola under arms on September 8. The resolution did not specify the reason for the call, but Lane didn't have to be explicit. Obviously this force was intended to march on Missouri and destroy the guerillas.

That Lane meant more that a campaign against Quantrill was made clear as he followed his resolution by criticizing Missouri politicians and Schofield for a "conservative" policy that protected Missouri at Kansas's expense. Everyone knew from history, Lane said, "that guerillas cannot exist without the sympathy and collusion" of residents of the lands they operate from. His audience was enthusiastically behind him; when he called for "extermination of the first tier of counties on the border of Missouri" to eliminate Quantrill's bands, someone called out, "And the second tier, too!"

General Schofield reported on this meeting to his superiors, stating that the main speakers, including Lane, had used "violent and inflammatory" rhetoric in their remarks. He feared "great danger of an indiscriminate slaughter of the people in western Missouri, or of a collision with the troops, under General Ewing, in their efforts to prevent it."

Schofield conceded that public outrage was as much a driving force behind the meeting as wild speeches. "The people of Kansas were, very naturally, intensely excited over the destruction of one of their fairest towns, and the murder of a large number of its unarmed citizens," he wrote in his report. But it was "greatly unjust to the people of Kansas, in general, to say that they shared in this desire for indiscriminate vengeance." Nor was there a lack of "unprincipled leaders to fan the flame of popular excitement and goad the people to madness, in the hope of thereby accomplishing their own selfish ends."

Schofield arrived in Leavenworth on September 2 and met with Governor Carney and some of his allies. Carney was "opposed to all unauthorized movement on the part of the people of Kansas, and willing to co-operate" with Schofield and Ewing. After meeting Carney, Schofield met with Lane, "the recognized leader of those engaged in the Paola movements." Lane, wrote Schofield, told the general it was necessary to make "a large portion of Western Missouri a desert waste, in order that Kansas might be secure against future invasion." Lane proposed giving Ewing "the services of all the armed citizens of Kansas to aid in executing this policy."

"This, I informed him, was impossible," said Schofield; "that whatever measures of this kind it might be necessary to adopt must be executed by United States troops; that irresponsible citizens could not be instructed with the discharge of such duties."

Lane "then insisted that the people who might assemble at Paola should be permitted to enter Missouri 'in search of their stolen property.'" Lane was willing to allow Schofield to take command of them and offered his personal pledge that they would "strictly confine themselves to such search, abstaining entirely from all unlawful acts." Schofield replied "that nothing would afford me greater pleasure than to do all in my power to assist the outraged and despoiled people to recover their property, as well as to punish their despoilers." He believed, however, that any such search would be "fruitless." The property that had not already been recovered was now "far beyond the border counties" with the men who had stolen it. Schofield added that he "had not the slightest faith" in his ability to control such an expedition.

"General Lane desired me to consider the matter fully," he wrote later, "and inform him, as soon as possible, of my decision, saying if I decided not to allow the people the 'right' which they claimed, he would appeal to the President." Schofield felt that Lane had not made his promises to him in good faith, because he thought he would be the one to blame when the expedition inevitably descended into "murder and robbery." Furthermore, Schofield expressed satisfaction that Lane would not "carry out his scheme in opposition to my orders" and that "the vast majority of the people of Kansas were entirely opposed to" the expedition.

To ensure that nothing did happen, Schofield issued an order on September 4 that stated, "The militia of Kansas and Missouri, not in the service of the United States, will be used only for the defense of their respective States. They will not be permitted to pass from one State into the other, without express orders from the district commander."

One of the soldiers in the Ninth Kansas Cavalry, Albert Greene, was a witness to the Paola meeting of September 8. Writing some fifty years later, Greene recalled that Ewing dispatched Col. William Weer with a company of the Ninth to prevent Lane's expedition from going forward. According to Greene, Weer only wanted ten men to accompany him, but Ewing insisted on sending seventy-five. Greene noted that the men in the ranks were "Lane men" while the officers were "anti-Lane," including Weer. Yet the men respected Weer and followed his orders.

As reported in the *Leavenworth Conservative* three days after the Paola meeting, Lane began by telling his audience that this was the most important occasion on which he had given a public address. Kansans had overcome "the slave-power of the Government" and were serving in the Union army in numbers proportionately well above the new state's small population. But now all over Kansas, "the women and children are terrified, the men stand sullen and confused, not knowing what to do."

At that point a heavy rain began to fall on the gathering, and the event declined from there. Already the turnout was modest. General Schofield wrote in a message to Washington that there were only "a few hundred people" in attendance. When Colonel Weer arrived he marched his command to the front of the speakers' platform, forcing those seated in the front to move back.

In spite of the rain and the meager showing, Lane continued to speak. His remarks followed the tone he had taken in Leavenworth days earlier. He decried Schofield's "conservative" and "defensive" policy and called for a pursuit of "the wolf Quantrile [*sic*] to his den." Years later Albert Greene called Lane's address "wild, incoherent, and bloodthirsty," wrote that Lane called all Missourians "wolves, snakes, [and] devils," and demanded that Missouri be made "a burning hell." Yet according to the *Conservative*'s report, the speech was not so provocative.

Neither did it contain two incidents Greene described. At one point Weer stood up and faced the crowd, turned, and "looked Lane straight in the eye." Once Weer sat back down Lane told his audience that Schofield wanted them to "go back to their desolate homes empty-handed." Members of the audience laughed at that, and Lane quickly ended his speech.

The second happened later that night, while Charles Jennison and other radicals were speaking. When their listeners roared with approval at their more inflammatory addresses, Lane again took the stage. "God damn Missouri," he shouted, "I want to see her destroyed—her men slain and her women outcasts." It was all he said, but that was enough to whip the crowd into a frenzy. "I fully believe if there had not been a military force present they would have started for Missouri that night," Greene claimed.

For the *Conservative*'s rival in Leavenworth, the *Daily Times,* Paola was the signal to stop quoting Lane and start disputing him again. In its issue of September 12 it called the meeting "Lane's Paola Fizzle" and accused him of having opposed Carney's home-guard recruits. Lane, they said, was trying to make "political capital" out of the Lawrence raid.

The course of Lane's activities from the aftermath of the Lawrence massacre to the meeting in Paola have been a source of his enemies' attacks. They would accuse him over the years of planning a massive raid of plunder into Missouri, either for his own benefit or to satisfy a thirst for revenge among the public. Lane's actions do indeed raise questions, but perhaps not the questions his foes asked, or might want to ask.

The first question that arises is why would Lane choose Paola as the stepping-off point for a vengeance raid against Missouri. The town is hardly centrally located. Paola is about forty miles from Lawrence, fifty miles from Leavenworth and Fort Leavenworth, sixty miles from Topeka, seventy miles from Atchison, and eighty miles from Fort Scott. Really, Paola is close only to the Missouri border, which is about twelve miles away. However, Fort Scott, Olathe, and Wyandotte are all just as close to the border, with the latter two being only ten miles from Leavenworth. In fact, if a location convenient to the majority of Kansas citizens was a criterion, Lawrence would have been a far better choice.

Why wasn't Lawrence chosen as the gathering spot? The destruction—the burned buildings, the widows and orphans, the graves of the dead—would be laid out before the eyes of those considering joining the raid. There would be no better place to inflame passions against Missouri than in the town that had so recently suffered so much at the hands of the Missouri bushwhackers. True,

Lawrence would have had no accommodations for such a meeting, but few towns in Kansas could have housed the gathering, except Leavenworth.

Leavenworth, too, would have been a better choice than Paola, and not just because of its size. It was already being radicalized by Mayor Anthony, so an enraged mob would have been right at hand for Lane to assume the leadership of. The fort would have had the arms and supplies Lane's invaders needed to carry out their assault. So would have Fort Scott.

If the location of the meeting seems odd, so, too, does the day the meeting was set for. September 8 fell on a Tuesday that year and was about two and a half weeks after the attack on Lawrence. Why not choose September 5, a Saturday, or September 4, a Friday, exactly two weeks after Lawrence? It seems strange to select a week-day to gather an army of outraged Kansans for an invasion of Missouri and even stranger to gather that mob in a town far from the population centers and main military posts in the state.

Unless that was exactly Lane's intention.

Lane knew how to read public opinion, so he could not have helped but notice the anger of the people in the wake of the Lawrence massacre. Within a day or two he also knew about Ewing's Order No. 11 forcing the evacuation of the Missouri bor-der counties and Schofield's backing of the order. It would have been clear listening to the crowds that such an order, harsh as it obviously was, could not possibly satisfy their rage at Missouri in general and the guerillas in particular. Lane might also have sensed that Ewing and Schofield were going to be very unpopular men until things quieted down. After all, they were supposed to be the military men keeping Quantrill's raiders at bay, and they had failed spectacularly.

To Lane, the situation might have seemed like this: Ewing and Schofield were going to deal with the guerilla problem as best as they could, but their solution would take time to implement. The people, enraged at the death and destruction, were unlikely to have the patience to wait. There were already calls among the mob for retaliation. Lane had two choices of action: defend the gener-als against a tide of anger, a tide that would rise before it fell, or go along with the angry mob.

Had Lane chosen the generals and caution, he would have been going against his populist instincts. He certainly would have become as unpopular as Ewing and Schofield became. Siding with them might also have seemed to the public, at least in the heat of the moment, as a sign of weakness on his part. Lane knew he had political enemies willing to pounce on any weakness; in fact he was probably already suspicious of Carney's ambitions for his Senate seat.

But Lane was not stupid. He had to have been aware that an invasion of Missouri by a mob of angry Kansans was not going to affect the Confederacy. Deep down he might already have felt that his 1861 expedition had played some small part in creating the guerillas in the first place. Even if he had no such remorse, he had to have known that leading a mob at this point would not be excused by President Lincoln, for it appears that Lincoln was somewhat exasperated by the political jockeying in Kansas. Had Lane led a mob into Missouri, he would have put Lincoln into the position of either backing a mob or backing legitimate authorities. Lincoln would almost certainly have supported the latter, and Lane's relationship with Lincoln, and the power he derived from it, would have been lost.

In addition, it might have occurred to Lane that if he did not take control of the mob, someone else probably would. Mayor Daniel Anthony was already taking on powers he had no right to, delighting the radicals in Leavenworth. Lane could not have been sure that Jennison and other former Jayhawkers were plotting to resume their raids on Missouri, and if those men failed to take charge of the mob, the mob would choose its own leader. That leader could very well have been a man not even Lane could charm.

So perhaps what Lane did was create a third choice: go with the mob and their anger—even stoke it a little—but go no farther than that. He could tell the mob what it wanted to hear, that a vengeance attack on Missouri would come; however, by setting the assembly for that army of revenge far enough ahead, but not so far out that anyone would get suspicious, passions could cool. A weekday would be ideal as well as an out-of-the-way place to assemble, since the inconvenience was certain to diminish the turnout.

If that truly was Lane's decision, then it was a stroke of genius. It allowed him to remain popular with the people while avoiding any serious confrontations with Schofield, Ewing, Carney, or Lincoln. He could ride the wave of public sentiment without having to actually perform any action. His rivals would howl, but when nothing came of the meeting, their ammunition against him would disappear. He would come through the greatest outrage of the Civil War with his power and popularity intact. And since that is what actually happened, one has to wonder if that is exactly what Lane intended.

As the Paola movement sputtered, General Ewing began his own effort at a crackdown on the Confederate guerillas in Missouri. On August 25, Ewing had sent a draft of an order he wanted to issue to General Schofield. Ewing told his superior that he was now "pretty much convinced" that the Union strategy during the previous two years had failed. Only through "devastation of the districts which are made the haunts of guerrillas will be sufficient to put a stop to the evil."

Later that same day Ewing decided to issue a new general order, Number 11. It began, "All persons living in Jackson, Cass, and Bates Counties, Missouri, and in that part of Vernon included in this district . . . , are hereby ordered to remove from their present places of residence within fifteen days" of August 25. The citizens would have to "establish their loyalty to the satisfaction of the commanding officer of the military station nearest their present places of residence." If they did so, they would receive a certificate and "be permitted to remove to any military station in this district, or to any part of the State of Kansas, except the counties on the eastern border of the State. . . . All others shall remove out of this district."

Schofield believed in Order No. 11 completely, telling his superiors that when he visited the "various points in the counties affected by General Ewing's order," he became "fully satisfied that the order depopulating certain counties, with the exception of specified districts, was wise and necessary."

Order No. 11 did calm the situation both in Kansas and Missouri. It was just tough enough to satisfy many Kansans and prevent them from taking the law into their own hands. Initially it forced the evacuation of some twenty thousand Missourians, Unionists, and Confederate sympathizers. But until October there were no more guerilla invasions of Kansas, and that incursion was a military engagement in far southeast Kansas. By November the order was rescinded, and many on both sides returned the following spring.

Unfortunately for General Schofield, any rise in his own stature in Kansas thanks to Order No. 11 crashed by the end of September. He put out a declaration of martial law "against all persons who shall utter or publish any facts or misrepresentation of facts calculated to create insubordination or distrust among the soldiers or people, or weaken the military authority." He was immediately denounced by several Kansas newspapers, including one of Jim Lane's sharpest critics, the *White Cloud Chief*, edited by Sol Miller. Miller's piece, called "Schofield's Last Grunt," was picked up by the *Leavenworth Conservative*. Schofield sent clippings to General Halleck in Washington, "asking your opinion whether it [the *Conservative*] is a proper subject for the application of martial law."

On September 30, Lane led a delegation of Kansas and Missouri men to the White House to demand that Lincoln remove Schofield. Lincoln listened while one of them presented an address on the matter. The address criticized both Schofield and the governor of Missouri. Lincoln agreed to consider their sentiments but refused to take any immediate action. During the discussion that followed, Lane asked Lincoln if he thought it was "sufficient cause" for a general to be removed because he had "lost the entire confidence of the people." Lincoln replied that he did not and that it was not "a very strong reason for his removal."

"General Schofield has lost that confidence," Lane said.

"You being judge!" the president shot back. Lincoln refused to budge on the Schofield matter and Lane went away unhappy.

Though the two politicians were in disagreement about Schofield, they were still allies in the overall struggle. Lincoln viewed Lane and his fellow Western radicals as valuable. A month after the meeting Lincoln told his personal secretary, John Hay, that Lane and the radicals were "nearer to me than the other side, in thought and in sentiment." He explained, "They are utterly lawless—the unhandiest devils in the world to deal with—but after all their faces are set Zionwards."

Schofield's popularity continued to decline, for Quantrill got back into the news on October 6 with an encounter with no less than General Blunt. While Blunt was moving his field headquarters to Fort Smith on October 6, Quantrill led his men on an attack on the small fort at Baxter Springs. Just at that moment Blunt and his escort arrived in the vicinity. At first Blunt's men assumed that the raiders were troops sent out from the fort to meet them. But when they approached, the guerillas opened fire. Blunt's escort, largely comprised of new recruits, broke immediately and tried to flee. Blunt and his officers were forced to ride for their lives. Eighty-nine of Blunt's men were killed, many murdered after surrendering.

After Baxter Springs, President Lincoln also seemed to be losing confidence in the job Schofield was doing. He might also have been aware at how unpopular the general was becoming. On January 1, 1864, Schofield was sent to Tennessee and replaced by Samuel Curtis.

In spite of having achieved Schofield's ouster, Jim Lane's political future as 1864 began was far from certain. A variety of plans were in the works to knock him down. Lane was going to need all his political skill to survive the coming battles.

XIII.

The 1864 Elections

As the election year of 1864 began, Jim Lane had to deal with an uprising in Kansas that threatened his place in the Senate. At the bottom of it was Gov. Thomas Carney. The governor had come to envy the power Lane held in Washington. His ambition grew until he was willing to do whatever he could to oust Lane and get himself elected to Lane's Senate seat.

Sol Miller in White Cloud had already taken note of the growing rivalry between the governor and the senator. In a piece in the July 23, 1863, issue of the *Chief,* under the title "A Gay Fight," Miller claimed to be a "disinterested spectator" of the Carney-Lane feud. Of course he was no such thing. He wrote that Carney's nomination was "disgusting" but the governor was "entitled to the support of every citizen of the state." Lane, on the other hand, wanted to either "control the State Government" or to "disgrace it." He had humiliated the state with Charles Robinson's impeachment, and Miller was certain Lane would do it again to Carney.

Carney had one opening if he desired to replace Lane. When Lane was chosen senator in 1861 it was to a four-year term, while Pomeroy received the standard six-year term. This assured that the elections of senators would not fall in the same year in Kansas, as set out in the U.S. Constitution. Lane's term was set to expire in 1865 when state legislators elected at the polls in 1864 would meet. But there was nothing in federal law that stated when a legislative election for senator could be held. That was the opening Carney aimed for.

There were rumors floating around Kansas in 1863 that Lane would press for an election as early as 1864. The speculation was that he hoped to have some of the legislators friendly to him carry over in the 1863 off-year polling, along with adding a few more friends to his list. But for a variety of reasons that balloting did not go his way. As the year came to a close, Lane was denouncing any early election as bogus. However, Carney took up the idea for his own purposes, and on February 9, 1864, he managed to get the state legislature to elect him as the new senator from Kansas.

The speed at which Carney moved can be seen in two letters written by one of Lane's supporters, a legislator named Rogers, to James Redfield, another Lane man. On February 1, Rogers told Redfield that the early election issue had come up "much sooner than I expected and with more force than I had looked for." Two days later Rogers predicted that Carney "will be elected by a large majority in spite of every thing that the friends of Lane can do." Rogers was sure Lane could not get "over twenty votes in the House and not more than five in the Senate."

In 1879 the *Topeka Commonwealth* ran a story about this extraordinary election. Building on material from Carney's private secretary published recently in another newspaper as well as from an interview with Carney, the story revealed some fascinating aspects of the incident. Apparently, Carney initially received encouragement from Salmon Chase in the fall of 1863, when Carney visited Washington and had dinner with the Treasury secretary. Carney agreed to give Chase's suggestion some thought but was not inclined to take it seriously.

What changed his mind, and the minds of his Kansas allies, was a letter from Pomeroy that arrived early in February 1864. Pomeroy stated in the letter that several "leading Republican Senators" had held a caucus to offer support for Carney to replace Lane. Based on that comment Carney and his friends engineered the election. When word of the election got to Washington, Pomeroy told Carney that he was certain "the next Legislature" would "ratify the action of the present one." This no doubt stunned Carney, for the statement seemed to suggest that the vote that had just been held was not as legitimate as he and his allies had believed.

As soon as the legislature adjourned, Carney raced to the nation's capital to discern the truth of the situation. He spoke to the senators Pomeroy had first mentioned, and each one not only expressed surprise at what Carney had done and told him that no caucus had been held, but also said that such a ballot might set a precedent that would threaten their own seats. Carney realized that everything Pomeroy had written earlier "was a lie manufactured by Pomeroy out of whole cloth." What's more, according to the *Commonwealth* piece, Carney discovered that Pomeroy was worried about the prospect of "a Senator from Leavenworth" defeating his reelection bid and had backed out. With no hope left of getting Lane's seat a year early, Carney abandoned the effort and decided to try again after the 1864 elections were held.

The piece the *Commonwealth* ran was from a story in Sol Miller's *Chief*, by then being printed in Troy. While the Topeka newspaper was preparing the article for its publication, its editor allowed John Speer to take a look at it. Speer wrote a letter to the newspaper with his comments about what had happened, and his letter ran under the article.

The first thing Speer said in his letter was that when he heard rumors of Lane favoring an early election in the summer of 1863, he spoke to Lane about the matter. "To me," he said, "Lane had on more than one occasion denied it." To that end Speer prepared a strong denunciation of the idea for the August 20 issue of the *Tribune*. Speer took his editorial to Lane to confirm Lane's views on the question. The next day, of course, was the day of the Quantrill raid. Speer hoped that at least one issue still existed that could prove the editorial he was describing had been written and printed.

There does seem to be proof of this article, oddly enough, from the anti-Lane *Leavenworth Times* of November 8, 1863. In responding to a piece in a pro-Lane Topeka newspaper, the *Times* stated that at the Leavenworth meeting after the Lawrence massacre, a resolution was passed rejecting the notion of electing a U.S. senator that winter. Carney was not interested in an election for that office in early 1864, according to the *Times*, but in unfounded attacks, pro-Lane papers claimed otherwise. "Governor Carney, in our belief," the *Times* editorial stated firmly, "is utterly opposed to the exercise of 'one man power.'"

To further back his account, Speer related an effort Lane had undertaken to convince a Lawrence man to run for a seat in the state House that summer. When Lane and Speer met with the man, Lane acknowledged to the reluctant candidate that he was not a friend, but Lane was not looking for another legislative ally. "I believe an effort will be made to elect Carney this winter," Lane said, "and all I want is some man from my own home who will oppose such a d——d outrage." The candidate confirmed to Lane that he was opposed to Carney's election. He did indeed run, was elected, and opposed Carney's scheme.

Speer concluded his letter with the claim that he knew nothing of what had transpired between Carney and Pomeroy, but he presumed the story was true. "I have no doubt also, that Mr. Carney's friends were led to believe that Lane purposed his own election at the same session that Carney was elected," Speer said; "but if he did, he deceived me, and not only me, but all his intimate friends with whom I have ever conversed."

A letter written by none other than Charles Robinson the December before the voting seems to confirm Speer's account. The letter, from the former governor to his wife, was written from Lawrence on December 27, 1863. On the third page of the missive Robinson said, "The legislature will probably attempt to elect a Senator in Lane's place early this winter. It is claimed to be largely anti-Lane."

Yet in 1889 Sol Miller returned to the matter and placed Lane squarely at the root of the farce. He alleged that Lane had indeed wanted an early election and only backed out when he saw that the new legislature contained more enemies than friends. Miller ignored the 1879 account that named Pomeroy as the architect of the plan and Carney as his dupe, even though Miller had been the first to publish the story. Miller, like so many of the men who despised Lane, would never allow evidence to get in the way of his hatred, even after twenty-five years had passed.

At the time, though, Carney's supporters thought the special election was a good idea. The *Council Grove Press* endorsed it on February 8, and the following week one of the area's legislators exulted over his vote, claiming that Lane was "played out." On February 25 the *Freedom's Champion* in Atchison advised that bells be tolled to celebrate the political death of "Jeems Henry." The *Times* in Leavenworth praised the election, expressing the hope that it would take away Lane's "cunning" and therefore leave him "helpless as a rotten tree."

If anyone other than Carney was exultant at Lane's defeat, it was Sol Miller in White Cloud. In the February 18 issue of the *Chief* he wrote that Lane's friends had deserted him. In the following week's issue he accused Lane's political allies of being engaged in fraud. The next week he reprinted a piece from the *State Journal* in Lawrence that alleged Carney was the honest man and Lane the fraud. But two weeks after that, on March 17, Miller's tone changed slightly. He published a piece claiming that almost every newspaper decrying the election was a Lane organ; however, he began that piece with the statement, "That there are many persons in the State who are honestly opposed to the Senatorial Election, we have no doubt; and their opinions are entitled to respect."

This remark may have reflected the fact that not everyone who opposed Lane supported the actions of Carney and his allies. A letter printed in the February 13 issue of the *Osage Chronicle* of Burlingame came from a Carney supporter who was now "antagonistic" toward him for usurping the voting rights of the people. The *Olathe Mirror* of February 20 was ambivalent about the legality of the effort. The *Emporia News,* in early 1864 no Lane friend, expressed concern that the election would "excite the people and make politics boisterous and bitter."

An author known only as the "Spectator" wrote to the *Nemaha Courier* in Seneca that the vote was "a verdict against Jim Lane." In the issue in which the letter appeared, that of February 13, the newspaper itself said it was opposed to any election for senator "until the proper time arrives." A week later the newspaper asked of Carney's friends, "Have these self-constituted guardians of the people contemplated the amount of feeling, earnest and bitter, which might better have remained latent, that will necessarily be developed by this premature action of theirs?"

Sure enough, Lane's allies howled bitterly at the election. In the February 4 issue of the *Daily Tribune,* John Speer accused Carney of trying to create a "Carney party." Three days later he wrote, "Let the schemers and swindlers work. A day of reckoning will come."

On February 7 the *Conservative* began to speak of the "Carney Fraud" and four days later reported of a meeting in the city that passed resolutions calling the election "an infamous fraud."

Public opinion rapidly turned against the governor. Within days "indignation meetings" were being held around Kansas, as noted in the *Nemaha Courier* and elsewhere. Although there was an effort to rally support for Carney in Manhattan in mid-March, the damage was done. By the end of April, Carney told a gathering in Topeka that he had "resigned" as senator. Around that same time the *Emporia News* noted that Carney and his allies were now on the "outs."

> The great object of the Senatorial election last winter was to kill off or rebuke Lane. And yet that very thing has done more to strengthen Lane than anything that ever took place in this State. We say this as one who has always desired and worked for that gentleman's overthrow, politically. The leaders in the Carney movement committed a great political blunder, and now they see it and acknowledge it. . . .
>
> Well, they richly deserved their fate, and they must blame nobody but themselves. The infatuated leaders in the Carney election did the work. They could not possibly have done better service for Lane. Many that had worked always with the anti-Lane party, hard and honestly, advised against them and warned them, but in vain. Their grasping after the political power of the State overrode their judgment, and now they find themselves flat on their backs.

With Governor Carney temporarily chastised, the man who seems to have instigated the mess was weakened a short time later. Sen. Samuel Pomeroy blundered into an effort to depose President Lincoln as the nominee of the Republican Party. Pomeroy was to pay dearly for the error.

As recounted by William Zornow in 1951, in December 1863 a meeting was held in Washington to support Salmon Chase, the secretary of the Treasury, in his bid for the Republican nomination for president. Chase had spent the year allying himself with the Radical Republicans in Congress, and in December the Chase campaign got underway.

A national committee was assembled to work for Chase's nomination, and Senator Pomeroy became its chairman. Pomeroy seems to have had few radical sentiments of his own, which should have kept him away from Chase, but Zornow speculated that his motivation was resentment at the Lincoln-Lane relationship. Lane continued to get the patronage, Pomeroy did not, and he might have believed that a change at the White House would turn this around.

Pomeroy quickly went to work promoting the Chase candidacy. In late January 1864 he and his committee put out an anonymous pamphlet called *The Next Presidential Election*. It insisted that Lincoln should not be reelected in the fall, hinted that the democracy would be destroyed if he was, and claimed that Lincoln was not "an advanced thinker" who understood "the spirit of the age."

Unfortunately for Chase and Pomeroy, the pamphlet backfired and brought them considerable criticism. However, the Chase faction failed to realize this and days later released what became known as the "Pomeroy Circular." (Although this second document had his signature, Pomeroy is not thought to have been the actual author.) It too denounced Lincoln, but it also heaped praise on Secretary Chase.

Like the earlier paper, the circular had the effect of harming Chase's effort and boosting Lincoln's standing. By the end of February, Chase even had to write to Lincoln claiming ignorance of the circular and offering to resign. The state legislature in Chase's home state of Ohio threw its support to Lincoln. Radical Republicans distanced themselves from both documents. Pomeroy retained his seat, but any relationship he had with the president was gone forever.

Jim Lane, too, had at first been reluctant to support Lincoln's bid for a second term. As noted by W. O. Stoddard in 1884, Lane sympathized with those from Kansas, as well from Missouri and Nebraska, who regarded Lincoln as a "selfish tyrant" who did not take their interests into account and who ruled them "through ignorant and merciless military 'satraps.'" Such sentiments may have been a holdover from the unpopular administration of Gen. John Schofield.

Lincoln knew that Lane would be crucial in getting votes for him, and not just in the Western theater. Perhaps with this in mind, Lincoln put Samuel Curtis, who had been district commander before Schofield, back in charge of the Union military effort in Missouri and Kansas in January 1864. Curtis was still popular in the region, especially with the radicals and Lane was able to claim influence in the decision. To express their pleasure, and possibly with a nod from Lane, the Kansas legislature became one of the first state legislatures to pass a resolution endorsing Lincoln's renomination.

Following this political maneuvering came a Grand Council meeting of the Union League of America. The Union League was formed in 1862 as a loyal secret society to support the Union war effort and to combat secret groups of rebel sympathizers in the Northern states. At the council meeting in early 1864, as W. O. Stoddard put it, "hot-headed and free-tongued representatives of every faction of the Republican party inimical to Mr. Lincoln" showed up and spoke.

After several had vented their anger against the president, the grand corresponding secretary spoke. He was "too red-hot angry to speak well," but all the same he was able to demonstrate that the men complaining about Lincoln's actions were for the most part complaining about him following their advice. Apparently humiliated and humbled by this "stunning defense," the dissenters backed down and the "tide turned as if by magic." The Grand Council adopted a resolution of support for Lincoln and his administration.

Among those whose opinions were turned at that meeting was Jim Lane. According to Stoddard, he walked up to the secretary, held out his hand, and said, "You've made at least one convert. I'll stand by Old Abe through thick and thin, after this."

Lane took up Lincoln's banner in the Senate on February 16, 1864, when a bill came up for colonizing Texas with freed slaves. Early in the war, Lane said, he had urged "the necessity of an emancipation proclamation" and "the arming of the blacks." He admitted,

> [H]ad either of these measures been adopted at that date, a counter revolution would have been inaugurated in the house of our own friends. . . . In my opinion, when the history of this Administration comes to be written, the proudest page therein will be the record of the fact that Mr. Lincoln had the self-possession,

the wisdom, and sagacity to restrain himself and his friends from issuing the emancipation proclamations and arming the blacks until public sentiment was well nigh ripe to sustain him.

Lane's remarks were directed at those Republicans, known as Radical Republicans, who thought Lincoln was not harsh enough with the Confederacy. They had wanted the end of slavery as a war aim from the beginning and were still unhappy that Lincoln had taken as long as he had to issue the Emancipation Proclamation. They were also splitting with the president over the policy of Reconstruction, the readmission of rebel states into the Union. Lincoln wanted to press Reconstruction while the war was going on to, as James McPherson phrased it in his Civil War history, "convert lukewarm Confederates into unionists as a means of winning the war." The Radicals preferred to postpone any rebuilding efforts until the war ended, but if it was to occur, then they wanted harsh terms for it.

Because of his connections on both sides of this split, Lane was an ideal advocate for Lincoln's campaign for a second term. He had the radical credentials. He had been advocating emancipation since 1861. He had even taken to the battlefield to fight against slavery. Lincoln's supporters could argue that if the Jayhawker was a Lincoln man, then other radicals ought to get behind the president as well.

Lane appeared at the Cooper Institute in New York on March 30 to give a speech entitled "The People's Choice." Lane told his audience, mainly members of the Union Lincoln Campaign Club, he was there to "aid you in coming to a correct conclusion in the exercise of the right of suffrage." To that end he began by telling them that in April 1861, while "the hears of men were failing them and perplexity overspread the land," only "one man" was "cool and collected in the midst of universal excitement": Abraham Lincoln.

He continued, saying that every "reasonable man" would admit that a change in the office of president could change war policy and therefore undermine the war effort. But why should the occupant of the president's office be changed, he questioned. Lincoln had overcome losing the "ripe experience of the South" and was now "able to hold such a steady helm" in the middle of the storm raging throughout the nation. Those causing the disruption in the nation, Confederate "traitors," ought to be "compelled" to submit to the man they voted against. In addition, the nation's foreign relations had "never been managed so successfully."

After making these points Lane went to the heart of the argument some within the Republican Party were making against Lincoln's renomination. "The principal pretext" that men such as Chase and Pomeroy were using was that the president did "not come up to their standard of radicalism." To that, Lane demanded "special attention" be placed on the Emancipation Proclamation, and to those who said it ought to have been issued earlier than it was, he said that such talk "betrays the ignorance of the situation and the danger that would have resulted from the premature issue of those papers."

"We must not flatter ourselves that the battle is to be won without unity of action," Lane said, "for our enemies are active and united on the general ground of opposition, whatever else may be their differences. It is their policy to disparage our strong men, to underrate the noble deeds of our political friends, and to overrate the qualities of their own." Therefore it was only loyal for Republicans to fall in behind the man at the center of rebel criticism, President Lincoln.

Lane told his audience that Lincoln had the full support of the soldiers in the field, because Lincoln had made their needs his "first care." The army had good generals such as Grant in command, and political support for them should not be wanting in "the hour of the country's need." The nation had to triumph in order to beat back imperialism and monarchism, and the best man for the job of leading the nation was Lincoln, "to assume a bold and decided stand for the great principles of civil and religious liberty."

Despite Lane's impassioned speeches on the president's behalf, once the Chase candidacy failed, some Radicals threw their support to a third-party rival, John C. Frémont. Nevertheless, by the time Frémont's party met in Cleveland on May 31, most Republicans had decided to back Lincoln. It did not help Frémont that the Democrats involved themselves in his election bid and tried to use it to their ends while Frémont went along seemingly unaware that he was being used. His movement quickly broke down and most Radicals denounced him and got behind Lincoln.

Lane was among the many men who met with Lincoln in the days leading up to the Union League meeting and the Republican convention in Baltimore, set for June 1864. W. O. Stoddard wrote that the Lane-Lincoln meeting "was somewhat protracted," but no one knows what was said. Considering that Lane was set to speak at both gatherings, he may have allowed Lincoln to review his planned remarks or obtained suggestions from the president about what he should say at the convention.

Jim Lane went before the National Grand Council of the Union League of America on June 7, 1864. During a stormy session Lane asked to be recognized by the chair. Once he was, wrote Stoddard, "he stood in silence for a moment, until he had deliberately turned around and looked all over the room." He had captured his audience, and then he addressed them.

> For a man to produce pain in another man by pressing upon a wounded spot requires no great degree of strength, and he who presses is not entitled to any emotion of triumph at the agony expressed by the sufferer. Neither skill nor wisdom has been exercised in the barbaric process. For a man, an orator, to produce an effect upon sore and weary hearts, gangrened with many hurts, worn out with many sacrifices, sick with long delays, broken with bitter disappointments; so stirring them up, even to passion and to folly, demands no high degree of oratorical ability. It is an easy tiling to do, as we have seen this evening. Almost anybody can do it.
>
> For a man to take such a crowd as this now is, so sore and sick at heart and now so stung and aroused to passionate folly; now so infused with a delusive hope for the future as well as with false and unjust thoughts concerning the past; for a man to address himself to such an assembly and turn the tide of its passion and its excitement in the opposite direction; that were a task worthy of the highest, greatest effort of human oratory. I am no orator at all, but to precisely that task have I now set myself, with absolute certainty of success. All that is needful is that the truth should be set forth plainly, now that the false has done its worst.

His audacity won over his listeners. His recounting of Lincoln's deeds while president turned them. As he changed their minds, he posed a question to the assembly.

> I am speaking individually to each man here. Do you, sir, know, in this broad land, and can you name to me, one man whom you could or would trust, before God, that he would have done better in this matter than Abraham Lincoln has done, and to whom you would be more willing to intrust the unforeseen emergency or peril which is next to come? That unforeseen peril, that perplexing emergency, that step in the dark, is right before us, and we are here to decide by whom it shall be made for the nation. Name your other man!

Lane wound down to a stirring conclusion:

> We shall come together to be watched, in breathless listening, by all this country—by all the civilized world—and if we shall seem to waver as to our set purpose, we destroy hope; and if we permit private feeling, as tonight, to break forth into discussion, we discuss defeat; and if we nominate any other man than Abraham Lincoln we nominate ruin! Gentlemen of the Grand Council of the Union League, I have done.

Stoddard believed that this address helped to cement support for Lincoln when the Republican Party convention met the next day, June 8. What part Lane played in the convention itself seems murky. None of the newspapers in Kansas allied with Lane carried accounts of his deeds there. In the *New York Times'* report of the session, Lane is only recorded as having taken part in two debates on the admission of convention delegates.

In contrast to the inactive role the newspaper reports imply, Leverett Spring stated in his article on Lane's career that it was Lane who aided in the selection of Lincoln's running mate, Tennessee politician and Unionist Andrew Johnson. Spring wrote, "The question, who shall be the candidate for Vice-President," had been "anxiously debated in Republican circles." Lincoln was believed to be for "the selection of a southern Unionist," namely Johnson. He added that not only did Lane claim "to have secured the nomination" for Johnson but that he also "urged him on the convention at Baltimore."

Lane's work at Baltimore was almost immediately overshadowed by stories circulating that a few weeks earlier he had been attacked by a woman on the streets of Washington. Lane gave differing versions of the event. He said to some that the woman was a political fanatic of some sort. To others he hinted that she was a spurned lover. While speaking in Manhattan, Kansas, in mid-August, Lane claimed that the woman was "perhaps 55 or 60 years old" and a frequent visitor to the White House. On the day in question she was forced to leave and was later told that Lane had been "instrumental" in removing her. While Lane was on his way to his Washington residence she met up with him and "used her tongue freely upon Mr. Lincoln, Mr. Stanton and upon myself. I bowed to her and walked off."

John Speer, in the June 23 issue of the *Weekly Tribune*, noted that the initial accounts of the incident also reflected some confusion. He took note of two pieces in a newspaper in Springfield, Illinois. The first claimed that Lane had been "assaulted" by "a young woman whom he had seduced." The second, written by the same correspondent, amended the first with the facts that the "'young woman' [was] fifty-two years old and subject to fits of insanity." Speer wrote that the newspapers in Kansas opposed to Lane were trumpeting the original story as true. "Will those journals who published the first report, which is now proved a false story, publish this second report, proving the first to be a base slander upon our Senator?" he wondered.

Apparently not, for the most bizarre account of this event appeared in the *State Journal* of Lawrence on September 29. It claimed that the attack was for Lane's "lecherous practices." This allowed the newspaper to recall other similar incidents that involved Lane and women. One was an affair with a "Mrs. Lindsay" that allegedly resulted in the attempted duel at the Topeka Convention of 1855. Another was with a "Mrs. Buffum" who "demanded pay[ment] for her services," and when the impoverished Lane failed to provide money, she challenged him to a duel and chased him "through the streets with a pistol." The *Journal* even claimed that Lane had a room in Washington "for purposes of assignation." Of course these charges came with little proof, and the *Journal* admitted that the incidents involving the first two women had happened early in Lane's residence in Kansas.

What is not in dispute is that on his return to Kansas from Baltimore, Lane stumped for Lincoln. On July 25, Lane gave a strong pro-Lincoln speech in St. Louis in which he denounced Frémont and suggested that the Democratic nominee for president be Jefferson Davis. Late in September he appeared in Indiana in support of the president, causing the Democratic newspaper in Lawrenceburg to shrilly call him a "notorious character," "the murderer of Jenkins," and the friend of John Brown, the "abolitionist, traitor, nigger stealer and horse thief."

Although Jim Lane did impressive work for Lincoln, and in spite of the mistakes Carney and Pomeroy had made, in Kansas during the summer of 1864 his reputation was once again in decline. Allegations of corruption against him and his favored general, Blunt, had caught up with him. The charges against Blunt seemed to have more substance, for if not based on actual evidence, the fact that they had been circulating for nearly a year gave them weight. The accusations would prove damaging to both the general and the senator.

The charge first surfaced with the hated John Schofield. In July 1863 he wrote to the assistant adjutant general of the army stating that he had received "from various sources" "reports of fraud, corruption, and maladministration in the Department and District of Kansas." These reports were still "circumstantial" and Schofield said he was unable "to frame specific charges against particular individuals." He asked for "a court of inquiry" to investigate the matter.

An inspection committee was sent to the region. After the war Blunt claimed that this "smelling committee" produced and signed a report previously agreed upon at a meeting with Schofield that "was not only false in every particular, but infamous in its character." He said that they had refused to meet him at Fort Smith, "where I was lying, confined to my bed by sickness." He added, with little or no proof, that the committee's "talent for drinking whisky was remarkable."

By October 1, 1863, Schofield felt that he had to remove Blunt from command. Unfortunately for Schofield, just days later Blunt and his escort were ambushed at Baxter Springs. Any sympathy Blunt might have garnered as a result of this event started to erode by the next month. On November 2, Col. William Weer reported to Schofield, "Blunt has gone to Fort Smith with a large

Government train, 200 wagons, loaded with contraband of war . . . The goods are to be sold to rebels." On November 24 a Kansas officer reported that another suspicious wagon train was heading to Fort Scott. "The teams were used in bringing sutlers' goods to this place; they are now loaded with cotton. . . . From what I can learn," he wrote, "a portion of the same has been purchased at a very small price, and the balance captured; and, from all appearances, I should think some one high in military rank was engaged in the operation."

None of these complaints resulted in Blunt's ouster, which may have emboldened him, for he quickly took advantage of a technicality. While the town of Fort Smith was part of the Department of Arkansas, the actual fort at Fort Smith was part of Samuel Curtis's department. Curtis informed his superiors that this seemed odd and asked for a clarification of the situation.

In early April 1864 reports went to Gen. Henry Halleck, still in overall command of the Union army, that Blunt was interfering in supply trains going through Fort Smith. Blunt was so out of line that the quartermaster could do nothing without Blunt's order, "not even to the issuing of a pair of pants." The men from the Department of Arkansas, said their commanders, "will be compelled to report to General Blunt or starve."

On April 17, Blunt was ordered to report to Fort Leavenworth for new orders. He was later transferred to Fort Larned; his humiliating mandate was to chase after the Plains Indian tribes. Blunt was out of the war, and if it was not due to corruption, his defenders would have been hard pressed to explain why, especially since it was Curtis, and not Schofield, who had exiled him.

Those opposed to Lane eagerly picked up on the charges against Blunt, including Sol Miller at the *Chief*. On September 8 he printed two diatribes against military corruption. In the first, titled "Discontent and Its Cause," Miller alleged that the reelection of Abraham Lincoln was in doubt in part because of the rampant corruption in frontier military affairs. Miller wrote flatly, "The great head of this fraud and corruption is James H. Lane." He even compared the officeholders Lane had installed with King George III's "swarms of officers" who harassed the thirteen colonies.

The second piece was called "On It." In that Miller listed some of the prominent figures whom he believed were on the take. Blunt was first of these, of course; he had "amassed a fortune of $500,000." Lane was "on it" as well, with a "corruption fund of $100,000" for his reelection. Miller also claimed that two generals who had opposed Blunt's actions were, if not "on it," then aware of what was going on and tolerating it. This suggests that either the generals had changed their characters in six months or that Miller was not as well informed as he claimed.

Lloyd Lewis, speaking about Lane in the 1930s, thought little of such allegations. "His whole life belies the charge of bribery, for he never cared for money," Lewis said. "Jim Lane would rather bind fifty farmers in the spell of his oratory than win a fat fee arguing a case before twelve jurymen."

Yet it could not have helped Jim Lane that national events were also turning out less than ideally for those who supported President Lincoln. Union military efforts appeared to be floundering on several fronts. The Democrats were about to nominate the still-popular George McClellan as their presidential candidate. It would have been surprising that, as these events damaged Lincoln's reelection chances, they would not have also had an impact on Lane's own prospects.

Problems on various battlefields were the most trouble to Lincoln and his supporters. In the spring Ulysses Grant had been appointed lieutenant general and general in chief. He came east to supervise Gen. George Meade and the Army of the Potomac in their operations against Lee and the Army of Northern Virginia. Grant left Sherman in the west to conduct a campaign to capture Atlanta and split the Confederacy. Other Union generals were to lead their own campaigns to tie up Confederate armies in less important theaters. As President Lincoln said, "Those not skinning can hold a leg."

But, as James McPherson noted, "the leg-holders bungled their jobs." As for Meade and the Army of the Potomac, they entered a series of bloody battles that seemed to accomplish little but cause Union casualties. In the Shenandoah Valley, David Hunter, the man Lane had feuded with over the Texas expedition in early 1862, came to grief against Confederates there. Sherman achieved more success in his campaign to take Atlanta, but he and the

Confederate commander, Joseph Johnston, avoided large battles in favor of maneuvers. By July he was on the outskirts of Atlanta. However, without battles that made for good newspaper stories, a public perception arose that Sherman was not having much success.

It was under the pressure of national and state events that the Republicans of Kansas met in Topeka on September 8 to agree on a slate of candidates. The nominee for governor was Col. Samuel Crawford. He had been in the army since 1861, rising steadily and most recently having commanded one of the black regiments Lane had raised. Crawford in his autobiography said he was reluctant to run for office, that he "preferred the army," but decided to accept the nomination.

The nominee for Kansas congressman was Sidney Clarke, much to the chagrin of Lane. According to an 1887 story in an Emporia newspaper, Lane had wanted A. C. Wilder to be Kansas's sole representative to Congress. Though Lane was accused in some circles of having betrayed Wilder in favor of Clarke, Lane had been convinced that Clarke's nomination would reflect badly on his chances at reelection. In the long run Clarke overcame Lane's opposition and would be a loyal follower, but at the time it was another black mark against Lane.

Five days after Clarke's nomination, two opposing conventions were held in Topeka. One was for the Republicans who were against Lane. The other, according to Samuel Crawford, consisted of "mugwump Democrats." Initially the anti-Lane Republicans threw their support behind Lincoln, but then they met with the Democrats to nominate a state ticket. Their choice for governor was Solon Thacher (with John J. Ingalls as lieutenant governor) and for congressman, A. L. Lee from Doniphan County.

According to John Speer, Jim Lane recognized that the Republican ticket aligned with him was weak. Although he did not attend the state convention, "all the mistakes of nominations were laid" at Lane's feet. Lane thought the nominations were "very unfortunate" and Speer admitted that "the opposition had selected a strong ticket."

Naturally enough, the state's newspapers were split along the same old lines. Pro-Lane papers like the *Conservative* of September

16 told their readers, "Decide whether you wish to vote for men who made a bargain and sold themselves to Copperheads." The day before, the *State Journal* in Lawrence had predicted defeat for Abraham Lincoln, and on September 17 the *Times* in Leavenworth claimed that Lane's "sinking fortunes" might bring down the president.

As the month of September came to a close Jim Lane appeared to be dead in the water. Republicans in Kansas were too divided, the criticism of Lane too loud, and Union prospects too uncertain for him to imagine that his days as the king of Kansas politics would last past the fall. But, as the old saying goes, it's always darkest before the dawn.

Back on January 16, 1864, Samuel Curtis had returned to take command of the Department of Kansas. A few weeks later he had a new superior, when William Rosecrans was put in charge of the Department of the Missouri. Joining them two months later was Alfred Pleasonton, who had led the Army of the Potomac's Cavalry Corps. These three men, along with a fourth, would end up part of a group of officers who were given the chance to rescue the failing political fortunes of Jim Lane.

That fourth man was the old Confederate war-horse on the frontier, Sterling Price. Throughout the summer of 1864, Price raised an army in southern Arkansas to carry out a campaign to retake Missouri, the dream he had held onto since being ousted from his home state in early 1862. When Price started his latest campaign on September 1, he had between twelve thousand and fifteen thousand men. It was late in the month, September 27, before Rosecrans knew Price was on the move. Price's movements were only revealed when he ran into his first major Union force, about one thousand men under Thomas Ewing, Jr., at Pilot Knob. Although outnumbered Ewing had heavy artillery, and he inflicted serious casualties on the Confederates. Price decided a few days later to change his destination from St. Louis to Jefferson City. His men attacked the Missouri capital but failed to take it. When Union armies in the state began converging on his force, Price decided to march on Kansas City.

Jim Lane was in St. Louis at the beginning of October, but as

Gen. Sterling Price tried in the fall of 1864 to retake his home state of Missouri for the Confederacy. He hoped his campaign would upset the chances of Lincoln's reelection. Instead his effort allowed Lane to redeem his sinking reputation. *Image courtesy the Kansas State Historical Society.*

soon as news broke of the battle to the south he returned to Kansas. Lane consulted with General Curtis about the situation. He offered his services, and on October 10, Curtis accepted, assigning him to the post of volunteer aide-de-camp. On that same day General Blunt returned from exile and became commander of the District of Southern Kansas and a division commander in Curtis's army. For the second time in their careers, Lane and Blunt would serve together in the Union army.

Blunt later noted that Curtis spent a week arguing with Carney about calling out the militia of Kansas to deal with Price's army. Carney had refused on the belief that Curtis was acting on Lane's behalf "for political purposes." For days Carney declared "that there was no enemy in Missouri" and "that Kansas was not in danger." Blunt wrote after the war that he and Lane went so far as to ask Curtis to issue the proclamation calling out the militia himself.

On October 9, Charles Robinson, serving on Carney's military staff, wrote to his wife that the "rebels are in [Missouri] in earnest & coming this way." Lane's other political enemies were less certain of the situation. On October 6, Sol Miller wrote in the *Chief* that Curtis had "entered into a conspiracy with Lane" to call out the militia so they would be absent on election day. Then, just a week later, Miller noted reports that Price's men were near Lexington, Missouri, and that no one was sure if he would head south or west. Generally speaking, most of the anti-Lane newspapers picked up on the notion that there was no danger and the call-up was to interfere with the election to Lane's benefit.

This discord finally culminated in a meeting in Shawnee on October 17 during which an effigy of Lane was burned. The *Conservative* wondered on October 21, "Is this the way that this pro-slavery faction are going to paralyze our military strength?" A few weeks later the *Emporia News* called the event "a bacchanalian spree" and asked, "Who is the patriot and soldier? The men who hung Lane in effigy or the man who marched to the front and [did] his duty as a soldier?"

Jim Lane arrived at Curtis's headquarters at Olathe on October 10, and from then until October 14, Lane was a member of Curtis's staff, helping the general position his men. Because of the militia situation, Curtis decided to keep his forces in a defensive position along the Big Blue River, between Kansas City and Independence. Information on Price's movements was still not coming in, so Blunt asked Curtis for permission to undertake a reconnaissance. Curtis granted Blunt permission, and late on October 16, the general headed east. Lane was ordered to accompany Blunt as a member of his staff.

Blunt learned from citizens and irregular militia that the rebels had taken Sedalia. A foray by some of Blunt's men to Warrensburg brought intelligence that Price was near Waverly and that soldiers under Rosecrans were in pursuit of his army. Blunt asked Curtis for reinforcements with the hope that he would be able to link up with some of Rosecrans' men and take the overall Union command against Price. He occupied Lexington on October 18 in anticipation of such an assault, but because Carney and others were making "much trouble with the militia," Curtis told Blunt that he could not send him reinforcements.

Having sent out a reconnaissance force from Lexington, Blunt decided to stage a brief stand to gauge "the enemy's strength and intentions." Engaging the enemy along the route from Lexington, Blunt's men kept up a fighting withdrawal until nightfall. Lane wrote in his official report that Blunt was personally "under fire" during the engagement, "inspiring" his men by example. His men stopped the following morning at the Little Blue River, nine miles east of Independence.

There was a bridge over the river at this point. Blunt's first thought was to resist Price here with all the men he had, but as Curtis wanted Blunt to leave only "two or three squadrons" of cavalry there, Blunt decided to compromise. He left Col. Thomas Moonlight and the Eleventh Kansas there with four cannons.

When the rebel troops arrived, Moonlight's men kept up a stubborn resistance. Though Blunt argued to Curtis that leaving such a small group of soldiers to defend the position was a mistake, Moonlight's men put up enough of a fight to convince Curtis otherwise. What was supposed to be a minor holding action turned into the Battle of the Little Blue, lasting most of October 21. During the battle, Blunt returned and brought fresh troops, including Jim Lane. According to Richard Hinton, another member of

Blunt's staff, Lane at one point during the battle even picked up a carbine and joined a line of skirmishers. The Union troops held back Price's men until late in the day, when most of the Confederate army came up. At that point the Union soldiers fell back to the Big Blue River, where the rest of the Union force was deployed.

On the morning of October 22, Price began to move against the Union position along the Big Blue. The Confederates tried to cross the river at Byram's Ford, but to no initial success. However, other attacks enabled them to flank the Union line. With their line in trouble, the Union troops pulled back to positions around Westport. There was some good news during that day: Gen. Alfred Pleasanton, leading the advance units of Rosecrans' army, had reached the Confederate rear.

The following day, October 23, was the Battle of Westport. Curtis's men attacked the Confederates along Brush Creek, while Pleasonton's men hit the Confederate right and rear. Price's lines broke under the pressure, and soon his men were in a confused retreat from the Kansas City area. The separate commands of Curtis and Pleasonton linked up at Little Santa Fe that night.

Lane was present when Curtis, Blunt, and Pleasonton met that night in a local farmhouse. Lane wrote in his official report that Pleasonton wanted to follow Price along a route leading toward Harrisonville, Missouri. Curtis preferred a more direct pursuit of the Confederates. The generals agreed on Curtis's plan, and preparations were made to continue after Price the following day.

Union forces attacked the rebels at Mine Creek in Kansas on October 25, smashing Price's rear and capturing one of his subordinate commanders, Gen. John Marmaduke. Blunt kept a small part of Curtis's army close on Price's heels as Price took his army out of Kansas and through Missouri on his way to Texas. Blunt's men made contact with the rebels at Newtonia, Missouri, on October 28. Though outnumbered, Blunt attacked anyway. At one point his men were almost out of ammunition and in danger of losing the battle. At about that time fresh troops arrived to push the Confederates farther back.

Then Rosecrans, apparently misinformed as to the situation in the field, ordered Curtis to break off the pursuit of the

Confederates. Curtis appealed to General Grant that this order contradicted standing orders. Grant agreed and ordered Curtis to resume the chase. Time had been lost and the remnants of Price's army managed to escape ultimate destruction.

All the principles wrote reports of the Price campaign, including Jim Lane. He largely stuck to the facts of the campaign as he knew them. He ended his official report as a politician might, by "expressing the thanks of the people of Kansas for the gallant defense made of our State."

> Devastation, ruin, and rapine threatened our border towns; an insolent and hopeful foe had placed himself, almost without interruption, within a day's march of our chief city; his avowed purpose was to sack and burn wherever he touched our soil. He was met, checked, beaten back, and finally put to rout by the skill and energy of the commanding general, and the indomitable, persistent, and dogged fighting of volunteers and militia. It would be impossible to mention particular instances of meritorious conduct, where all did so well, without seeming injustice to some, and I therefore reluctantly refrain from doing so. The States of the great Northwest, whose troops participated in this brief but important campaign, have added another to the long list of brilliant achievements won by them during the war. To the militia of my own State, who sprang to arms with the alacrity of other days, at the approach of the foe, I will be permitted to tender special thanks. Going out without the hope of fee or reward, some have fallen, others have been maimed for life, while all have testified their devotion to the common cause, and their love for our gallant young State; to one and all of these let us be ever grateful.

What is remarkable about that statement, and about Lane's report overall, is the omission of any reference to the militia mess of early October. The most likely reason Lane said nothing about it was that by saying nothing he made himself seem like a statesman. He left criticism to friendly newspaper editors.

In the end the "insolent and hopeful foe" had been beaten once and for all. Price's goal of retaking Missouri for the Confederacy was probably unrealistic from the start. Even with his army swelled by guerillas, Price lacked the manpower to hold much territory.

Any hopes he might have had of diverting Union strength away from other theaters was dashed as well. It turned out that there were enough Union forces in the region to deal with Price's army and to deal with it handily. Indeed, the chief beneficiary of Price's failed campaign was not the Confederate government, rebel armies to the east, or Peace Democrats in the North, but Jim Lane, who had from the start of Price's invasion vocally advocated the use of the militia in stopping the Confederate advance. Thanks to Price, and with assistance from Thomas Carney, Lane was able to recover all that he had lost by the fall of 1864 and then some.

On October 27 the *Conservative*, under the heading "Lost," offered a "liberal reward" for a copy of a proclamation Carney had written the previous week. In the proclamation Carney had decried the battles just fought as "humbugs" and "Jim Lane Frauds." "The said document can be of no use to any but the author," the *Conservative* said, but since it was evidence of Carney's "bravery, loyalty, and disinterestedness," it was no doubt worth the price to obtain it. The piece would not be the last to expose Carney's behavior during the crisis.

In the November 3 issue of the *Daily Tribune*, John Speer asked his readers, "Does any man doubt, that without the call for the militia, Kansas would have been literally burnt over?" In that same issue he claimed that the opposition to Lane supported only "any other man" against him, and that they "would rather have some Barrabas who is a thief and a robber."

When the *Times* printed an alleged comment from General Pleasonton that if "the people of Kansas think they are indebted to me," they should "beat Jim Lane," the *Fort Scott Monitor* produced an actual letter from the general to the *Conservative* expressing that he had "never intimated any preference" for or against Lane. This was followed by a letter from Pleasonton to Lane in which he thanked Lane "for the opportune assistance you frequently rendered me." The story concluded by wondering if Kansans would "endorse" the "slanders" printed in pro-Carney newspapers and answered, "We think not."

And they did not. Samuel Crawford carried twenty-eight of the thirty-five counties Kansas had at the time. In the state legislature, Lane's candidates took more than enough seats to assure him reelection to the Senate. Jim Lane had pulled off an amazing turn-around in the span of about a month.

It is interesting to note what Lane's critics later wrote about what happened during the Price campaign. Leverett Spring, for example, said nothing about Carney's reluctance to call out the militia, the unflattering rally against Lane and Blunt, and Lane's service during the emergency. Spring did write that the Kansas forces were "gallant" but "undisciplined," but he gave no explanation as to why they lacked discipline. He claimed that the actions at Lexington, Little Blue, and Big Blue showed that the Kansans were unable to deal with Price, and that the success at Westport was far more due to Pleasanton's cavalry than to the Kansans' attacks. Yet in his article on Lane's political career he wrote that Lane's "energy, his enthusiasm and knowledge of the country appear to have contributed materially to the success of the operations."

Friends of Lane were not so circumspect. John Speer wrote in 1896 that in the summer of 1864, Lane was in a "melancholy mood" over his prospects. Once the emergency arose, however, Lane "dropped all political work" and took to his duties. Lane "saw his opportunity" and "made the most of it," and when it was all said and done, Speer wrote succinctly, "Lane's enemies elected him." He was reelected senator with eighty-two votes in his favor against "16 aimlessly scattering" and two "not voting."

Although the outcome of the Price campaign had a profound effect on Lane's standing in Kansas, good news from other military theaters may have also had an impact. First there was Sherman and Atlanta. In mid-July, Confederate president Jefferson Davis replaced Joseph Johnston with John Bell Hood. Hood tried attacking Sherman to keep him from taking Atlanta but only succeeded in losing men he could not afford to lose. During August, Sherman slowly encircled the city. Before he could be completely cut off, Hood retreated, and on September 2, Sherman's army captured Atlanta. A month earlier the Union navy captured Mobile, Alabama. Just over a month later, Philip Sheridan in the Shenandoah Valley turned a Confederate surprise attack at Cedar Creek into a rousing Union victory.

These events maintained the split in the Democratic Party

between War Democrats and Peace Democrats. The War Democrats favored continuing the Union military effort, but they disliked Lincoln's management of it. The Peace Democrats wanted the war halted and negotiations begun with the Confederates, even to the point of allowing slavery to continue to exist.

The two wings of the Democratic Party did come together to nominate George McClellan as their candidate for president. McClellan initially favored the Peace Democrats, but the fall of Atlanta forced him to reconsider. McClellan and the Democrats had, as James McPherson put it, the "taint of peace without victory." Though the Democrats tried to tarnish Lincoln and the Republicans with the evils of racial equality, with events going their way and their opponents in confusion, Lincoln and his party swept the election.

A year that had begun with his political future in doubt had ended with the Grim Chieftain the single most powerful man in Kansas. All that remained was for Jim Lane to decide how he would wield that power, and to what purpose.

XIV.

Triumph and Tragedy

Lane had made many promises to many men to secure his reelection to the Senate. Naturally some of these promises overlapped, but none so dramatically as the one a Missouri politician told of in a Topeka newspaper in 1888. Lane had promised, among other things, the post of marshal to some seventeen members of the Kansas legislature. Of course they all followed him to Washington demanding the post be given to them. "Lane was at his wits' ends for excuses," until he "determined on a radical course."

He gathered the applicants together one night. They probably knew each other and what Lane had promised them, but none knew why Lane had called them together. When all were present Lane spoke to the group. "I was in a tight place last winter and I promised each of you the marshalship for the district of Kansas," he admitted. He asserted boldly,

> What I did last winter, I did with the purest motives. I thought the state of Kansas needed me in the senate, and it was with that idea that I made those promises which I cannot now fulfill. If I have deceived you gentlemen, I believe that heaven will forgive me. But you, gentlemen, who should have voted for me from the purest and highest impulses—you were actuated only by sordid motives. You voted for me for a price and I do not think you are worthy in the sight of heaven of any recognition or consideration. . . . I renounce all of you, and in the interest of the state of Kansas I will select an entirely new man for the position that you all covet, and have him appointed marshal.

With that Lane dismissed the men for the night.

Railroad matters were not so easy for Lane to ignore. Back in 1862, Lane had put forward what the *Kansas State Record* called at that time a "Kansas Railroad Bill." The bill was to grant right of ways through federal land in Kansas to several railroads. One was the Leavenworth, Pawnee & Western. When Thomas Ewing, Jr., left that company to join the Union army, he turned control of it over to John C. Frémont. Frémont hired Samuel Hallett, a New York banker and railroad executive, to start construction. Frémont and Hallett changed the name of the road to the Union Pacific, Eastern Division, and construction began in 1863.

Hallett was a voluble man who wanted the railroad completed. He did not intend to waste time dickering with local officials. So when the leaders of Leavenworth could not come to any agreement with him over bonds, Hallett simply moved the road's starting point south to the sleepy village of Wyandotte. (In later years, when Wyandotte became Kansas City, Kansas, and it and Kansas City, Missouri, became railroad centers, this move would prove prescient.)

Hallett planned to bypass both Lawrence and Topeka so as to maintain as straight a route as possible. This would of course hurt both towns, and Jim Lane jumped to their defense. In 1864 he was able to assemble a petition asking that the two cities be reached, obtain the signatures of thirty-six U.S. senators, and receive Lincoln's endorsement for the petition. Hallett ignored the petition, then demanded that Lawrence vote the railroad three hundred thousand dollars in bonds. Lane responded by passing a bill in Congress authorizing the railroad to connect to the towns. Again Hallett refused to relocate the planned line.

Hallett and new company president, John Perry, then paid a visit to Lane in Washington. They told Lane, who was lying on his bed, and John Speer, who had been sent from Kansas to help Lane's lobbying effort, that they would not change their route until Lawrence voted for the bonds. Lane sat up, his eyes flashing with anger, and told the railroad men, "Before you get a dollar out of that burned and murdered town you will take up every stump and every old log you have buried in your grade to save money, and stone ballast every rod to Lawrence; and even then, when you get your first subsidies, let Jim Lane know!"

Speer confessed in 1896 that he was concerned about Lane's outburst and told the senator so. To that, Lane replied, "They will want to see me worse to-morrow than they did to-day." Sure enough, within a few days Hallett backed down. The railroad was built to connect both Lawrence and Topeka. Speer believed Lane alone deserved the credit for that outcome.

Jim Lane was more closely tied to another railroad, the Lawrence-based Leavenworth, Lawrence & Fort Gibson. The LL&FG became important to Lawrence because it was one of the projects that was supposed to make the city a regional center of commerce. The LL&FG was to run south to the Texas gulf coast and the port of Galveston.

Lane's first action to assist the LL&FG was to introduce a bill into Congress in December 1862 giving a land grant to the company. The bill was signed into law by President Lincoln on March 4, 1863. The following year Lane took a more active role in the management of the railroad. Then in June 1865, Lane's friends elected him president of the company.

Lane personally led a campaign to bring investment capital into the LL&FG to start construction. On September 12 the people of Lawrence and Douglas County voted overwhelmingly in favor of county bonds to support the project. Not long afterward, three of the four counties along the route, as well as two counties along a proposed branch line southwest to the Santa Fe Trail, had also voted for construction bonds. I. E. Quastler, who wrote about Lawrence's efforts to become a railroad center, believed that Lane's involvement was essential to these early successes of the LL&FG.

Though busy with his railroad pursuits, Lane found time during this period to aid one of his former foes from the territorial days. The buildings of the Shawnee Indian Mission, the former territorial capital, were in disrepair at the end of the Civil War, and the last superintendent, Thomas Johnson, was unsure what he would do with the mission he had grown to love in years of service to the tribe and the government. Lane used his influence to assist Johnson, a former proslavery man, in getting patents on three of the buildings. Johnson was murdered by outlaws on January 2, 1865, but his family kept the buildings as their home. They remained in the family for decades, until a preservation effort began after World War I. In 1927 the Kansas State Historical Society took control of the old mission buildings, and today they comprise the Shawnee Mission State Historic Site, adding to the accomplishments of Jim Lane.

On April 14, 1865, just days after Robert E. Lee had surrendered his army to Ulysses Grant, President Lincoln was shot by actor and Southern sympathizer John Wilkes Booth. Lincoln died early the following day. The nation's mood, so uplifted by Lee's surrender and the prospect of the end of the Civil War, was crushed by the assassination.

Jim Lane, too, was devastated by the blow. Several days later it was reported in the *Leavenworth Conservative* that he "was bowed down with the deepest grief when he first heard the loss" of Lincoln and "wept like a child."

> It is well known that the personal relations of [Lane and Lincoln] were of the most intimate, confidential character [the Conservative noted]. They were close, personal friends; and while representing somewhat different views as to the policy of treating rebels, each had the fullest confidence in, and the greatest respect for, the opinion of the other; and their intercourse was always marked by the greatest harmony and warmest friendship. The President at one time told us that while he was compelled to dissent from General Lane's radical views, he had the highest respect for them, and that circumstances had more than once compelled him to adopt and follow them.

Initially the nation rallied behind the new president, Andrew Johnson, as the last Confederate armies surrendered and the nation moved toward readmission of the former Confederate states. Before 1865 had ended, however, a split developed between Johnson, who tried to carry out a policy in line with the moderate views of Lincoln, and Republicans in Congress who wanted a harsher policy toward "traitors." For Jim Lane this presented a choice of political alliances: President Johnson or the Radical Republicans, as the congressional faction came to be known.

The choice required some consideration on his part. After all,

Lane was a populist; his appeal to public sentiment was what launched him into power and kept him there. But with the Civil War over and slavery dead as a political issue, it would have been hard for Lane to ascertain popular will. Perhaps because initial public support was behind the new president, Lane chose to ally himself with Johnson.

That choice makes sense for another reason. Lane's power base in the Senate was due to his control over federal patronage. It was his ability to reward supporters with federal jobs that made him friends and allowed him to keep them during the ups and downs of politics. What's more, patronage politics had been going on since his father's time. With no readily apparent popular sentiment for Lane to latch onto at the war's end, he fell back upon the other kind of politics he knew.

One sign of the conflict between the Radicals and Johnson appeared when Lane spoke in Leavenworth on January 5, 1866. The main theme of Lane's address was a pending bill in Congress that would give voting rights to black men. More generally Lane talked about Reconstruction, and to that end, Lane said, he was traveling through Kansas to "consult" with the public on Reconstruction policy. He presented resolutions to be voted on that supported Johnson's plans and told his audience that the president "has faithfully carried out the policy of his predecessor." He assured them that Johnson would not allow former rebels who would not now be loyal to the government to enter that government. He also said that the president supported laws that would protect the rights of the newly freed slaves.

But Johnson's support did not extend to a federal voting rights law, and Lane argued that it shouldn't. "States have rights subordinate to the constitution," Lane said, and among those was the right to determine who could and could not vote. "If Congress has the power to extend the right of suffrage to any class of people," it "may extend that right to all, and may withdraw or modify it at will," infringing on the rights of the individual states. Though he backed Johnson's stance to prevent federal protection of black suffrage, Lane obviously supported the ideal of equality among voters, for later he added, to the applause of the audience, "I laugh to scorn any man, especially any Kansas man, who would advocate the extension of suffrage to the colored man in the Southern States and deny it to him in his own State."

After Lane's speech one man struck a note of discord at the meeting. He said that the matter of Reconstruction had been referred to Congress by the president, and "the people were content" to leave it there. He added that he was "opposed to the manufacturing of public sentiment" to change this situation. The *Conservative* of January 7 reported that Daniel Anthony rose to agree, but he was followed by James Legate, who "in a masterly speech of ten minutes" beat back the opposition.

A few months later sentiment had changed drastically. On April 17 the *Conservative* accused Johnson of not fully carrying out Lincoln's Reconstruction policy. The trouble was over Johnson's veto of the suffrage bill, now known as the Civil Rights Act of 1866. A Lawrence meeting a few days earlier passed resolutions decrying the veto and Lane's vote against the bill. On the nineteenth, the *Conservative* reported that a meeting in Fort Scott had a similar outcome. The following day, April 20, a piece claimed that the majority of Kansas newspapers were siding with Congress and against the president.

Yet Lane eventually voted to sustain Johnson's veto of the bill. Lane ally J. H. Shimmons, writing in a Lawrence newspaper in 1891 of Lane's last year, said that Johnson believed the bill was too extreme in its grant of universal voting rights. Shimmons noted that radical politicians in Kansas and in Washington had at first assumed Lane was on their side, but when Lane's son James, Jr., told Shimmons that Lane's vote was up in the air, Shimmons became worried.

Shimmons wrote that he had been hesitant to advise Lane against voting to uphold Johnson's veto, but his conversation with the younger Lane changed his mind. He joined Charles Adams, John Speer, and Josiah Miller in sending Lane a telegram on April 5, 1866. "For God's sake do not vote to sustain the president's veto," it began. "If you do it will be the great mistake of your life and your political ruin."

Lane had already promised Andrew Johnson his support. Nevertheless, with telegram in hand Lane went to the White House the next day. Shimmons wrote that Lane "begged to be released from the promise." Johnson refused to release Lane, and the senator was compelled to vote to uphold Johnson's veto of the bill.

William Cutler provided another explanation for Lane's vote. He wrote in 1883 that Lane "thought he saw the popular tide drifting" toward Johnson's stance, "and with his accustomed alacrity he anticipated what he believed would prove the popular sentiment of the people. For once he was deceived."

Lane critic Leverett Spring in 1898 presented a surprisingly balanced view of Lane's vote. He called the bill "an extreme, ill-advised measure," and when an Ohio senator "assailed the President in the most violent language," Lane ended his connection with the Radicals. When Spring wondered if Lane had "made a mistake in his defense of President Johnson," he answered, "Certainly not unless we measure his conduct by the standards of a blind partisanship. The scheme of reconstruction which he advocated was preferable to the rough-shod programme of the radicals."

John Speer also wrote about this vote in his biography of Lane. He said that Lane had told him he'd acted as he had in part to try to "conciliate the President with the Republican Congress." That the work seemed to be failing was getting to Lane, and Speer said Lane had told an associate that perhaps he should go "to an asylum for the insane." John Shimmons, in his 1891 piece on Lane, wrote that he met Lane in June before the senator returned to Kansas. Lane told Shimmons that on the April day he'd talked to Johnson he had "suffered more mental torture" than on any other day of his life and "that he prayed to God that [Shimmons] would never see such a day."

In Kansas, Lane was attacked bitterly for his alliance with Johnson. On June 4 the *Leavenworth Daily Bulletin* pronounced that there was a "Lane-Johnson party" opposed to more loyal Radical Republicans. Five days later, when word came that Lane might be changing his support, the *Bulletin* accused him of "pretend[ing] to return to his old faith." On June 15 it opined of a "cool, deliberate plan" by Johnson to "assassinate the Republican Party" and charged Lane of being a coconspirator.

Lane's choice to support Johnson had consequences in

Washington as well. Leverett Spring wrote that his decision "gave offense to former friends," the Radical Republicans he had once been allied with. They promptly began to look into "discreditable rumors" about Lane, such as an accusation of corrupt practices associated with Indian contracts. A reporter threatened to publicize these charges, and this sent Lane into a depression, Spring claimed. Lane friend John Shimmons wrote that it was not one reporter but three who were trying to do in Lane: William A. Phillips of the *New York Tribune;* R. J. Hinton of Boston; and Henry Villard of Chicago.

Lane did put up a fight, as John Speer noted in 1896. Lane "denied utterly" the truth of the story. He even got George W. Dietzler to swear out an affidavit supporting his denial. At a meeting between Lane and Carney in Washington, Leverett Spring said the former governor told Lane the story was "nothing" and did not "amount to much."

> "Doesn't amount to much!" Lane repeated in a very excited and tragic manner [Spring wrote]. The next morning Carney returned and found Lane in a pitiable plight—half-clad, his hair erect and bristling, his small, sunken, snaky eyes burning like live coals, his "sinister face, plain to ugliness," figured over with desperation, and raving that two sunshine friends whom he suspected of treachery must be sent for at once, the one to receive a challenge, the other a cowhiding.

At seeing Lane this way, Spring said that Carney, who had reconciled with Lane since his unsuccessful attempt at the Senate seat, and another friend of Lane's "bestirred themselves to refute the newspaper charges." One of them wrote an oath supporting Lane's side, then both wrote a speech for Lane to give in the Senate to defend himself. Lane gave the speech on May 29 and afterward was quoted by Spring as having said, "The speech was just the thing. It was one of the happiest little efforts of my life."

Two weeks later Lane returned to Kansas. Carney, meanwhile, met with a senator who had what Spring called "copartnership papers" regarding an Indian trading company and a canceled check made out to Lane in the amount of twenty thousand dollars. This caused Lane to head back to Washington. In St. Louis on June

19 he met with Carney and asked, "Do you think that I had better resign? Do you suppose Johnson would give me a foreign mission? Could I be confirmed?" John Shimmons later wrote that around this time he urged Lane to break with Johnson.

Lane managed to get some of his friends, including Mark Delahay and Gov. Samuel Crawford, to put out a statement of support. The statement expressed regret for "the present difficulty between the President and Congress" and objected to the president's veto of the civil rights bill, but backed compromise legislation. The purpose of this statement seems to have been to allow Lane not only to continue to balance both sides, but also to get out of his promises to Johnson and change course.

Lane knew he was in trouble over his alliance with the president. A letter from a friend, Ward Burlingame, clearly revealed his situation. Burlingame reported from Leavenworth that "a majority of the people unmistakably sympathise with Congress" in the dispute, and Senator Pomeroy and Congressman Clarke were apparently angling to be "enemies" of Lane and Johnson. Burlingame was confident that both could be dealt with, but he urged Lane, "We must run in the radical groove."

The pressure of the battle between Johnson and Congress was getting to Lane. Noted William Cutler, "He was debilitated in physical health and in the depths of despondency. His mental condition rapidly grew worse, and on his arrival at St. Louis, it was deemed imprudent to continue the journey [home to Kansas] further, as his delirium was such as presaged the worst form of insanity."

The *Daily Tribune* of Lawrence reprinted an account from the *St. Louis Democrat* of Lane's state of mind in that city. The St. Louis paper spoke to a doctor who met with Lane. The doctor said that Lane had complained to him of feeling dizzy, of being unable to sleep, and of having "sinking sensations." The doctor tried treating Lane's symptoms, but Lane got worse, so the doctor urged him to return to his home. Lane got as far as Leavenworth.

Near Leavenworth, Lane was taken to a farm run by his brother-in-law. On Friday, June 29, John Speer went to see how his old friend was doing. Speer wrote three decades later that when he saw Lane, he joked that he had heard that Lane was "dangerously ill" but that he "could see he was worth a dozen dead men yet." "The

Samuel Crawford was not well-known when Jim Lane tapped him to run for governor of Kansas in 1864, but his bravery during Price's raid catapulted him to victory in the fall election. However, his friendship with Lane was strained when many Republicans turned against Andrew Johnson while Lane remained tied to the president. *Photograph courtesy the Kansas State Historical Society.*

pitcher is broken at the fountain," Lane replied. "My life is ended; I want you to do my memory justice; I ask nothing more." Speer tried to encourage his friend, but since there seemed nothing he could do, he returned to Lawrence. Two days later Jim Lane tried to take his life.

Verres Smith said that the suicide attempt happened this way. At the house he was staying at Lane noticed a revolver on the mantel. On Sunday, July 1, 1866, his hosts were to take a carriage ride and Lane was to join them. Just before stepping into the carriage, Lane told them that he had forgotten his handkerchief. He went back inside, snatched the gun, and hid it when he boarded the carriage. He went along with them, and when they returned home he suddenly jumped out of the carriage. He said "in a loud and cheerful voice, 'Good-bye, gentlemen!'" He put the barrel of the pistol in his mouth and pulled the trigger.

Lane's prospects at first appeared dire. He had shot himself in the evening and immediately became unconscious. The *Conservative* reported two days later that around noon the following day he recovered slightly, but there was no improvement during the afternoon, and at 11 P.M. on July 2 it was thought that Lane would not last longer than twenty-four hours. Surprisingly, the next day there was a report of further slight improvement in Lane's condition.

On July 5 the *Topeka Leader* reported that while the "probabilities are against his recovery," there was a chance that "he may [yet] live." While the next day an erroneous report circulated that Lane had died, a brief item in the *Daily Tribune* on July 7 stated that Lane was "still improving." He had even been able to sit up "for a short time" the day before. On July 10 the *Conservative* reported that although Lane's friends "were quite confident of his recovery," the doctors attending him "hardly dare hope for such a favorable result." That day his condition took a turn for the worse and at five minutes before noon on July 11, 1866, Jim Lane's life came to an end. Because of the July heat Lane had to be buried in Lawrence on July 13, two days before his funeral.

The Reverend Hugh Fisher delivered the funeral sermon, which was printed in its entirety in the *Daily Tribune* on July 21. Fisher compared Lane to other great men of other ages who were misunderstood in their time. He reviewed Lane's career and some of his accomplishments. He also made this telling statement: "We are all more familiar, too, with the foibles of our own *families* than others, and it is very unbecoming to publish these things in the ears of others, who perhaps have as many and great faults as have we. We should all be careful of the reputation of those who belong to us." Fisher concluded his sermon with "Do justly, love mercy and walk humbly with thy God."

Why did Jim Lane choose to end his life? To some degree the explanations provided have depended upon the writer providing the answer.

Charles Robinson and his friends thought they knew. One of them, Samuel Smith, wrote to Robinson on August 5, 1866, saying that Lane's suicide was "his own verdict on his life & actions." Not even a pro-Robinson author as ardent as *Leverett Spring* would go that far. He wrote in the late 1890s that a "fatal despondency" came over Lane due to his loss of power, "and Lane, unable to find a better solution, cut the knot of his perplexities by suicide."

William Cutler went somewhat further, speculating that it could be attributed to "the intense disappointment, humiliation and grief consequent on the desertion of his friends. . . . This alone, to a man of Lane's temperament, was sufficient to dethrone reason." To Lane "life had no further charms, and, with reason shattered, he fled from the dark forms which disappointment conjured, to the oblivious rest of the shadowy hereafter."

Lloyd Lewis picked up on that theme, saying, "Jim Lane shot himself because with the end of the Civil War, he saw his whole world gone, his era dead, his age vanished. He was the pioneer, the adventurer, the restless hunter for new horizons, and the glories of that time had vanished. He was a revolutionist, and the revolution had been won and was thenceforth to be in the hands of the corporation lawyers. He was a fighter, and the war was over."

Noble Prentis, writing about Lane in 1888, considered the ideas that there was a "suicidal mania" in Lane's head and that Lane killed himself to avoid disgrace. Without supporting or discounting either theory, Prentis asked, "Is it possible that his iron heart was broken?" John Speer said much the same thing eight years later. "An overworked man," he wrote of Lane, "reason dethroned, he took his own life." Jim Lane was just too despondent to have done anything else.

It was Abelard Guthrie who had written in February 1862, "There seems to me a species of insanity in some of [Lane's] eccentricities." Lane's actions during his life and his suicide have continually raised the question of whether or not the Grim Chieftain was mentally unstable. His enemies certainly believed Lane was crazy in a very dangerous way. But his allies also wondered about Lane's mind.

John Speer thought his friend had "suicidal tendencies." He wrote years later that shortly after the Lawrence massacre Lane took Speer to a spot where he had hidden from Quantrill's men. Lane told Speer that some of the raiders had come close to that spot. He then showed Speer "a delicate penknife" with "one small blade." Lane said that if his capture had been imminent, "I intended to thrust that little blade up into my brain to escape torture."

To explain his suicide, along with his emotional highs and lows, Craig Miner and others have recently speculated that Lane might have been manic-depressive. Commonly called manic depression, the mental illness known as bipolar disorder is defined by alternating manic and depressed moods. Patients suffering from this illness can fall into deep states of despair then rise to optimistic and energetic periods of extreme excitement. As patients get older the peaks and valleys get more extreme, and mental health professionals are warned to watch for signs of suicide.

The symptoms of bipolar disorder seem on the surface to fit what is known of Lane's emotional life. He was often described as energetic when confident, but when things looked bad he appeared to believe all was hopeless. He was clearly deeply depressed when he killed himself. As some mental health professionals and historians believe that Abraham Lincoln also suffered from bipolar disorder, any historical stigma attached to this diagnosis of Lane ought to be reevaluated, making such a view neither a negative nor a positive attribute.

The trouble with any such diagnosis is that it is not based in absolute knowledge. It is relatively easy to characterize Lincoln's mental state a century and a half later, for aside from his own substantial correspondence, several of those around Lincoln kept detailed diaries of his day-to-day life. From this material it is possible to assemble a picture of Lincoln's mental health that is as clear as if a modern-day professional had the chance to examine the president. By contrast, little of Lane's own writing survives and no one close to him kept a daily diary. Any attempt to attribute a given illness to Lane has to be done with a very incomplete record.

And the record itself might be deceiving. This author is not convinced that Lane's suicide threat before the 1861 senatorial election was serious. As to the incident during the Quantrill raid, any threats on Lane's part were probably less about depression and more about avoiding a gruesome death. There is no evidence that Lane underwent any depressive state before or after his whirlwind of activity in 1855. Bipolar disorder might explain the many fights Lane had, but so might a bad temper, sensitivity to personal insult, or a need to appear tough in a tough environment.

Overall history lacks enough evidence to conclude that Jim Lane suffered from any specific mental illness. There are too many gaps in time from too few sources with too much bias to put together a clear picture. The only thing that can be said with any accuracy is that in the spring of 1866 Lane fell into such a deep state of despair that he believed there was no way to escape his troubles except by ending his life.

The death of Jim Lane created problems for those he left behind. His widow, Mary, lived on for almost two decades. Although she died in Ohio on July 21, 1883, she was buried in Lawrence on July 24 alongside her husband. His daughter Ella died young, in 1874; his son James Lane, Jr., lived until 1893; Thomas Lane lived to 1922; and Anna (Annie) lived to see 1928. Lane's children, as well as Anna's husband and child, are buried with him.

The story does not end there, as author Mark Plummer noted in 1962. Lane's death left Kansas with an empty seat to fill in the U.S. Senate. Governor Crawford, who himself wanted to run again for governor in the fall, faced the challenge of nominating Lane's successor. He knew that the Kansas Republican Party was still fractured and therefore viewed the appointment of Lane's successor as both an opportunity and a challenge. The right candidate could

Jim Lane's grave at Oak Lawn Cemetery in Lawrence. He is buried alongside his wife, his children, and their families. Even death could not end the
controversy over Jim Lane, as debate over his reputation has continued
among his supporters and critics for almost 150 years. *Author's photograph.*

bind the party to his renomination; the wrong choice would turn him into another one-term governor.

There were several possible candidates for Lane's seat. One was John Speer, another was James Blunt, a third was Thomas Carney, and a fourth was the Reverend Hugh Fisher. Each one of these men had their own supporters. Most of Lane's allies supported Speer; veterans liked Blunt; Carney was backed by a group of important Leavenworth businessmen; and Fisher was championed by several churches.

To the surprise of just about everyone, Crawford appointed Edmund G. Ross on July 19 and formally announced the appointment the next day. Edmund Ross had served with Crawford during the Civil War, and he was partner of Speer's in the *Kansas Daily Tribune*. Nothing else seemed to point Crawford to him, except that unlike all the other named candidates, Ross had no enemies.

There was a storm over the Ross appointment, but it quickly blew over and Crawford was able to get renominated for governor, largely because his foes could not organize. By the fall most of those who had criticized the appointment rallied behind Crawford. Crawford was handily reelected, and he used his new-found popularity to give Pomeroy another six-year term and to get Ross formally elected by the state legislature to fill the last four years of Lane's term.

That rise in Crawford's standing would last little longer than a year. Radical Republicans in Washington continued to attack President Johnson, and those attacks culminated in an effort to impeach Johnson in the spring of 1868. Ross largely supported the Radicals, but when it came to the matter of impeachment, he famously stood his ground and voted not guilty, defeating the impeachment of Johnson. The vote stunned Crawford and led to a storm of attacks for choosing Ross.

History, however, has vindicated Ross's vote against the articles of impeachment. His action is seen as a courageous stand against an attempt by Congress to usurp the presidency for political purposes. Ross is viewed as a man who boldly stood up for what was right instead of what was popular. There is even a belief that Ross single-handedly preserved the office of the presidency itself. It is all but certain that had Crawford appointed anyone but Ross to Lane's seat, Johnson might have been removed from office.

This raises an intriguing question. Ross had aligned himself with the congressmen and senators who supported the impeachment trial before it took place. He only broke with them on the impeachment vote. Jim Lane had chosen to side with Johnson in the president's battles with the Radical Republicans. He therefore would have been certain to oppose the impeachment from the start. Had Lane lived another two years, would his likely opposition have made the Radicals unsure of their ability to remove Johnson? Would that have dissuaded the Radicals from even trying to impeach Johnson?

Those questions have no answers, but they do make one thing very clear. James Henry Lane had a very great influence on national events in the last decade of his life. He had power, and others had to take that into account in dealing with him. That, more than anything else, made him controversial in his time and continues to do so to this day.

XV.

Debating Jim Lane's Legacy

More than seventy-five years after James Lane was buried, America was in the midst of another war. World War II saw the nation fighting across the globe and needing to provide materials to its allies. America had to expand its army, navy, and air force to cope with the situation and drive to victory. Expansion of the navy meant more ships, and those ships needed names. Kansas was not left out when new ships were commissioned for the war effort.

Senator Lane was not forgotten when this process got under way, and in 1943 a vessel was named in his honor. However, that ship was not a cruiser, a carrier, a destroyer, or even a frigate. The *James Lane* was a Liberty ship, a cargo ship that could be erected quickly to move men and supplies from America's home front to where they were needed. The *James Lane* was one of almost thirty Liberty ships to bear the names of important Kansans or Kansas natives. In fact, another ship was named for his rival, Charles Robinson, and another for his replacement, Edmund Ross. By the time of the Second World War, Lane's name was not the most prominent among those ships; more people would have known who the ships *William Allen White, Wyatt Earp, James B. Hickok, Amelia Earhart,* or *Cyrus K. Holliday* were named for than the *James Lane*.

How Lane came to be ignored by history is another fascinating aspect to his story. It involves a continuation of the Lane-Robinson struggle, waged between Lane's friends and Robinson and his defenders. It carried on as historians took sides in the effort to pre-serve and interpret Kansas history and the places these men had in

it. The controversy began in the years after Lane's death, proceeded through the twentieth century, and appears to be going on to
this day.

"Where a man stands in history depends upon who keeps the
record," noted Lloyd Lewis in 1938. "[M]ore than that, it depends
upon who lives to keep the record. If you are a favorite of the lit-
erary men, the history professors, the clergy, you have a head start
toward a place in history." Where Jim Lane stands in Kansas history in the nearly century and a half since his death is an almost-forgotten tale of the interpretation and reinterpretation of history. It
serves as a testament to the man, to his enemies, and to the idea
that history can sometimes be as much an art (or a form of propaganda) as a science.

In writing about F. B. Sanborn, a New England supporter of the
Kansas struggle and a biographer of John Brown, William
Connelley claimed that after an 1879 meeting of territorial pio-
neers, those who had been in the New England Emigrant Aid
Company began their campaign to revise history. "It was believed
necessary to destroy the characters of both Lane and Brown," he
said, "that the work they did in Kansas in aid of freedom might be
discredited and condemned." In that same article he stated that
Sanborn had predicted that Connelley "would incur the wrath" of
the anti-Lane faction as he took to the cause of Lane and Brown.

Lloyd Lewis, the man who addressed the Kansas State Historical
Society in 1938 about Lane, observed a similar phenomenon and
explained the reason. "New England never liked Kansas' most
influential citizen of the 1850's and 1860's," he said.

> So much of the importance of New England in history is due
> to its early corner on the literary men, the book publishers, the
> college professors. We are not yet free, as a nation, from the his-
> torical prejudices of the New Englanders. For the sake of objec-
> tivity there are still too many midland biographers and historians
> and professors blandly adopting the historical viewpoints of New
> England—a natural thing, perhaps, for men whose dream it is to
> be called some day to a full professorship at Harvard.

What's more, Lewis noted, "The New Englanders outlived Lane."
Lane "used every wile and trick in the realm of politics" to protect

Kansas during the Civil War, and there might have been "nothing he would not have done for the union." But that could also be said of Abraham Lincoln. People wanted to "believe that Lincoln saved the union with beautiful words and tears." They didn't want to admit that Lincoln would stoop to Lane's level, or perhaps more properly, that Lane rose to Lincoln's. "Lincoln is martyred and goes into history too noble, too exalted to be linked any more with Jim Lane, who committed suicide," Lewis said. "Yet, when both were living, Lane may be said to have been President Lincoln's political viceroy in Kansas and sometimes, perhaps, in the whole regions west of the Mississippi river."

Lewis's address hit on another reason the New England faction in Kansas tried to knock down Lane. "Lane was for the masses, the rag tag and bob tail, so the conservatives didn't admire him, although they frequently couldn't resist him." Largely comprising those masses were those whom Lewis called "midlanders," who didn't care "much about slavery except that they did not want it where they were, cutting the price of labor." This was not moral opposition to slavery, but economic opposition. The New Englanders viewed slavery as a sin, while the Midwesterners viewed it as unfair competition. The New England abolitionists wanted the contest in Kansas to be a moral struggle of right against wrong; yet what seems to have turned the tide in the conflict between the Free State forces and their proslavery foes was the increasing movement of antislavery Midwesterners into the territory. Their numbers could not be overcome by creative fraud at the ballot box. By the same token, they did not oust slavery from Kansas with moral arguments, which is what the New Englanders had hoped would happen. Following this line of reasoning, it becomes easy to see why the New England abolitionists would have hated Lane, the most prominent of the midlanders, and tried to bring him down.

In Lewis's view, this antipathy toward Lane was more directly tied to how Lane faced the proslavery forces. At their disposal was "the powerful political machine" of Sen. David Rice Atchison. They also had the backing of Franklin Pierce's administration. The abolitionists' leader, Charles Robinson, "although he learned something of politics," lacked "the training to match Atchison and the payrollers of the federal machine in politics." But then came

Lane, who "knew the tricks with which to overcome Sen. Davy Atchison from Missouri; he knew the ruses with which to outlast, outmaneuver the whole administration machine from Washington." But "because his methods weren't of the purest, nor his devices of the most admirable variety, the idealists among the New England colonists disliked him." The New Englanders preferred Charles Robinson, a Massachusetts native who had been on the frontier but had not been tarnished by it.

Their man had little to show for all their support. After all it wasn't Charles Robinson who rallied the North to the cause of making Kansas a Free State in the summer of 1856, it was James Lane. It was not Robinson's name that spread fear through the ranks of the Border Ruffians, it was Lane's. Lane became a powerful senator; Robinson, a failed one-term governor. Lane warned Kansas of the Price invasion of 1864 and served honorably during the fighting. Robinson and his allies called Lane's warning a political ploy and then did almost nothing during the battles that resulted from the invasion.

One inference that can be drawn from how Robinson, his widow, and his allies struggled over the former governor's place in state history is that they knew he had a tarnished reputation. Charles Robinson became the leader of the Free State movement almost by acclamation. But then came James Lane, a Democrat with fuzzy views on slavery, and almost overnight he gained a status and influence almost as high as Robinson's. Lane became the man of the hour in 1856, while Robinson was kept under house arrest in Lecompton. Not even a murder charge stopped Lane from becoming senator in 1861. While Lane gained the confidence of President Lincoln and the power of patronage, Robinson walked into a cheap scandal and was cast out of office. Robinson allied himself with Governor Carney in 1864, only to see both their names turned to mud in the wake of Sterling Price's failed campaign.

After the war was over and Lane had committed suicide, Robinson reentered politics and tried several times to return to power. The first of these attempts came in 1867 when two state constitutional amendments came up for public votes. One was to give the ballot to black men, a movement also known as universal manhood suffrage. The other, women's suffrage, would give women the right to vote. The Republicans in Kansas had put up the first amendment, and the Democrats threw in the second in hopes of blocking the Republican act.

Robinson cast his lot with the second amendment, although he supported both, and used his time to lobby for women's suffrage. Though several other prominent Kansans and national feminist leaders traveled the state to support the amendment, Robinson and other former politicians were accused of supporting the measure to get back into office. Ultimately, both amendments were defeated, and some blamed Robinson for promoting a side issue that killed universal manhood suffrage.

Later that year Robinson left the Republican Party and joined the Independent Reform Party. This party had what might be called a proto-Populist stand on national issues. It supported such ideas as state regulation of railroad corporations and the direct election of U.S. senators. For a brief time the party considered Robinson as their gubernatorial candidate, but he opted to run for a state senate seat to represent Lawrence. His Republican opponent was Lane's good friend John Speer. The two men conducted a bitter campaign that Robinson managed to win.

The next time Charles Robinson made headlines was in 1880 when an amendment to prohibit the sale of alcohol came up for a vote. Although personally he was a temperance man, he decided publicly that he could not support the proposed law. He believed that such a law would regulate societal morality, and regulating morality would hinder social progress. While in the light of history his stand seems quite logical, at the time it was highly unpopular. Robinson himself was accused of being a tool of the liquor interests. Considering the traditional connections between the abolitionist movement and the temperance movement, no doubt people were stunned by Robinson's stance. It probably did not advance his reputation when the amendment passed in the fall election.

Nor must it have helped when, pushed by his progressive views and opposition to prohibition, Charles Robinson joined the Democratic Party in the mid-1880s. He was their candidate for governor in 1886 and again in 1890. Both times he lost, the second time coming in third behind the Republican and Populist candidates. Although Robinson had populist leanings, in the 1890s he simply could not make any accommodation with the Populist Party because of their support for prohibition.

Modern Robinson biographer Don Wilson regarded that stubbornness as Robinson's major flaw. Once Robinson made up his mind about something, wrote Wilson, "he showed little patience with people or groups who disagreed with him." Sol Miller went further, for in January 1889 he claimed that Robinson had so soured on the Republican Party that after the war he would "advocate principles that he does not believe in." Robinson was not merely stubborn, said Miller, but vengeful toward the party that Lane once controlled.

Before he died Robinson took one last vengeful swipe at his "unscrupulous antagonist" by writing his memoirs, *The Kansas Conflict*. Merrill Peterson, author of a recent book about the twists and turns the John Brown legend took, called the work a "self-serving memoir," an assessment as accurate as any. In it Robinson claimed that his strategy of resistance kept slavery out of Kansas. But he went further, and at times to quite a disturbing degree. He alleged that Lane's vote for the Kansas-Nebraska Act was a vote "to open to Kansas to slavery" and that Lane was a secret supporter of the proslavery movement. Of the five pages he devoted to the Topeka convention of September 19, 1855, half was spent on Lane's duel.

When Robinson turned to the subject of the Jenkins murder, as William Connelley pointed out in 1925, he relied on decidedly biased sources. Part of Robinson's account came from Lane enemy James Blood, another from the administrator of the Jenkins estate, and a third from Ely Moore, Jr., the son of one of the proslavery men who had beaten a Free State man to death in early 1856. Robinson even quoted a letter that suggested the claim dispute had been decided at the time of the Jenkins shooting, which the facts clearly contradict.

Of Quantrill's attack on Lawrence, Robinson wrote that the guerilla leader had only 175 men, that Lane was in complete control of military affairs along the border in 1863, and that his and Plumb's men far outnumbered Quantrill's early in the Union pursuit of the raiders. Perhaps the oddest and most unpleasant "fact"

Robinson put forward was that his property was spared because Quantrill said that the former governor had done "all he could to preserve peace on the border." One has to wonder at what survivors of the Lawrence massacre thought about such a statement from Charles Robinson.

The Kansas Conflict became one of many books and articles put out by Robinson and his supporters to increase his stature and to diminish Lane. The first volley in this history war appears to have been fired in June 1879 with conflicting letters in the two *Tribune* newspapers of Lawrence. The first was in the weekly paper. In that issue was a letter from Eli Thayer, one of the Emigrant Aid Company's founders, to the Kansas State Historical Society. Thayer's letter suggested that credit for liberating Kansas from slavery should go to his company and to the leadership of Charles Robinson.

A few days later in the *Daily Tribune*, John Shimmons, one of Lane's old friends, shot back. Shimmons wrote that many men deserved the credit, including Robinson, Thayer, Lane, and John Brown. Shimmons then noted that it was not Robinson who prevented a conflict with the U.S. Army over the capture of the Free State prisoners in 1856, rather it was Lane's actions. Once Lane's campaign ended he marched on Lecompton, attacking and defeating parties of proslavery men that summer, and Shimmons claimed it was due to these victories that the proslavery authorities released the prisoners.

In the mid-1880s Shimmons exchanged oratorical fire with Robinson himself. The fray was carried out in the columns of another Lawrence newspaper, the *Daily Herald*. It began in December 1883 with Robinson writing about the killing of Gaius Jenkins. Robinson's account was biased and far from the facts. He alleged that Lane had shot Jenkins while the other was drawing water from the contested well, that Lane was tried in a court of his "partizans," and that as senator, Lane used his influence to win his land claim case. Unfortunately, when Shimmons responded to this in February 1884 he spent more space on Lane's achievements than on refuting Robinson's errors.

A few years later Leverett Spring, a professor at the University of Kansas, published *Prelude to the War for the Union*. The book was a history of Kansas largely focused on the territorial period. Spring was inclined far more toward Robinson's view of events and was generally contemptuous of Lane and his actions. There were some who appreciated Spring's book, but not everyone thought highly of it. Noble Prentis, in his well-known article on Lane first published in the *Olathe Mirror* in 1888, quipped that Spring, by going near the Lane-Robinson feud, had smoked "a cigar in a powder magazine." The "mild-mannered professor" was "blown clear through the state by the explosion." When Spring resigned his post at the University of Kansas, a Topeka newspaper went so far as to comment, "The loss of the professor would be more generally mourned if he had not attempted to write a history of Kansas."

Perhaps the best comments on Spring's book, and on Charles Robinson's efforts to boost his standing, came from one Ewing Herbert. In 1894, Herbert wrote a piece about Jim Lane in a northeastern Kansas newspaper. Much of Herbert's writing contains colorful anecdotes about Lane, but there were some sharp observations. He noted that in the ongoing Lane-Robinson feud, those who wrote about either man were "too frequently blinded by political differences." One of those, alleged Herbert, was Professor Spring, who "merely compiled the personal recollections and opinions of Gov. Robinson." Half a paragraph later he wrote:

> One who has lived in a Lane atmosphere cannot agree with Dr. Robinson. When death retires that eminent Kansan from politics—for it seems only death can do it—Lane and anti-Lane controversy may be buried with him, but much has been said that will not be forgotten. The dying Kansan bequeaths his likes and dislikes, his hates, his loves, to his sons, so that no feud is certain of end.

When Robinson died later in 1894 his widow, Sara, took up the cause of restoring her husband's reputation. She did so with a zeal that at times bordered on mania. She was determined not to allow the facts as she saw them either become lost or altered by the opinions of those who did not share her view of her husband and his contribution to the state's history.

Sara Robinson had taken some part in the battle between the Free State movement and their proslavery opponents. In 1856 she wrote a book about the conflict which supported the view that the

Free State faction was righteous and their opponents a band of ruffians and slave drivers. She even traveled east to plead her husband's case when he was arrested and charged with treason. Yet by the time Charles Robinson died she had stepped out of politics, taking no part in either the temperance or the women's suffrage movements. Starting in 1894, wrote a recent scholar, her "one obsession was Kansas history."

Her effort began when she had her husband's book, *The Kansas Conflict*, reprinted in 1898. She then encouraged Frank Blackmar, a sociology and economics professor at the University of Kansas and executor of the Robinson estate, to write a biography of her husband. She wrote letters to state and national newspapers decrying books and articles that praised John Brown and James Lane. Her denunciations of Brown and Lane led her into a feud with three important members of the Kansas State Historical Society: early secretary Franklin G. Adams, his successor George Martin, and president and later secretary William Connelley. She directed additional ire at F. B. Sanborn and Noble Prentis for their positive pieces on Lane and Brown.

Blackmar finished his biography around 1902, but when he told Mrs. Robinson that he intended to have the book published by Crane and Company of Topeka, she balked. Crane had published, among others, John Speer's biography of Lane and Connelley's book on Brown. She even offered Blackmar five hundred dollars to take it to an Eastern publisher. Blackmar demurred, and the book was published by Crane. It was well received by Robinson's friends and allies and not surprisingly was reviewed poorly by those who thought his views inaccurate.

The year Blackmar's biography was published, Sara Robinson financed a book by George W. Brown, editor of the *Herald of Freedom* and longtime Robinson supporter. The book was basically an attack on William Connelley, and Connelley replied with a pamphlet the following year. Connelley became so enraged with what Sara Robinson was doing to promote her husband that he privately wrote to a friend that she was "old and feeble of mind" and suggested that she knew what she was saying about Brown and Lane was untrue.

Perhaps more troubling to those with whom she disagreed, and to those who are today interested in that period, was what she did for the tenth edition of her own book, *Kansas: Its Interior and Exterior Life*. The book had gone through several editions after being published in 1856, but by 1899 its sales appeared to have gone dormant. Sara Robinson undertook to get it back into print in order to continue her struggle to promote Robinson's role in state history. Rather than simply trying to get new copies printed, she rewrote parts of the manuscript to both improve her husband's standing and to diminish Lane and Brown. Although she insisted that the changes were facts, questions remain to this day on that score. Did she invent some things? Did she "remember" some events and comments and "forget" others? She does appear to have allowed her increasingly partisan view of the conflict between the Robinson and Lane factions to color her narrative. It is possible that by tinkering with the appendix to that edition, she tried to turn what was a personal reminiscence into a scholarly history.

One of Sara Robinson's most strenuous opponents was author and historian William Connelley. Among his efforts to resist her view of state history was his biography of Lane, which was published in 1899. Connelley's book was not a full biography, but a limited treatise focused on Lane's life during the territorial period and his work for Lincoln's renomination. Connelley conceded that Lane had faults: he "was a politician before he was a statesman"; his "political methods were not always honorable or just" and he could be "unscrupulous"; and he could be "extremely bitter" toward his enemies, including Governor Robinson, whom Connelley said Lane had "deeply wronged." However, "his services to Kansas and to humanity far outweigh his faults were they multiplied a hundred fold," Connelley added.

Three years before Connelley, Lane's closest friend had also responded to the Robinson drumbeat. John Speer published his biography of Lane in 1896, which covered a great deal more of Lane's life than Connelley's book. Speer's work contained many personal anecdotes about his friend and included some correspondence from Lane's own hand. Speer strenuously defended Lane from the attacks of others, including devoting one whole chapter to the Jenkins shooting, citing sources to prove that it was not a "cold-blooded murder" and that Lane's case for the land had merit.

What is more interesting about Speer's biography is the way he handled Lane's attackers. One example is John Ingalls, who by the early 1890s was a senator himself and was writing about Kansas history. In one piece Ingalls mentioned Lane, the 1864 election, and his suicide in 1866. He wrote that Lane had "presumed too far upon the toleration of a constituency which had honored him so long and forgiven him so much." Lane had "apostatized once too often" and "to avoid impending exposure" by scandal killed himself.

"This is a most unjust accusation," countered Speer, in that it attacked "the man whose voice is silenced by death" and implied "frequent acts of dishonor." Lane was never charged with any crime, outside of the Jenkins shooting, never dealt in fraudulent bonds, never stole contributions to Kansas, and was never court-martialed, Speer insisted. What Speer did not do was counter Ingalls' volley by telling readers of Ingalls' place on the Carney ticket in the 1864 election. He did not impugn Ingalls' character with guilt by association to Carney's reckless acts during that campaign. By not resorting to insults and allegations, Speer may have been trying to present Lane's side of the Lane-Robinson dispute in a better light than had Robinson's supporters, who employed such incendiaries along with or in place of factual evidence.

Speer's book was followed some three decades later by Wendell Stephenson's more scholarly biography of Jim Lane. Stephenson found a great deal of source material in Indiana that clarified some details of Lane's life. Stephenson's book was also largely free of the invective that had characterized much of the writing about Lane since his suicide. It was by and large a balanced book but it did lean slightly in Lane's favor. Yet there were some significant omissions in Stephenson's book, namely that little space was given to the Gaius Jenkins shooting, and the Quantrill raid and Lane's actions during and after were only mentioned in passing.

More important was the absence of any real commentary about the division between Lane's friends and enemies. Occasionally Stephenson mentioned the Lane-Robinson feud, and in one of his chapter notes he wrote that Leverett Spring was "perhaps too severe in his criticism of Lane," but that was the extent of his discussion on the biases impacting history's perception of the statesman. This may have been due to the influence of William

Connelley, who at the time was acting as secretary of the Kansas State Historical Society. Connelley had been an active participant in what has been called a "history war," and he did allow Stephenson total access to the Lane materials he had been collecting. As a result, Stephenson might not have been willing to tackle the feud and antagonize the man who had given him so much help and encouragement.

As it was, Stephenson's work was published at a time when Lane's star was falling. Despite her questionable actions, Sara Robinson's view of the history war between her husband and Lane prevailed in the decades after her death. By the time Lloyd Lewis spoke to the Historical Society in 1939, Lane was seen as a corrupt, radical opportunist, while Robinson was looked upon as a statesman who helped save Kansas from slavery. Lewis was unable to change that perception, and it was given further credence with two books published in the 1950s, Alice Nichols' *Bleeding Kansas* and Albert Castel's *A Frontier State at War.*

Nichols' book, though thoroughly researched, often adopted a conversational tone, almost to the point of chattiness. She took the side of the Robinson faction, calling Lane "a perfect specimen of *chameleon politico,*" writing at one point that Lane was "ever the actor in search of an audience" and at another that Lane "was an orator who used every trick of the trade, even resorting to logic when necessary." A reading of both the text and her chapter notes reveals that she seems to have accepted at face value the tales about Lane's planned attack on the Lecompton convention and about the Danites. In one of her chapter notes, Nichols even went so far as to call Leverett Spring "the only impartial historian of the period."

Castel's book, although more scholarly, was no more friendly to Lane than Nichols' book had been. He described Lane as "a cynic who posed as a zealot, a demagogue who claimed to be a statesman." Robinson, on the other hand, was "quiet and dignified," though Castel conceded that he had "tremendous self-pride," which he said was both a strength and a weakness. Castel suggested that the rivalry was intense on both sides, claiming that "Lane's hated of Robinson verged on insanity."

When it came to the bond scandal, Castel wrote that there was no evidence that Robinson "had any financial share" in the bond sales. Despite stating that Robinson's "reputation never wholly recovered" from the scandal, Castel said the fact that he was not removed from office had "blocked" Lane. Castel also wrote that in the wake of Robinson's fall, Lane became a full recipient of the graft in the military supply system during the war.

On the matter of Lane's recruitment of the two colored regiments, Castel said very little beyond the facts. He did not directly tie the Lawrence massacre to Lane's Osceola raid. Though Lane did come into some blame for the massacre, that was for his interference in Carney's attempt to raise a home-guard regiment and was one of seven factors Castel said contributed to Quantrill's success. Castel wrote that when it came to the Price raid of 1864, Lane's enemies made numerous blunders that assured his faction of victory in the elections that followed. Yet at the end of his book, when he came to the matter of Lane's suicide, Castel chose to quote a friend of Robinson's who wrote, "His suicide was his own verdict on his life & actions." Castel's history of Kansas during the Civil War would be the cornerstone of the accounts that followed, and his view of Lane would continue the Robinson version of events.

Another book that mentioned Lane, published before the Nichols and Castel works, is worth noting here. W. G. Clugston's *Rascals in Democracy* came out in 1940 and was largely devoted to critiques of Kansas anti-populist conservative politicians and those who promoted moral legislation like prohibition while living less than moral lives themselves. Clugston devoted only seven pages to Lane's life and career, and those pages contained no new information about him, but the book is remarkable for two reasons: first, it proved that colorful writing about Lane often overruled the facts, and second, it contains perhaps the most incredible misstatement about Lane's life ever published.

Clugston asserted without much proof that Lane "had no honest convictions about anything." He quoted only John Ingalls on Lane's speaking style. He spent a great deal of time on Lane's admittedly dodgy religious beliefs but said nothing about Lane's evolving views on slavery. More disturbing was Clugston's confused chronology. He wrote that Lane was a "stooge of the railroads that were building towards the west," then discussed the 1861 senatorial contest, ignoring the fact that Lane did little for any railroad until after he was elected senator.

This inaccuracy in the order of events leads to Clugston's massive error, his comments about the Gaius Jenkins shooting. Implying that Lane shot Jenkins in 1865 or 1866, he called Jenkins "one of [Lane's] old associates in land speculations." Clugston even wrote, "Lane shot and killed the man in cold blood." Clugston told the tale well enough, but anyone with any familiarity with Lane's life would have recognized the author's obvious mistakes and misinterpretations. It seemed that by this time, colorful commentary about Lane was more important than the facts.

Interestingly, the most prominent and possibly most prolific of the Kansas author-historians of the day wrote nothing directly about Jim Lane. James C. Malin was a professor at the University of Kansas; served for many years in editorial posts for the *Kansas Historical Quarterly*, the Kansas State Historical Society's main publication; contributed numerous articles to the publication; and wrote several books about Kansas history. Malin only touched on Lane tangentially in one of his most well-known works, *John Brown and the Legend of Fifty-Six*, published in 1942.

Malin's massive book was an attempt not so much to review John Brown's life but to analyze the positive and negative writings about Brown in the decades since his death. Brown's stature was declining during that period, as author Merrill Peterson has recently noted, and Malin fell in with the prevailing view that Brown was a religious fanatic devoted to inciting civil war. Malin had "no sympathy whatsoever for John Brown," Peterson wrote; nor did Malin "make an effort to understand the man."

The first part of Malin's opus dealt with the contemporary view of Brown, in which the author attempted to prove that Brown was "a bit player" in Kansas history. The second part dealt with the growth of the Brown legend nationally and in Kansas. Malin pointed out the contradictions in the claims of Brown supporters, as well as those of Brown's critics. Ultimately, Malin concluded that the outcome of the struggle in Kansas was due to the efforts of moderates like Robinson, and one prominent reviewer praised his book for stripping away the "hero worship" of John Brown.

Caught up in the backwash of Malin's attack on Brown was Jim Lane. Malin commented very little about Lane personally. He did attribute to Lane the radical leadership of the Free State movement, classifying him as one of the architects of Free State violence in 1856. However, with his focus so directed on Brown, Malin seemed to give short shrift to Lane and his place in the territorial struggle.

Other state histories published over the next few decades followed this view. In *This Place Called Kansas,* Charles Howes associated Lane with John Brown, Charles Jennison, and James Montgomery as the Northerners who fought fire with fire in the territory. William Zornow, in his 1957 history of the state, did give Lane credit for the founding of the Republican Party in Kansas but accused him of using a "trick election" to oust Robinson in 1861 and of using "his military position to fatten the business interests of Leavenworth." These views continued to an extent in Robert Richmond's book, *Kansas: A Land of Contrasts.* In his section on Bleeding Kansas, Richmond called Lane "a militant supporter of the Topeka government." When it came to the Civil War era, Richmond wrote that Lane was part of the radical faction of the Republican Party in Kansas while "the conservative element" was led by Charles Robinson. Finally, in his brief account of the bond scandal, Richmond said that when Lane "took a hand in the bond investigation many Kansans felt that the whole business was his idea to eliminate Robinson as political competition."

It was not until 1962 that a new biography of Jim Lane was published, *Rider on the Wind* by Kendall Bailes. Bailes took an approach to Lane that was at times favorable and at others balanced. He viewed Lane as very much a man and a politician of the American frontier of the nineteenth century. It was because of that characteristic, he believed, that Lane was able to rise to prominence in Kansas politics from 1855 to 1865.

Bailes' work seems to have circulated throughout Kansas better than previous Lane biographies. However, the book appears to have been self-published, which may have worked against its being taken seriously by state historians. Bailes also relied a great deal on reminiscences, quoting only a few contemporary letters and almost no period newspaper reports. His book does contain gaps in Lane's life, as it says nothing on Lane's work to raise black regiments or to direct the Union war effort against slavery. Perhaps because of these flaws Bailes' book was unable to break the standard assumptions about Lane.

The first modern biography of Lane's rival, Charles Robinson, came out in 1975. Author Don Wilson was sympathetic to his subject from the first. He began the preface to his book by stating that for "more than a century" Robinson was a figure "secondary" in Kansas history to Lane and John Brown. Wilson made no connection between Robinson's time in California and his policy in territorial Kansas. Nor did be believe that Robinson had done anything wrong during the imbroglio over the sale of state bonds. Wilson did criticize Sara Robinson for her efforts to lionize her husband after his death and blamed Charles Robinson's stubborn nature for his inability to regain public office after the Civil War, but Wilson gave Robinson the credit for the defeat of slavery in Kansas and cited him as a stronger influence on the state than Jim Lane.

In 1976, Kenneth Davis had a history of Kansas published as part of an overall series of state histories to coincide with the nation's bicentennial. Davis, who had grown up in Manhattan, had returned to the city the year before the book was released to serve as a visiting professor at Kansas State University. His book can be seen as the point where the established views of Lane, Robinson, and their feud started to change.

When Robinson first appears in Davis's book, the author describes him as a man of "generally sound judgment, much calculating shrewdness, a notable self-control, and an equally notable self-esteem." However, Davis also characterized Robinson as argumentative and as having "highly developed acquisitive instincts." A few pages later, when Lane enters Davis's narrative, he is depicted as a man with "a special genius for self-dramatization," a powerful gift of oratory, a "shrewd understanding of his particular constituency," and a "freedom from scruple." Davis also wrote that Lane was "chronically indigent" and was a man that "gave the impression of hotly frictional electric energy."

Overall, Davis's approach to both men was balanced. Lane's sudden rise to leadership of the Free State movement in 1855 was met by "an increasingly resentful Robinson," Davis said. The author resurrected the fact, long since forgotten, that the opposition of the nonabolitionists in the Free State movement was as much racial as it was moral. Lane's stand on the black law at the Big Springs convention was to offer it as "a mere instruction" to a state legislature, Davis wrote, rather than forcing its inclusion in the constitution to pacify that part of the movement. He credited Lane as a moderating influence over the people of Lawrence in the Wakarusa War, keeping them from launching their own attack on the Missourians surrounding them.

Davis also went after the old Robinson charge that associated Lane with John Brown. Lane, he wrote, tended to gather "the violent passions of his followers" and dissipate them "into harmless channels" where and when such violence "might otherwise have been actually effective." Lane's "ferocious reputation derived from his words rather than his deeds," Davis noted. Brown, on the other hand, was "a fanatic" who had "a hatred of slavery and slaveholders." Davis claimed that Brown had "a crazy glitter" in his eyes and a lineage "darkly tainted by hereditary insanity."

But the author did not give credit to Lane for everything. When Lane and Brown joined forces in August 1856 and open warfare seemed imminent, Davis gave Lane some acknowledgment for the diffusion of the crisis, but most of the responsibility he gave to Col. Phillip St. George Cooke for being a fair military man and Gov. John Geary for getting Lane and Brown to leave the territory. He did not attribute the defeat of slavery in Kansas to Lane, nor to Robinson, but to the Kansas voters who soundly rejected the Lecompton constitution.

Perhaps most interesting in Davis's history is his treatment of Governors Robinson and Carney during the Civil War. Although he accused Lane of a "full and ruthless exploitation" of Robinson during the bond scandal, he also wrote that Robinson's administration had a "vulnerability" and a "culpability" in the bond sales. State laws were "most certainly broken" and the bond sales "netted substantial profits" to Robinson's friends, which Davis believed doomed his career. The author wrote that Carney's downfall began when he was tempted by Pomeroy's "oily piece of deceit" to obtain "by trickery" Lane's Senate seat. Carney unwisely sided with the anti-Lane faction in 1864, said Davis, and paid for it when Lane's warnings of the Price raid proved true.

In spite of these favorable evaluations, Davis showed some bias against Lane. Writing of the shooting of Gaius Jenkins, he said it was true that Lane killed a man in a land-claim dispute but was acquitted; Davis gave no mention of self-defense. The two commanding officers he named in the Lane Brigade were the "notorious Jayhawker" James Montgomery and the "cruel, rapacious, [and] unscrupulous" Charles Jennison. Lane's "sacking of Osceola" gave "a decided impetus" toward Quantrill's campaign and the eventual massacre at Lawrence. Davis even agreed with Albert Castel's view that Lane's suicide "was his own verdict on his life & actions."

Indiana journalist Bob Markwalter wrote a piece on Jim Lane in 1981 for a newspaper near Lane's hometown. It was a largely fair view of the man, pointing out the many contradictions of his life and actions. It also contained a quote that puts some of the negative works about Lane into perspective. "He was a man of so many sides," Markwalter said of Lane, "no one—save perhaps Lincoln—knew which was real."

And so matters stood until author and business history professor Craig Miner undertook the writing of a new Kansas history in the late 1990s. His book, published in 2002, presented an even more balanced version of the feud between Lane and Robinson. Indeed, before getting too far into the battle, Miner wrote, "It is certain that Lane was more of a statesman and Robinson more of a stinker than is generally communicated."

Miner also examined the close ties between Abraham Lincoln and Lane. He pointed out that Robinson was "Lincoln's personal and political enemy," which colored Robinson's perspective on the Lane-Lincoln relationship. He also wrote that "a great myth of Lincoln as sainted martyr" arose after Lincoln's assassination, affecting how the relationship was viewed. Miner added that Lincoln appreciated the "political loyalty and effectiveness" of Lane, that Lane was "a populist who took care of his friends," and that "Lane was a great speaker and Lincoln needed one."

Just as important as his book was an article Miner wrote about Lane and Lincoln for *Kansas History,* the current main publication of the Kansas State Historical Society. In the piece Miner pointed out the similarities between the two, as well as the evidence that

Lane was as useful to Lincoln as the president was to the senator. Almost as important to understanding them, wrote Miner, was that both men were subject to bouts of melancholy. "Is it too much to suppose that the two men, both tall, both carelessly dressed, both homely, and both magnetic partly due to their mysterious emotional volatility, found an understanding?" he asked his readers. Lane was a powerful man, Miner concluded, in spite of his flaws, and during the worst crisis the nation had faced, Lincoln needed powerful men to obtain victory.

What seems remarkable about Lane's reputation in the decades since his death is his continual association with the most radical elements of the Free State movement and the Civil War Republican Party. Many of Lane's nineteenth-century enemies often lumped him with the most radical of abolitionists, John Brown, but on the issue of slavery Lane's stance did not turn radical until late in the territorial period, and possibly not until the war started. Lane's view of slavery through much of the 1850s reflected that of his Western constituents. Brown's views on the issue were far closer to those of the New Englanders. In spite of this disparity Lane's name and Brown's became tied together as part of the radical faction of the Free State party.

The association is probably due to both men's willingness to fight the proslavery forces in the summer and fall of 1856. It may also be attributed to Lane's taking up the most radical of causes during the war, the enlistment of black soldiers into the Union army. It is just as likely that those who never liked Lane also came to loathe Brown. Brown had the blood of the Pottawatomie Creek murders on his hands. His fame after Harpers Ferry eclipsed the reputations of the actual leaders of the Free State movement. Morality mixed with ego to turn men like Charles Robinson against the image of John Brown the extremist martyr. So how did Brown and Lane become linked in their minds?

Probably because of their rivals' fears for their own reputations as leaders of the movement, especially Robinson's. Anyone who delved beneath the surface of the Brown legend would discover that he was not the leader of the abolition effort in Kansas Territory. That effort might direct them toward Jim Lane; after all, Lane was a fighter but did not have a massacre attached to his record. By contrast Robinson had neither battles nor dramatic speeches to his credit, nothing to show actual leadership except the title of governor. What better way to diminish Lane than to associate him with the violent fanatic John Brown by fixing "radical" to Lane's name? Both had employed violence in their lives, so as long as the hows and whys behind each man's actions were ignored or twisted, the connection might work. No doubt the connection was further enhanced because the word "radical" came to have even more negative connotations during the Victorian Era. Thus it was that Lane and Brown, the clever Free State politician and the puritanical abolitionist, were shaped into a pair of wild-eyed antislavery killers.

It might also be that the critics of Lane who often tied him to Brown were products of their era. Not only did Victorians come to view "radical" as a pejorative, but so too the word "ambitious." That word and its variants became associated with the robber barons, businessmen who often did anything to make money. Those men could be ruthless and were hungry for power, financial and otherwise. They became unsavory characters, as did anyone who was thought to share those traits. Lane was certainly ambitious and wanted power. In the minds of his foes and critics perhaps those desires, instead of simply being part of his character, became character flaws that marked Lane as a man unworthy of admiration.

As for the more recent critics, their writings may also shed more light on them than on Jim Lane. He was without a doubt a populist who moved crowds with fiery oratory, but during the mid-twentieth century a sinister aspect attached itself to the image of the rabble-rousing politician. Slowly that image came to be associated with dangerous demagogues, the ideology of fascism, and the anarchy of mob politics. Even the word "populism" has become tarnished in some quarters by being defined as appealing to the lowest of the political spectrum. Would it be surprising then that authors and historians with a dim view of crowd-moving oratory directed toward the masses might have little good to say about Jim Lane?

Is there anything positive to say about Jim Lane? What was his effect on Kansas? What is his legacy? In answering these questions, it might do to keep in mind this statement from William Connelley:

> In a reformatory revolution such as the fathers of Kansas inau-
> gurated, the prudent man, the conservative man,—I had almost
> said the just man,—cannot lead. He is hedged about with a
> scrupulous regard for conventionalities and obsolete ritualisms
> imposed upon his age by some advance in the upward growth of
> man in a long-gone preceding age. He does not discern that soci-
> ety is about to exercise its highest right, and readjust itself to the
> higher plane made necessary by the changed environment.

In short, it is hard to picture how things in Kansas might have turned out had Lane not taken part. Who else could have bridged the gap between the antislavery Westerners and the New England abolitionists? Perhaps John Speer, but he did not have the plat-form of a former congressman. Certainly not resentful New Englanders like Charles Robinson and George W. Brown.

Who was free to rally the North to the Free State cause in the summer of 1856? Andrew Reeder was, but considering that few mention or remember that fact suggests he was not up to that task.

Who would have taken control of the Free State forces that autumn? John Brown probably, but that prospect should not be comforting to anyone. Brown was a true believer. He might not have stopped at a few well-publicized victories. He might not have stopped at the Kansas-Missouri border. Who knows where that path would have led for the Free State movement, the region, or the United States?

Which of the Free State men turned Republicans in Kansas would have turned from black law to support of blacks in the Union army had not Lane turned first? And what of prominent national Republicans? How many of them who shared Lane's stat-ed views on slavery, emancipation, and the enlistment of freedmen accepted Lincoln's slow change of mind on those issues? How many of them voiced their acceptance? How many did so before Lane spoke up?

This is not to say that Lane was the lever that moved the world, far from it. He had his faults, and at times they obstructed any good intentions he had. The promises his life held went unful-filled in part because of the mistakes he made and the enemies he created or sustained. In the full scope of American history, he was not as crucial a figure as his friend Abraham Lincoln, but without

Lane present, events in Kansas Territory probably would have occurred very differently, and probably not for the best for Kansas or for the nation.

Important men are not always great men, and great men are not always important men. That James Henry Lane was an important man there can be no doubt. That he was a great man, well, the debate may rage until the end of time. I suspect he would prefer importance to greatness. If that is so, then I believe he made the best choice for himself, and that was the best for us.

Bibliography

BOOKS

Bailes, Kendall E. *Rider on the Wind: Jim Lane and Kansas.* Shawnee Mission, KS: The Wagon Wheel Press, 1962.

Bauer, K. Jack. *The Mexican War, 1846-1848.* New York: Macmillan, 1974; reprint, Lincoln: University of Nebraska Press, 1992.

Brewerton, G. Douglas. *The War in Kansas (A Rough Trip to the Border Among New Homes and a Strange People).* 1856. Reprint, Freeport, NY: Books for Libraries Press, 1971.

Britton, Wiley. *Memoirs of the Rebellion on the Border, 1863.* 1882. Reprint, Lincoln: Bison Books, University of Nebraska Press, 1993.

Hay, John. *At Lincoln's Side: John Hay's Civil War Correspondence and Selected Writings.* Edited by Michael Burlingame. Carbondale: Southern Illinois University Press, 2000.

Castel, Albert. Civil War Kansas: Reaping the Whirlwind (originally published as *A Frontier State at War: Kansas, 1861-1865*). Ithaca, NY: Cornell University Press, 1958. Reprint, Lawrence: University Press of Kansas, 1997.

Chaffin, Tom. *Pathfinder: John Charles Frémont and the Course of American Empire.* New York: Hill & Wang, 2002.

Clugston, W. G. *Rascals in Democracy.* New York: Richard R. Smith, 1940.

Connelley, William E. *James Henry Lane.* Topeka: Crane & Company, 1899.

——. *A Standard History of Kansas and Kansans, Volume Two.* Chicago and New York: Lewis Publishing Co., 1918.

Collins, Robert. *General James G. Blunt: Tarnished Glory.* Gretna, LA: Pelican Publishing Co., 2005.

Cordley, Richard. *A History of Lawrence, Kansas.* Lawrence, KS: E. F. Caldwell, 1895.

Crawford, Samuel J. *Kansas in the Sixties.* 1911. Reprint, Kansas Heritage Press, 1994.

Culter, William G. *History of the State of Kansas.* N.p.: A. T. Andreas, 1883.

Davis, Kenneth S. *Kansas, A History.* New York: W. W. Norton & Co., 1984.

Etcheson, Nicole. *Bleeding Kansas: Contested Liberty in the Civil War Era.* Lawrence: University Press of Kansas, 2004.

Fish, Reeder M. *The Grim Chieftain of Kansas, and Other Free-State Men in Their Struggles Against Slavery.* Cherryvale, KS: Clarion Book and Job Print, 1885.

Fisher, Rev. H. D. *The Gun and the Gospel.* 2nd ed. New York and Chicago: Medical Century Company, 1897.

Fitzgerald, Daniel. *Ghost Towns of Kansas: A Traveler's Guide.* Lawrence: University Press of Kansas, 1988.

Gaeddert, G. Raymond. *The Birth of Kansas.* Lawrence: University Press of Kansas, 1940.

Gihon, John H. *Governor Geary's Administration in Kansas.* Philadelphia: Chas. C. Rhodes, 1857.

Gladstone, T. H. *The Englishman in Kansas, or Squatter Life and Border Warfare.* 1857. Reprint, Lincoln: University of Nebraska Press, 1971.

Goodrich, Thomas. *Black Flag: Guerilla Warfare on the Western Border, 1861-1865.* Bloomington: Indiana University Press, 1999.

Goodrich, Thomas. *Bloody Dawn: The Story of the Lawrence Massacre.* Kent, OH: Kent State University Press, 1991.

——. *War to the Knife: Bleeding Kansas, 1854-1861.* Mechanisburg, PA: Stackpole Books, 1998.

Hinton, Richard J. *Rebel Invasion of Missouri and Kansas and the Campaign of the Army of the Border Against General Sterling Price in October and November 1864.* 1865. Reprint, Ottawa, KS: Kansas Heritage Press, 1994.

History of Dearborn, Ohio, and Switzerland Counties, Indiana. Chicago: Weakley, Harraman & Co. Publishers, 1885.

Howes, Charles C. *This Place Called Kansas.* Norman: University of Oklahoma Press, 1984.

Ingalls, John James. *A Collection of the Writings of John James Ingalls.* Edited by William E. Connelley. Kansas City, MO: Hudson Kimberley Publishing Co., 1902.

Johnson, Robert Underwood, and Clarence Clough Buel, ed. *Battles & Leaders of the Civil War.* New York, 1888.

Malin, James C. *John Brown and the Legend of Fifty-Six.* Philadelphia: American Philosophical Society, 1942.

———. *The Nebraska Question, 1852-1854.* Ann Arbor, MI: Edwards Brothers Inc., 1953.

McPherson, James M. *Battle Cry of Freedom: The Civil War Era.* Oxford, England: Oxford University Press, 1988.

Mechem, Kirke, ed. *The Annals of Kansas, 1886-1925.* Vol. 1. N.p.: Kansas State Historical Society, 1954.

Mildfelt, Todd. *The Secret Danites: Kansas' First Jayhawkers.* Richmond, KS: Todd Mildfelt Publishing, 2003.

Miner, Craig. *Kansas: The History of the Sunflower State, 1854-2000.* Lawrence: University Press of Kansas, 2002.

Monaghan, Jay. *Civil War on the Western Border, 1854-1865.* New York: Bonanza Books, 1955.

Nichols, Alice. *Bleeding Kansas.* New York: Oxford University Press, 1954.

Nicolay, John G., and John Hay. *Abraham Lincoln: A History.* Vol. 5. New York: The Century Co., 1890.

Oates, Stephen B. *To Purge This Land with Blood: A Biography of John Brown.* New York: Harper & Row, 1970.

Perry, Oran, comp. *Indiana in the Mexican War.* Indianapolis, 1908.

Peterson, Merrill D. *John Brown: The Legend Revisited.* Charlottesville: University of Virginia Press, 2002.

Quastler, I. E. *Railroads of Lawrence, Kansas.* Lawrence, KS: Coronado Press, 1979.

Rawley, James A. *Race & Politics: "Bleeding Kansas" and the Coming of the Civil War Era.* Philadelphia: J. B. Lippincott Company, 1969.

Richardson, Albert D. *Beyond the Mississippi: From the Great River to the Great Ocean.* N.p.: American Publishing Company, 1867.

Richmond, Robert W. *Kansas: A Land of Contrasts.* N.p.: Forum Press, 1989.

Robinson, Charles. *The Kansas Conflict.* 1892. Reprint, Freeport, NY: Books for Libraries Press, 1972.

Robinson, Sara T. L. *Kansas: Its Interior and Exterior Life.* N.p., 1856.

Ropes, Hannah Anderson. *Six Months in Kansas.* N.p.: John P. Jewett and Co., 1856.

Speer, John. *Life of Gen. James H. Lane, "The Liberator of Kansas."* Garden City, KS: self-published, 1896.

Spring, Leverett Wilson. *Kansas: The Prelude to the War for the Union.* New York: Houghton Mifflin, 1885.

Steele, Phillip W., and Steve Cottrell. *Civil War in the Ozarks.* Gretna, LA: Pelican Publishing Co., 2000.

Stephenson, Wendell Holmes. *The Political Career of General James H. Lane.* N.p.: Kansas State Historical Society, 1930.

Villard, Oswald Garrison. *John Brown: A Biography, 1800-1859.* New York: Doubleday, Doran & Company, Inc., 1929.

The War of the Rebellion: A Compilation of the Official Records of the Union and Confederate Armies. Washington, D.C., 1881-1901.

Wilder, Daniel W. *The Annals of Kansas.* N.p.: George W. Martin, Kansas Publishing House, 1875.

Wilson, Don W. *Governor Charles Robinson of Kansas.* Lawrence: University Press of Kansas, 1975.

Zornow, William Frank. *Kansas: A History of the Jayhawk State.* Norman: University of Oklahoma Press, 1957.

ARTICLES

"Address of Ex-Governor James W. Denver." *Kansas Historical Collections* 3 (1885).

"Address of Ex-Governor Frederick P. Stanton." *Kansas Historical Collections* 3 (1885).

Ballard, David E. "The First State Legislature." *Kansas Historical Collections* 10 (1908).

Blunt, James G. "General Blunt's Account of His Civil War Experiences." *Kansas Historical Quarterly* 1, no. 3 (May 1932).

"Bypaths of Kansas History." *Kansas Historical Quarterly* 13, no. 2 (May 1944).

Cecil-Fronsman, Bill. "'Advocate the Freedom of White Men, as Well as That of Negroes': The *Kansas Free State* and Antislavery Westerners in Territorial Kansas." *Kansas History* 20, no. 2 (summer 1997).

Connelly, William E. "The Lane-Jenkins Claim Contest." *Kansas Historical Collections* 16 (1925).

——. "The Lane Trail." *Kansas Historical Collections* 13 (1913-14).

——. "Personal Reminiscences of F. B. Sanborn." *Kansas Historical Collections* 14 (1915-18).

Cordley, Richard. "The Convention Epoch in Kansas History." *Kansas Historical Collections* 5 (1896).

Cornish, Dudley Taylor. "Kansas Negro Regiments in the Civil War." *Kansas Historical Quarterly* 20, no. 6 (May 1953).

Cory, Charles E. "The Sixth Kansas Cavalry and Its Commander." *Kansas Historical Collections* 11 (1910).

Courtright, Julie. "'A Goblin That Drives Her Insane': Sara Robinson and the History Wars of Kansas, 1894-1911." *Kansas History* 25, no. 2 (summer 2002).

Cruise, John D. "Early Days on the Union Pacific." *Kansas Historical Collections* 11 (1910).

Dickson, Charles Howard. "The True History of the Branson Rescue." *Kansas Historical Collections* 13 (1913-14).

Elliott, R. G. "The Big Springs Convention." *Kansas Historical Collections* 8 (1904).

"Executive Minutes Kept During Governor Shannon's Administration." *Kansas Historical Collections* 3 (1885).

"The Frontier Guard at the White House, Washington, 1861." *Kansas Historical Collections* 10 (1908).

Gambone, Joseph G. "Samuel C. Pomeroy and the Senatorial Election of 1861, Reconsidered." *Kansas Historical Quarterly* 37, no. 1 (spring, 1971).

Gleed, Charles S. "Samuel Walker." *Kansas Historical Collections* 6 (1900).

"Governor Denver's Administration." *Kansas Historical Collections* 5 (1896).

"Governor Walker's Administration." *Kansas Historical Collections* 5 (1896).

Greene, Albert R. "What I Saw of the Quantrill Raid." *Kansas Historical Collections* 13 (1913-14).

Griffith, G. W. E. "The Battle of Black Jack." *Kansas Historical Collections* 16 (1925).

Henderson, Harold J. "Ships in World War II Bearing Kansas Names." *Kansas Historical Quarterly* 15, no. 2 (May 1947).

Hoole, William Stanley, ed. "A Southerner's Viewpoint of the Kansas Situation, 1856-1857: The Letters of Lieut. Col. A. J. Hoole, C.S.A." Parts 1 and 2. *Kansas Historical Quarterly* 3, no. 1 (February 1934); 3, no. 2 (May 1934).

Horton, James. "Reminiscences of Hon. James C. Horton." *Kansas Historical Collections* 8 (1904).

Johannsen, Robert W. "The Kansas-Nebraska Act and Territorial Government in the United States." *Territorial Kansas, Studies Commemorating the Centennial* (Lawrence: University of Kansas Publications, Social Science Studies, 1954).

"Kansas Chronology." *Kansas Historical Collections* 12 (1911-12).

"Kansas Quarter-Centennial." *Kansas Historical Collections* 3 (1886).

Langsdorf, Edgar. "Jim Lane and the Frontier Guard." *Kansas Historical Quarterly* 9, no. 1 (February 1940).

——, ed. "The Letters of Joseph H. Trego, 1857-1864, Linn County Pioneer, Part One, 1857, 1858." *Kansas Historical Quarterly* 19, no. 2 (May 1951).

"The Letters of Samuel James Reader, 1861-1863." Parts 1 and 2. *Kansas Historical Quarterly* 9, no. 1 (February 1940); 9, no. 2 (May 1940).

Lewis, Lloyd. "The Man the Historians Forgot." *Kansas Historical Quarterly* 8, no. 1 (February 1939).

Malin, James C. "The Topeka Statehood Movement Reconsidered: Origins." *Territorial Kansas, Studies Commemorating the Centennial* (University of Kansas Publications, Social Science Studies, 1954).

Miner, Craig. "Lane and Lincoln: A Mysterious Connection." *Kansas History* 24, no. 3 (fall 2001).

Moody, Joel. "The Marais Des Cygnes Massacre." *Kansas Historical Collections* 14 (1915-18).

Patrick, Jeffrey L., ed. "'This Regiment Will Make A Mark': Letters from a Member of Jennison's Jayhawkers." *Kansas History* 20, no. 1 (spring 1997).

Peterson, John M. "From Border War to Civil War: More Letters of

Edward and Sarah Fitch, 1855-1863, Part Two." *Kansas History* 20, no. 2 (summer 1997).

Plummer, Mark A. "Governor Crawford's Appointment of Edmund G. Ross to the United States Senate." *Kansas Historical Quarterly* 28, no. 2 (summer 1962).

Robinson, Charles. "Topeka and Her Constitution." *Kansas Historical Collections* 6 (1900).

Root, George A., ed. "The First Day's Battle at Hickory Point, From the Diary and Reminiscenses [*sic*] of Samuel James Reader." *Kansas Historical Quarterly* 1, no. 1 (November 1931).

Ross, Edith Connelley. "The Old Shawnee Mission." *Kansas Historical Collections* 17 (1926-28).

Smith, Charles W. "The Battle of Hickory Point, September 13, 1856." *Kansas Historical Collections* 7 (1902).

Smith, Nathan. "Letters of a Free-State Man in Kansas, 1856." *Kansas Historical Quarterly* 21, no. 3 (fall 1954).

Speer, John. "The Burning of Osceola, Mo., by Lane, and the Quantril Massacre Contrasted." *Kansas Historical Collections* 6 (1900).

Smith, Verres [Jacob Stringfellow]. "Jim Lane." *Lippincott's Magazine* (March 1870).

"Some Ingalls Letters." *Kansas Historical Collections* 14 (1915-18).

"Some of the Lost Towns of Kansas." *Kansas Historical Collections* 12 (1911-12).

Spring, Leverett W. "The Career of a Kansas Politician." *American Historical Review* 4, no. 1 (October 1898).

Stoddard, W. O. "The Story of a Nomination." *North American Review* 138 (March 1884).

Taylor, David G. "Thomas Ewing, Jr., and the Origins of the Kansas Pacific Railway Company." *Kansas Historical Quarterly* 42, no. 2 (summer 1976).

Thacher, T. Dwight. "The Leavenworth Constitutional Convention." *Kansas Historical Collections* 3 (1885).

"The Topeka Movement." *Kansas Historical Collections* 13 (1913-14).

Watts, Dale E. "How Bloody Was Bleeding Kansas? Political Killings in Kansas Territory, 1854-1861." *Kansas History* 18, no. 2 (summer 1995).

Woodward, Brinton W. "Reminiscences of September 14, 1856; Invasion of the 2700." *Kansas Historical Collections* 6 (1900).

Zornow, William Frank. "The Kansas Senators and the Re-election of Lincoln." *Kansas Historical Quarterly* 19, no. 2 (May 1951).

NEWSPAPERS

Arkansas City Traveler, April 3, 1878.
Atchison Freedom's Champion, June 12, 1858; February 8 and 25, 1864; January 19, 1865.
Atchison Union, November 5, 1859; March 24, 1860.
Brown County World (Hiawatha), March 2, 1894.
Council Grove Press, February 8 and 15, 1864.
Doniphan Crusader of Freedom, February 3, 1858.
Emporia Daily News, November 20, 1882.
Emporia News, February 13, April 6 and 13, 1861; January 25, June 21, October 4, 1862; February 13, April 30, November 12, 1864.
Emporia Weekly Globe, January 20, 1887.
Fort Scott Bulletin, July 26, 1862.
Fort Scott Democrat, June 10, 1858; March 16, 1861.
Fort Scott Monitor, March 16, 1861; November 4, 1864.
Herald of Freedom, June 30, September 8, 1855; January 19, 1856; June 13, 1857; July 25, September 5, December 5, 1857; May 29, June 5 and 12, 1858; January 15 and 29, March 5, October 22, 1859.
Kansas City (MO) Journal, September 14, 1879.
Kansas City Kansan, July 21, 1921.
Kansas City (MO) Star, May 25, 1913.
Kansas Daily Tribune, February 4 and 7, November 3, 1864; July 7 and 21, 1866; June 7, 1879.
Kansas Free State, September 3 and 10, 1855; March 24, May 5 and 19, 1856.
Kansas State Journal, April 11, May 9 and 16, June 6, July 18, October 17, 1861; October 9, 1862; August 4, September 15 and 29, 1864.
Lawrence Weekly Tribune, June 23, August 4, 1864; June 5, 1879.
Lawrence Daily Herald, December 7, 1883; February 22, 1884.
Lawrence Daily Record, February 3, 1891.
Lawrence Republican, September 3, October 22, 1857; June 10,

1858; January 20, February 17, March 17, May 5 and 26, October 27, 1859; March 21, April 4 and 25, May 2, 9, 16, and 30, July 16, November 16, 1861; January 9, 1862.

Lawrenceburg (IN) Independent Press, January 17, 1851; October 11, 1854; January 11, February 14, 1856.

Lawrenceburg (IN) Register, October 3, 1846; September 13, 1850; October 15, 1852; March 17, April 28, 1854; January 19, February 16, 1855; September 23, 1860; September 30, 1864; February 10, 1876.

Lawrenceburg (IN) Journal Press, "James H. Lane Saw Life as a Duel," by Bob Markwalter, June 23, 1981.

Lawrenceburg (IN) Union Press, July 12, 1866.

Leavenworth Daily Conservative, April 7, May 11 and 26, June 26, July 21, August 4, September 24, October 23, November 8, December 18, 1861; January 21, February 28, September 3, 20, and 30, October 2 and 10, 1862; September 11 and 23, 1863; February 7 and 11, April 23, July 31, September 16, October 21, 26, and 27, 1864; April 23, 1865; January 7, April 17, 19, and 20, July 3, 4, 7, 10, 11, 12, and 14, 1866.

Leavenworth Daily Bulletin, June 4, 9, and 15, 1866.

Leavenworth Daily Times, April 10, May 3, October 9, 18, and 20, November 16, 1861; August 5, October 8, November 2 and 4, 1862; August 26 and 28, September 12, November 8, 1863; February 12, September 17, 1864.

Leavenworth Weekly Conservative, May 9, 1861.

Leavenworth Weekly Times, June 12, 1858.

Lecompton Union, August 20, 1856.

Manhattan Independent, March 21, August 15, 1864.

Nemaha Courier (Seneca), February 13 and 20, 1864.

New York Daily Times, November 5, 1855; April 16, 1856; September 4, 1863; June 9, 1864.

New York Daily Tribune, April 19 and 25, 1861.

Olathe Mirror, February 20, 1864; June 14, 1866; June 7, 1888.

Osage Chronicle (Burlingame), February 13, 1864.

Oskaloosa Independent, November 20, 1864.

Ottawa Herald, December 22, 1916.

Prairie City Freemen's Champion, February 25, 1858.

Topeka Capital-Commonwealth, December 23, 1888.

Topeka Commonwealth, April 13, 1879; December 4, 1886.
Topeka Daily Capital, January 29, February 5, 1893.
Topeka Daily Kansas Freeman, October 24, 1855.
Topeka State Record, March 23, April 6 and 20, May 18, October 12, 1861; January 7, 1863.
Topeka Tribune, October 1, 1859; March 10 and 24, April 21, 1860; February 16 and 23, March 2 and 23, April 6, May 11 and 25, June 1, 1861; October 4, 1862.
Topeka Weekly Leader, July 5 and 12, 1866.
Troy Chief, January 23, 1879; January 10, February 7, 1889.
White Cloud Kansas Chief, August 27, 1857; March 25, April 1, June 17, 1858; April 19, 1860; April 11, 18, and 25, May 2, June 27, July 4 and 18, September 5, October 10, 17, and 24, November 28, 1861; July 3, August 6, 1862; July 23, 1863; February 18 and 25, March 3 and 17, August 11, 1864; September 8, 1864; October 6 and 13, 1864.

MANUSCRIPT COLLECTIONS

History, Constitutions, archives of the Kansas State Historical Society; Journal, #570, Samuel F. Tappan Journal of the Leavenworth Constitutional Convention.

Kansas Collected Speeches and Pamphlets. Archives of the Kansas State Historical Society. speech of James H. Lane, Springfield, Missouri, November 8, 1861; speech of Lane at Tremont Temple, Boston, November 31, 1861; speech of Lane in Washington, D. C., December 2, 1861; speech of Lane in the Senate, February 16, 1864; speech of Lane at the Cooper Institute, New York, March 30, 1864.

Thomas H. Webb Scrapbooks. Archives of the Kansas State Historical Society: Volume 5, pages 183-4, 192-3; Volume 6, pages 12, 196, 239, 243; Volume 7, page 186; Volume 8, pages 172-4, 247; Volume 11, pages 42-3, 55; Volume 12, pages 39-40; Volume 13, page 172.

James Abbott Collection. Kansas State Historical Society: Lane to Abbott, October 15, 1857; Abbott to his wife, December 22, 1857.

John Brown Collection. Kansas State Historical Society: James G. Blunt to the secretary of the K. S. H. S., October 12, 1877.

Delahay, Mark. Papers. Kansas State Historical Society: James Lane to Delahay, December 18, 1860; Lyman Trumbull to Delahay, February 16, 1861.

Ewing, Thomas Jr. Papers. Kansas State Historical Society: Thomas to Hugh Ewing, January 17, 1861; Ewing to Caleb Smith, January 21, 1861; Ewing to Thomas Corwin, January 22, 1861; Ewing to J. J. Coombs, January 22, 1861.

Gray, Alfred. Papers. Kansas State Historical Society: Marcus Parrott to Gray, March 12, 1861.

Abelard Guthrie Collection. Diary. Kansas State Historical Society: January 17, 18, and 30, 1862; February 4 and 27, 1862.

Ingalls, John J. Papers. Kansas State Historical Society: Ingalls to Father, February 23, 1862.

Lane, James H. Papers. Spencer Research Library, University of Kansas: James Lane to Mary Lane, June 21, 1848; Ward Burlingame to James Lane, May 18, 1866;.

Robinson, Charles and Sara. Papers. Kansas State Historical Society: Charles Robinson to Eli Thayer, April 2, 1855; Charles to Messrs Allen, Blood, Hutchinson & others, August 16, 1856; Charles to Sara, December 20, 1860; Charles to Sara, January 11, 1861; Charles to Sara, December 27, 1863; Charles to Sara, October 9, 1864; Samuel C. Smith to Charles, August 5, 1866.

———. Papers. History, University of Kansas, Kansas State Historical Society: Charles to Amos Lawrence, June 27, 1863.

D. Rogers Collection. Kansas State Historical Society: Rogers to James Redfield, February 1 & 3, 1864.

Wood, Samuel N. Papers. Kansas State Historical Society: A. J. Chipman to Wood, August 20, 1861.

Index